SINGLES

C0-EWY-056

Published in cooperation with the
NATIONAL COUNCIL ON FAMILY RELATIONS

Series Editor: **John Scanzoni**
Family Research Center
University of North Carolina, Greensboro

Books appearing in New Perspectives on Family are either single or multiple-authored volumes or concisely edited books of original articles on focused topics within the broad field of marriage and family. Books can be reports of significant research, innovations in methodology, treatises on family theory, or syntheses of current knowledge in a subfield of the discipline. Each volume meets the highest academic standards and makes a substantial contribution to our knowledge of marriage and family.

SINGLES: Myths and Realities, Leonard Cargan and Matthew Melko
THE CHILDBEARING EXPERIENCE: Fertility Attitudes and Behavior, Greer Litton Fox, ed.

Other volumes currently available from Sage and sponsored by NCFR:

THE VIOLENT HOME: A Study of Physical Aggression Between Husbands and Wives, *Richard J. Gelles*
ROLE STRUCTURE AND ANALYSIS OF THE FAMILY, *F. Ivan Nye*
SONS OR DAUGHTERS: A Cross-Cultural Survey of Parental Preferences, *Nancy Williamson*
CONFLICT AND POWER IN MARRIAGE: Expecting the First Child, *Ralph LaRossa*
THE AMERICAN FAMILY: A Demographic History, *Rudy Ray Seward*
THE SOCIAL WORLD OF OLD WOMEN: Management of Self-Identity, *Sarah H. Matthews*
FAMILIES AGAINST SOCIETY: A Study of Reactions to Children with Birth Defects, *Rosalyn Benjamin Darling*
ASSESSING MARRIAGE: New Behavioral Approaches, *Erik E. Filsinger and Robert A. Lewis, eds.*
SEX AND PREGNANCY IN ADOLESCENCE, *Melvin Zelnik, John F. Kantner, and Kathleen Ford*

301.417
C191s

SINGLES
Myths and Realities

Leonard Cargan
Matthew Melko

Published in cooperation with
the National Council on Family Relations

WITHDRAWN
The Library
Saint Francis College
Fort Wayne, Indiana 46808

SAGE PUBLICATIONS
Beverly Hills / London / New Delhi

85-1607

Copyright © 1982 by Sage Publications, Inc.

All rights reserved. No part of this book may be reproduced or utilized in any form or by any means, electronic or mechanical, including photocopying, recording, or by any information storage and retrieval system, without permission in writing from the publisher.

For information address:

SAGE Publications, Inc.
275 South Beverly Drive
Beverly Hills, California 90212

SAGE Publications Ltd
28 Banner Street
London EC1Y 8QE, England

SAGE Publications India Pvt. Ltd.
C-236 Defence Colony
New Delhi 110 024, India

Printed in the United States of America

Library of Congress Cataloging in Publication Data

Cargan, Leonard
Singles : Myths and realities.

(New perspectives on family)
"Published in cooperation with the National Council on Family Relations."
Bibliography: p.
1. Single people — United States. I. Melko, Matthew. II. Title. III. Series.
HQ800.4.U6C37 306.7 81-23343
ISBN 0-8039-1806-2 AACR2
ISBN 0-8039-1807-0 (pbk.)

SECOND PRINTING, 1983

CONTENTS

PART IV SINGLE AND MARRIED OUTLOOKS

DEDICATION

In the dedication for his book, *The Little Prince,* Saint Exupery apologized for dedicating his fairy tale for children to an adult. But, he explained, the adult was once a child.

Similarly, I would like to apologize for dedicating this book on singles to three marrieds. But then, they were once single.

Dave Cargan, Sidney Cohen, and Manny Sarko were catalysts in my academic efforts. In reality, then, this dedication is to humanistic persons rather than to persons of a particular civil status.

— Len Cargan

ACKNOWLEDGMENTS

Many people have contributed to this book, some of them without knowing that they were doing so. In mentioning the following, we are aware that there were others we have forgotten, who we will no doubt remember when we first read these acknowledgments in print.

Our thanks first to our secretaries, Shirley Mullins-Vanover and Betty Snow, who have often had to type and retype many drafts, not to mention drawing the tables and graphs. Earlier secretaries, Bev Wright and Kathy Kear, worked on the first versions of the questionnaire. The secretaries were aided by a number of students, notably Peggy Brunswick, Constance Smith, Leslie Loper, Theresa Bohn, Amanda Romero, Marietta Kelley, Anita Reynolds, Julie Rollins, and (especially) Donna Helfenstine.

Our work was made easier by the help of a number of university reference librarians, particularly Rich Tyce, Stephen Haas, Diane Marketti, Karen Kimber, and Howard Jarrell. We are also indebted to Art Mercer, who provided us with our printouts, Bruce Stiver, who did the graphs, and John Ferrara, who expedited the graphics production.

Many editors and faculty members have helped us by commenting on sections of the book, providing us with readers' comments, accepting papers, or just being encouraging. These include Bob Woodbury, Charles Webel, Bryant Robey, Ruth Brasher, Peter Stein, Elias Nigem, and Quentin Evans.

We were greatly helped by the members of *Interaction,* who gave us two hours of comments on our results, almost all of which appear somewhere in the book.

Finally, our punctuation and spelling were improved, and our thinking unfuzzed, by Mary Cargan and our editors at Sage Publications.

SERIES EDITOR'S PREFACE

As the students and I were wrapping up a recent semester's course on changes in sex roles, a woman in her mid-twenties said, "What about people like me?" She was single and on a career track, but we had not read much literature about "people like her" simply because there was not much available.

Since then, fortunately, there have been some publications attempting to fill the gaps in our knowledge about a rapidly growing segment of the population. The work by Professors Cargan and Melko is different from most of the other efforts because it targets a representative sample of singles and married persons and, in an in-depth fashion, compares and contrasts their differences and similarities. Furthermore, to expand their data base the authors drew an additional sample from a local singles' organization. Finally, they make considerable use of popular sources of information to illustrate and illuminate their findings.

The product is a highly readable and extremely informative book, though not everyone will agree with all of their interpretations. Nevertheless their materials do enable us to understand more clearly and fully than before some of the fundamental dimensions of the single lifestyle as it began to emerge during the 1970s. The authors would be the first to acknowledge that, during these fast-paced times, there is much about singleness they may have overlooked. It is their hope and mine that this book will stimulate a great deal of fresh thinking and research into a heretofore neglected — but increasingly vital — area.

* * * * *

This volume represents a change in the format of books sponsored by the National Council on Family Relations and published by Sage Publications. Though a dozen joint NCFR-Sage publications have appeared over the last decade under the series editorship of Jetse Sprey, Murray Straus, or myself, these publications have been done on an ad hoc basis, each being hidden in one or the other of Sage's many book series. With this volume, NCFR-sponsored books finally achieve their own identity in an official NCFR series — NEW PERSPECTIVES ON FAMILY. Books in this series will, as in the past, be rigorously examined by NCFR reviewers before publication to ensure the highest quality of scholarship. A substantial portion of the royalties on these books is donated to NCFR to support the work of the organization. By establishing a formal series, we hope to heighten the visibility of the contribution by NCFR to the study of marriage, the family, and related disciplines. I urge you to assist us in this endeavor by submitting your current scholarly work to be considered for the NEW PERSPECTIVES ON FAMILY series.

— John Scanzoni

PART I

Introduction

Chapter 1

BEING SINGLE ON NOAH'S ARK

Singles in the World of the Married

THE VALUES SYSTEM

America is a society of contradictory values. On the one hand, we regard highly the values of individualism, of being unique in thoughts and actions, of using Yankee ingenuity and inventiveness. These values have long been considered the cornerstone for America's development and are summed up in our emphasis on competition and on being different.

On the other hand, no society can function without a norm of conformity. There are times when it becomes necessary for individuals to subsume their personal needs and desires for the higher goal of the group, the organization, and the community. As we have become an organizational society in the twentieth century, there has been more need for cooperation and less scope for individual adventure and initiative.

Thus, we teach and value individual initiative, but learn in everyday society that individuality carried beyond very moderate limits can incur serious penalties. This contradiction is felt most strongly by minority populations. Among these minorities are not only racial and ethnic groups, but also groups that had not been perceived until recently as minorities: the poor, the handicapped, and the unmarried (O'Brien, 1973: 51).

Marriage is seen as instrumental in fulfilling such societal needs as socializing the infant into a person with human qualities, providing for our personal needs of affection and security, and maintaining life itself (Nye, 1967: 248). Despite the loss of many functions in regard to work, protective, educational, and recreational practices, the family is still seen as the provider of psychic well-being and as the "matrix for the development of personality" (Ackerman, 1972: 16). In addition, the things that people are seeking in marriage are among the best we need and want, and they are those things for which we have no reliable substitutes: love, stability, and loyalty (O'Brien, 1973: 51). Thus the state of marriage is thought of as the natural order of things, and those who do not conform threaten this order; the result is that there is little room in the system for the unaccompanied person (Duberman, 1977: 115).

STEREOTYPES ABOUT SINGLES

Such perceptions have led to the development of beliefs designed to perpetuate the dominance of pairs, beliefs in which marriage is seen as the positive choice, as something good; singleness implies the opposite idea, of a negative choice, a bad state (Deegan, 1969: 9). The single person is often perceived as one who, lacking a partner, is alone and not complete, "who is moving against the grain of the powerful norms defining marriage as the most desirable state adults can attain," and who comes to be seen as "unfit and deviant" (Bell, 1972: 89).

When students of marriage consider the possible reasons for not marrying (or, as they often put it, "failing" to marry), the reasons they come up with often seem to be negative: People do not marry because they are hostile toward members of the opposite sex or are homosexual; because they are immature, unwilling to assume responsibility, neurotic, or emotionally fixated on a parent; because they are unattractive or unhealthy; because they failed in the dating game, either because they are socially inadequate or because they became fixated on a lost love; because they were overfocused on economics, either perceiving themselves too poor to marry or perceiving marriage as a threat to their careers; because they were just unluckily isolated by geography, education, or occupation (for instance, illiterate lighthouse keepers); because they were overcome by some sort of "principled deviance"; or, if none of the above, their failure to marry must have been the result of an oversight! (See Kuhn, 1955: 521; Davis and Strong, 1977: 125.) Such lists "reflect our adherence to the ideal that everyone marry and that . . . anyone can" if they really want to (Duberman, 1977: 118) and omit the possibility that remaining single might have been a rational choice, as well as obscure the realities of singlehood.

In sum, "no matter how often it is called 'a positive, individual state,' the single life as . . . publicly drawn comes to this composite picture: the single is a poseur, a squanderer, a narcissist, a wastrel; he dances the hustle in the apartment house party room; loafs on his plastic sea horse in the . . . swimming pool; lives for lotions, balms and sprays; is a non-stop lover, drinker, laugher, and more (or less)" (Rosenblatt, 1977: 14).

Not surprisingly, the stereotype of the deviant single applies more to women than to men since it is women who are "saved" by marriage in an economy dominated by males. Thus, in an examination of single women as portrayed in literary fiction, Deegan (1969: 3) found that the women pictured were unmarried because they are unattractive, handicapped, or incompetent. Since marriage is the important factor, they are creatures pitied or ridiculed rather than admired, despite the fact that they are generally pictured as admirable people (Deegan, 1969: 111-112).

O'Brien (1973: 74) adds to this contradictory view of the single woman in America by noting that she is usually pitied, disliked, or ascribed a low status except when she is needed — in times of war, to nurse the wounded or to run the farms and factories. While the young single woman may be challenging and intriguing, prolonged singleness, like prolonged virginity, is suspect. At some point she becomes a spinster or an old maid. The terms have become archaic, but their meaning persists. It appears that it is difficult to believe that women are single because they do not want to be wives. Thus the "experts" tell us that women can only find love and sexual fulfillment within the bonds of matrimony, and so it is important for them to marry or remarry lest they face emotional and physical deterioration (Edwards and Hoover, 1974: 17).

No wonder Dorothy Parker was led to conclude:

> Men in single state should tarry,
> While women, I suggest, should marry.

But, Dorothy Parker notwithstanding, men have not entirely escaped social reprobation for bachelorhood. Singlehood for men has often suggested alcoholism, homosexuality, personality inadequacy, or psychopathology (Libby, 1978: 163). Even if they participate in the social mainstream, they may be pictured as workaholics or, if their enterprises are theological, as religious fanatics or recluses (Carter and Glick, 1970: 229). A contrary image, that of the Joe Namath kind of swinging single, nevertheless carries with it overtones of immaturity, selfishness, lechery, and social irresponsibility (Libby, 1978: 165; Stein, 1976: 2).

The stereotypes cited here are much entangled, some overlapping, some contradictory. It is worth pausing to try to sort them out, and to hear the reply of those being condemned: the singles.

Deviance. The stereotype is that singles are somehow abnormal. Marriage is a normal process and, at least between certain ages, a person normally should be married. The singles community tends to reply that, like the decision to marry, singlehood is a normal choice, and that the percentage of singles has grown so that among adults it constitutes a very substantial minority, which, if it keeps growing, may constitute a majority before very long. The very size of this group belies the claim of its deviancy.

Immaturity. Since marriage is a normal stage of development, the "failure" to marry or to remain married reflects some kind of immaturity. If a man, he may be tied to his mother's apron strings; if a woman, a spinster who has not experienced life. It may be that the single person has not reached the state of altruism, that he or she is selfish and unable to share. The singles community points to many singles who are obviously mature, experienced, and selfless, be it an Isaac Newton in the past or a current Ralph Nader.

Sexual deviance. Conjugal sexuality is normal. How does the single meet sexual needs? Either by swinging, a lecherous hopping from bed to bed; by sexual inversion, which is perceived as a developmental failure; by abstinence, which is unnatural; or by masturbation, which again is selfish. Often ignored is the fact that what is considered to be sexual deviance has been found to be extensive among both marrieds and singles (Kinsey, 1948; Hunt, 1974).

Freedom. The single is perceived ambiguously as freer than the married person, as having more time, since he or she is not burdened with family and children. For this reason, however, the single is also perceived to be less responsible, a swinger concerned only with having fun and looking after his or her own interests, a person lacking community ties and responsibilities; again, an immature and irresponsible person. (These separations for clarification inevitably call to be reconnected with other aspects of the situation.) Singles respond that since they have to do both housework and office work, they have less time than the married, but still assume their share of social responsibility.

Happiness and loneliness. Here we have a mixed set of stereotypes. On one hand the single is pictured as having more fun, getting out more, having more freedom to make choices, and having fewer worries; therefore, it would seem that the single ought to be happier than the nonsingle. On the other hand, the single is perceived as living alone, always having to initiate social relationships, and having no permanent person with whom to share; therefore the single is more lonely, and if more lonely, unhappier. Singles tend to respond that they share similar life problems with the married, and so are probably neither happier nor having more fun than marrieds. As for loneliness, they point out that many single people live with others, that many singles as well as marrieds do not depend on housemates for social needs, and that many marrieds are lonely, too. Other singles grant that loneliness is a problem, but one they are willing to confront in exchange for the advantages of being single.

Affluence. Since singles do not have children, and children cost tens of thousands of dollars each in this world, it is obvious that singles must be richer than marrieds. And singles seem to live from trip to trip — they are always taking vacations. They live in well-furnished apartments or condominiums, usually with a decorative woman or man spending the night, drinking French wine and listening to the stereo. Singles respond to this one with hoots and laughter, pointing out that either they do not have children, in which case they pay terrific taxes and are discriminated against by family economy sizes, or they have children, in which case they have to raise them by themselves on one income, with baby-sitter fees besides.

Workaholism. Since they do not have families, singles devote themselves to their careers with fanatical intensity that the married person, who has divided responsibilities, cannot match. The result is that they get the top positions in their organizations. If the top people are married, they are likely to get divorces anyway, either because they are married to their work or because they can afford it. Singles respond that there are some singles like that, as there are some marrieds (who may, indeed, be candidates for serial marriage), but there are also many charming singles who take their work in normal proportion to their lives, taking ample time for their friends and their hobbies. Besides, the married are the ones who get the promotions, since they are seen as more mature, restrained, and responsible.

Given these beliefs, it is not surprising that we are taught early in the socialization process that to be truly happy and fulfilled, it is necessary to become married and take on the responsibilities of a family. Marriage, then, is the social norm, and remaining unmarried or choosing against marriage leads to negative stereotypes, biases, and discriminations.

The world throughout history goes marching two by two. From Noah's Ark to the socialization process of today's society, two is the proper number, and in a world that counts by twos, the pressure to marry has been overwhelming.

THE GROWING SINGLES POPULATION

We have referred, in commenting on responses to stereotypes, to a singles community. Such a community exists in that there is a growing number of singles who are aware of themselves as such. They are attempting to transmit this awareness to a much larger category, who perceive of themselves as widowed, divorced, planning to remarry, planning to marry, or being unmarried and having no immediate plans for being married. Members of this category do not readily identify with one another. A college junior involved in the dating game would not be expected to see herself as linked in any community with her divorced uncle and widowed grandmother. But if she marries next year, she will more readily perceive, at least on a family occasion, that she, like her mother and grandmother, is a married woman. The word single, then, is becoming a label for a large and divergent category of people as a means of treating them on the basis of their one common characteristic — their nonmarriage status. It is a term coming into wide use as a replacement for the words spinster or bachelor, and applied to all who find themselves in this nonmarriage state, regardless of the reason — the never married, the divorced, the widowed.

Whatever the social pressures, it is clear that singles have been growing as a percentage of the population in America. The figures reveal that since 1960 there has been a marked increase of single households with a resultant decline in the nuclear family. Between 1960 and 1975, the number of adults between the ages of 20 and 34 who have never been married increased by 50 percent, while in the same period the divorce rate doubled. The number of people under 25 living alone has tripled in 7 years (1970-1977). The large increase in divorce is emphasized when it is noted that 39 percent of first marriages now end in divorce within 10 years, and 59 percent of second marriages end so within 5 years. In addition, the time interval between divorce and remarriage has increased and so the number of those divorced but not remarried doubled in the decade from 1963 to

1973. Thus there has been a slowdown of marriage and remarriage versus a speedup in the rate of divorce; the annual rate of first marriages has not been keeping pace with the growth of the prime age group for first marriages and the divorce rate is now at the highest point in our history. The result is that there are now over 52 million single adults aged 18 or over. Singles, including those raising children, now make up 1 out of every 3 households in the United States (U.S. News and World Report, 1977: 59).

Some demographers expect the nation to return to its traditional family orientation as soon as the big generation boom of the 1950s and early 1960s settles down. But others, noting that divorce and antifamily attitudes are spreading to other segments of the population, expect an expansion of singlehood. This depends on the extent to which young, unmarried people maintain their attitudes as they grow older. However, according to the Bureau of the Census, "proportionately more and more will be living independently, and more and more will be breaking up their marriage" for some time to come (U.S. News and World Report, 1977: 60; Newsweek, 1978: 76).

It is worth pausing to ask why the percentage of singles is increasing. Consider, first, why we marry. Reasons given by marriage authorities include the bond of love or sex, mutual aid in the struggle for existence, and the desire for children (Ackerman, 1972: 12). In noting the demographic reasons for the emergence of a singles community, however, we have indirectly indicated that over time, and especially more recently, factors have seemingly emerged that have made marriage less imperative as a means of providing children, mutual aid, or love.

In the industrial age, a series of changes has taken place that has undermined much of the logic behind these marriage imperatives. The process of urbanization and industrialization has reduced the percentage of people involved in farming occupations from more than 90 percent to fewer than 10 percent in many developed countries. The more recent development of the organizational structure has meant a decline in the percentage of people engaged in family businesses. Developments in medicine have reduced infant mortality and led to an increase in world population from 1 to 4 billion in a little more than a century. All of these factors greatly reduced the importance of the childbearing functions of the family. Then came the development of the effective means of preventing conception: oral contraceptives and outpatient sterilization.

There also have been changes in the need for mutual aid in the struggle for existence. National highway systems and air transportation have greatly increased mobility, which in turn has contributed to the undermining of the extended family and therefore, for many people — married and single alike — has created greater dependence on an extended community of friendships. Add to this complicated changes in attitudes that are partly independent of the change in family structure and partly reinforced by it: continued secularization of religion, a changing perception of the individual, and a widening perception of the rights of minorities that had not previously been perceived as such — women, the handicapped, homosexuals, and others.

For example, partly as the result of the women's rights movement, which has come out of larger social changes, and partly as the result of a general increase in concern about minority rights, which has been developing throughout the century but was accelerated by the world wars, greater attention has been given to equal opportunity hiring practices. This has provided women with greater opportunities for financial independence, and may also have reduced the perception of the single man as irresponsible and thus reduced pressure on him to marry or to remain married. Given that the alternatives to marriage have become more available, it may be that some women who two decades ago would have chosen marriage now prefer to remain single.

Another factor that may affect singleness among women is the increasing difficulty of finding eligible male partners, a result of what Glick called the "marriage squeeze." Until 1940, the male population in this country exceeded the female population, but since then there have been more adult women and by 1979 there were 8 million more women than men. In any given year, women in their peak marrying year (age 21) have outnumbered men in their peak marrying year (age 23). This situation has resulted in a younger but larger group of women competing for marriage partners from a smaller and older group of men (Glick, 1975: 17). Thus, partly due to social changes and partly due to demographic changes, women are not marrying as quickly or as readily as in the past.

Other factors that have emerged fortuitously have added to the independence of individuals from the need for marriage: the emergence of fast food restaurants, for instance, and, even more important, frozen foods, along with the development of laundromats, clothes that do not require ironing, and various convenience services. The increase in singles and the perception of them as a market resulted in the development of bars and clubs for singles, packaged vacations for singles, small cars, new insurance policies, and various other benefits that, in turn, provide further incentive to people to remain single (Stein, 1976: 38).

Also affecting the traditional appeal of marriage and family life for young people are the increasing divorce rate and criticism of this style of life by scholarly and mass media sources (Stein, 1978: 5).

In sum, there are many pressures that militate toward marriage, such as economic security, cultural pressures that idealize marriage, peer and parental socialization, and a desire for a family. However, there are also factors that make singlehood attractive in comparison to marriage, such as freedom from the restrictions of a binding relationship, self-sufficiency, increased opportunities for geographical mobility, and supportive groups (Kain, 1981: 3).

What is true for the never married is also true for the divorced. Traditionally, marriage has been seen as a relationship that restricts all intimate companionship with others. The usual concluding line of the marriage vows emphasizes the expectations of the couple — "till death do us part." Such expectations naturally lead to a reluctance to end the marriage and a sense of shame if divorce occurs. Be that as it may, there has also been an exploding increase in the divorce component of the singles category. Factors involved in this trend include liberalization and reform of divorce laws; changes in the role of women; challenges to many basic social institutions and values that have been supportive to more traditional family forms; a growing acceptance of the belief that divorce is a reasonable alternative to an unhappy marriage; and a decline in fertility rates, which allows for greater participation in the labor force and so contributes to women's economic independence (Albrecht, 1979: 857). Earlier marriages and longer life spans means that people are "now expected to make it together for two generations instead of one" — a feat Alvin Toffler calls "a rather astonishing bit of optimism in light of a rapidly changing society" (quoted in Ackerman, 1972: 15-16). Furthermore, the growing secularization mentioned earlier has led to a decline in religious and legal opposition to divorce. For these reasons Toffler believes that "we are moving toward a society based on temporary relationships rather than permanent ones" (Ackerman, 1972: 16).

According to Robert Bell (1972: 89), such changes have led

> to the point where the traditional institutions of marriage and the family are of much less significance for survival and physical well being, and adultery is no longer a threat to the economy given the loss or modification of so many traditional functions of marriage and the family. What is left? In effect, marriage — as it was known in the past — has, to a great extent, disappeared.

Finally, as a result of these changes, there has been a corresponding change of opinion among marrieds and singles alike about the single status. Attitude surveys show that in the past 20 years singlehood has been regarded with less hostility than in the past, while single women's evaluation of marriage has correspondingly dropped. Attitudes toward divorce are also becoming less rigid. By 1976, 80 percent of the respondents in one study approved of divorce, at least under some circumstances (ISR Newsletter, 1979: 4).

It is hardly surprising, then, that there has developed a perception of singles as an aggregate with common interests, and that this perception has lead to the defense of singles and a challenge to the stereotype of the single as irresponsible swinger, lonely loser, or even nonconformist. Thus an organizer of an exposition for singles states that whereas being single used to be "what you were when you were divorced or widowed," now "people are looking at being single as more than just passing through a stage"; and a coauthor of a marriage text notes that "clear across the board, it's easier being single" and that "they are losing the image of being life's lonely losers" (Newsweek, 1978: 76). In confirmation of this claim, a study by the Institute for Social Research (ISR Newsletter, 1979: 4) finds that marriage and parenthood are no longer viewed as necessary and that "people who do not choose those roles are no longer considered as social deviants." *Newsweek* (1973: 52) concludes that "singlehood has emerged as an intensely ritualized — and newly respectable — style of life."

The causes for the increase in numbers and new perceptions of singles are obviously complex. They are being explored at length by many social scientists and historians. Suffice it to say, for purposes of this study, that for complex reasons economic opportunities for singles, especially single women, have increased, and this increase has probably contributed to the development of the singles community. This growing community has been providing support and developing ideology for those who are considering remaining or becoming single.

This emergence of social and ideological support has led to singlehood's emergence as a viable and positive alternative to marriage (Libby, 1978: 165); that is, the postponement of marriage and childbearing by women at least appears to be part of a trend toward choosing alternatives to marriage — alternatives that may be preferred (Glick, 1975: 17). In sum, it is claimed that singlehood can provide a situation conducive to human growth and self-fulfillment, with marriage no longer necessary for emotional support, an active social life, or sex (Stein, 1976: 78-79).

A Comparative Study of Singles and Marrieds

CONTEXT OF THE STUDY

Actually, the statistics on singles are in a sense misleading. True, singles are increasing, but only if they are compared to what is considered the norm — the 1950s. As Skolnick and Skolnick (1977: 8) note, current demographic trends are regarded as an exception and "by implication, the family patterns of the fifties with their seeming stability and tranquility are taken as the normal state. In reality, the so-called radical ideas of the late 20th century recapitulated an earlier ferment surrounding women's rights, male and female sex roles, sexuality and the relations between the individual, the family and society." The depression and World War II interrupted these trends and led to the era of the fifties, with the emphasis on family togetherness, the baby boom, and the increased domesticity of women. It would appear, then, that the so-called norm perpetuated by the period of the fifties was a direct product of a special set of demographic, economic, and historical circumstances, and not the norm at all.

Though there is considerable reason to believe that the 1950s represent an anomalous period in the century, nevertheless the changes from that period are what we currently perceive. Since there is a natural lag between each step of the gradual development of awareness, the formation of hypotheses about that awareness, and the testing of these hypotheses, it is not surprising that social scientists really began to focus on the problem only in the 1970s. In the 1960s family sociologists "either ignored singles or relegated them to boring, out-of-date discussions of dating" (Libby, 1978: 164). Even in the seventies "they seemed to deny that change was possible in family structure, the relations between the sexes, and parenthood" (Skolnick and Skolnick, 1977: 3). Even now, it is difficult to classify singles as a category. Are they a subject for family studies, a transient category either waiting to get married or between marriages, or are they a subject for minority studies?

In any event, until recently singles have not been perceived as a distinct social entity "that has its own characteristics, dynamics and unique features" (Adams, 1976: 10). Where they have been perceived as such they often have been stoutly defended, usually by advocates from the singles community who draw support from personal experience. But only toward the end of the seventies do we begin to find studies that are designated to test whether singles are undesirable, lonely, or incomplete. And even these studies tend to be tentative, often with skewed samples drawn by family sociologists from their own students. And while such studies begin to measure attributes of singles, many still do not have control categories of marrieds with which to compare. So even if we find that a category of singles do have fun or are not lonely, we cannot tell whether they have more fun or are less lonely than marrieds. And, by the way, similar studies of marrieds usually do not make use of control categories of singles.

With serious study of singles only beginning, the negative stereotypes remain dominant, with consequences of serious and often unperceived discrimination. Because they are perceived to require less income, they pay a higher share of our nation's taxes. Because they are perceived to be immature, they have more difficulty obtaining home mortgages. Because they are perceived to be unstable or odd, they lose out to marrieds in seeking organizational promotions.

The stereotypes must be investigated. We need to find out if single people are really unstable, immature, poor risks, and, at the same time, better off when compared with marrieds. We need to find out if they are really selfish and uninterested in others. Do their outlooks mean they are lonely because of their aloneness, or are they happier with their fewer obligations? Are there factors in their family backgrounds that led to their choice of singleness, or is it a viable lifestyle, freely chosen, an alternative means of fulfilling personal goals? Are single people deviants, or are they normal?

HOW THE STUDY WAS CONDUCTED

In order to answer these questions, it was clear that we needed to get out of the classroom, out of the university, and into American society, but we felt there had not been sufficient comparative research to justify a national study. We were lucky enough to be near the city of Dayton, a metropolitan area considered by George Gallup to be one of the ten typical areas in the nation. He has referred to this area as "a barometer for the nation" (Dayton Journal-Herald, 1976: 1).

A probability proportionate to size (PPS) sample of 400 households was drawn from the Dayton metropolitan area, which consists of the eastern two-thirds of Montgomery County and the urbanized western areas of Green County in Ohio. After determining the total number of households in the sample area, the number was divided by 80 in order to determine an interval number. Selecting a random number between 1 and the interval number allowed for a random starting point. Using 1970 census data allowed for the selection of a block area in a census tract utilizing the above random starting number and adding the interval number until all 80 blocks were selected. Starting with another randomly selected number, 5 households were interviewed in each block. Based on previously determined randomized order, an adult male or female was interviewed. "Not-homes" and refusals were replaced by similarly randomly drawn households in the same block area. In this manner the desired 400 interviews were conducted. In order to avoid interviewer bias, the questionnaire was designed to be self-administered, and so consisted of 77 mostly closed-ended items (see Appendix I). Questionnaire administrators were present while the questionnaire was being answered in order to answer questions and as a means of dealing with the selected response of a mailed questionnaire. To ensure the probable inclusion of all segments of the population, all interviews were conducted in the evening or on weekends. Pretesting for validity and reliability was conducted with a group drawn from Interaction, a large singles organization in Dayton.

Once our sample data were in, we found it useful to make some subdivisions of categories. We already had divided singles into three categories: the never married, the divorced, and the widowed. It turned out, however, that the widowed constituted too small a percentage of our responses, and they had to be deleted. So, while the widowed are referred to in our historical chapters, they are not included in our contemporary study.

Having two categories of singles left, the never married and the divorced, we became aware that there were two parallel categories among the married: the once married and the remarried. When they change status, singles marry and the divorced remarry. Or to put it the other way, the married are the formerly single, the remarried are usually the formerly divorced (less frequently the formerly widowed). The breakdown reveals that 29 percent of the sample were never married (114), 9 percent were divorced (37), 55 percent were married once (205), and 11 percent were remarried (44; see Appendix II).

This breakdown gave us more flexibility, for sometimes we found that apparent differences between marrieds and singles turned out to be differences between the divorced and all the other categories. And, less frequently, distinctions could be made that cut across categories, so that never marrieds might be found to be more like once marrieds, while the divorced were more like the remarried.

While this questionnaire was being distributed, collected, and codified, we thought we would try to learn something about our present situation in relation to the past. So we explored the census data throughout the century and followed that with a thematic study of popular magazine articles over the same period, first comparing titles, then working out a thematic analysis of selected articles. The historical study does not go very deep, since it was intended only as a contextual backdrop for our current comparative study.

When our data had been codified via several independent variables and tested for significance with chi square, we encountered another question: Why had singles responded as they had? We needed some comments, some explanations, but our area sample had been anonymous, so we could not recover the singles who had filled out the original questionnaire.

So another set of questionnaires was mailed to the attendees of Interaction. The large response we received — almost 40 percent of the participants, 603 responses in all — provided support for our belief that singles have been a relatively ignored segment of the population; as many of the respondents noted, this was the first time that anybody had paid attention to them as singles, and they thanked us for this opportunity to respond to the questionnaire. Finally, we spent an evening with about 20 participants of this group in order to explore some of our findings in more detail with direct comments.

These additional data gave us a greater feel for the beliefs, feelings, and activities of singles since their statistical representation in the sample was based on their population numbers and consequently was not large. It also gave us some information on whether such an organization designed for singles helped them cope with their needs and problems. Would members of Interaction be happier, less lonely, think less about suicide, or be less inclined to get drunk than singles from our metropolitan study?

THEORETICAL CONSIDERATIONS

It was not our intention to develop an overall theoretical formulation about why people have chosen to remain single or to return to singlehood despite the apparent difficulties of resisting a societal norm. Our interest lay in testing the stereotypes and, in so doing, developing a description of singles, as compared with marrieds, that would reveal whether such stereotypes are wholly, partially, or not at all valid. It was expected that this approach would uncover areas of discrimination, and that the needs of singles as compared with marrieds would be better understood. While theoretical matters are left for discussion as they relate to particular topics in subsequent chapters, our guiding principle in formulating this study was the null hypothesis that the singles advocates would prove to be correct, and that there would be little difference between singles and marrieds. We expected that singles would prove to be no more deviant than the marrieds, that they would be as mature and as happy but no freer, richer, or more fanatical in their work. It was our expectation that most or all of the images about singles would prove to be myths, not realities.

Our plan for presentation of the data is simple. This part, of course, introduces the problem. Part II presents the historical contexts. Part III focuses on comparative lifestyles — do singles live differently from marrieds? Part IV is concerned with attitudes — do singles feel and perceive differently? Part V concludes by returning to the myths and realities — is the hypothesis correct? Are the stereotypes myths? Not to keep you in suspense: some are, some are not.

At a given point in history, it no longer may be necessary for a society to encourage its members to marry and procreate. But change is slow, and societies continue to hold on to comfortable but perhaps archaic beliefs. As noted, the single woman no longer has to prove herself by getting married; she no longer has to mark time at some economic way station; the single male no longer needs a wife to make his clothes and cook his meals; he no longer has to marry to meet his sexual needs. The options available as the result of greater economic opportunity, greater sexual freedom, and the women's (as well as other) rights movements may mean significant changes in American society. In short, singles of all lifestyles have begun the fight for the right to equal consideration. The result may be that some tomorrow the stigma will be removed from nonmarital cohabitation or homosexual unions, and the single will no longer be considered deviant by a society believing that all must marry. The ripples in the stream have begun and the result will be a changed social structure. Whether the change will be for the better or the worse, it is too early to tell; but as a means of making this determination, more information is needed on a scientific basis — hence this study.

PART II

American Singles Through the Century

Chapter 2

THE INCREASE IN SINGLES: 1960-1979

The Fall and Rise of Singles

Sheer numbers are important in terms of markets and available aggregates from which communities and associations might be drawn, but if you are trying to ascertain trends it is also necessary to consider percentages of population. When this is done, it is apparent that the percentage of singles had been falling throughout the century until 1960, and that even in 1979 the percentage of singles in the country had not recouped — it was still lower than it had been at any period before World War II (Table 2.1; all tables appear, numbered by chapter, in the "Tables" section). However, 2 assertions that appear frequently in articles about singles — that there are more singles in America than ever before, and that singles are a growing population — appear to be true. In 1979, the population of 68 million singles aged 14 or over was the highest in American history. Moreover, this population had increased by 27 million, nearly 70 percent, in the sixties and seventies (Figure 2.1; Table 2.4). Thus our perception that there are more singles around is borne out by the national statistics.

There are 2 periods of time that stand out in this first examination of the census data: a long drop in the percentage of singles from 46 percent to 32 percent between 1900 and 1960, and an apparent reversal of the trend (from 32 percent to 40 percent) between 1960 and 1979. Since this upward period has been the first such period in the century and, therefore, the first within the memory of most of us, we need to ask whether this

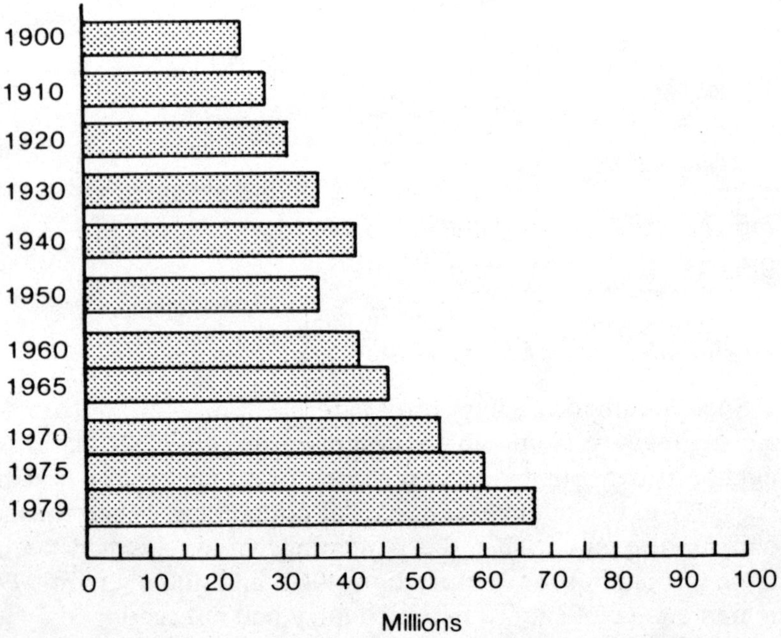

Figure 2.1 Number of Singles (in Millions) 1900-1979

Except for the years following World War II, the number of singles in the United States has been rising each decade.

2-decade increase represents an anomalous period in our social history or the early phase of a long-term trend destined to reverse the pattern of the first half of the century.

To say that singles have increased by 27 million in 2 decades does not tell us much. What we need to know is to what extent this increase is attributable to changes in outlook and lifestyle among the singles and to what extent the increase simply reflects an increase in population.

One simple answer is to consider singles, as a whole, as a percentage of population. At the 1960 level they constituted 32.7 percent of the population. By 1979, that figure had risen to 40 percent (Table 2.1). If the proportions had remained at the 1960 level, what would have been the increase in the singles population? It turns out that it would have been something over

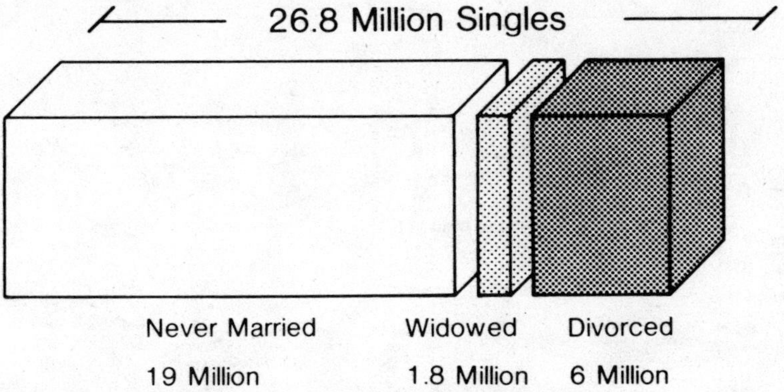

Figure 2.2 Increases in Singles (in Millions) 1960-1979
The largest increase in singles since 1960 has been in the never married.

14 million. Since the total increase was actually almost 27 million, it would appear that an increase of almost 13 million singles must be explained by reasons other than population increase.

But that is the simple answer. A more complete picture is provided by dividing the data on singles into the three subcategories used by the Census Bureau: the never married (called "single" by the Census Bureau), the widowed, and the divorced. We might expect that a greater percentage are remaining unmarried, since other options are opening up for singles; that, since people are living longer, there ought to be a higher percentage of widows and widowers; and, most strikingly, the percentage of divorced should be increasing since the divorce rate has been rising rapidly.

Are the Never Married Really Not-Yet Married?

Why did the percentage of never married increase between 1960 and 1979 after the long period of decline? One obvious reason would be an increase in the percentage of young people — those in the 14-24 age category — since a large percentage of

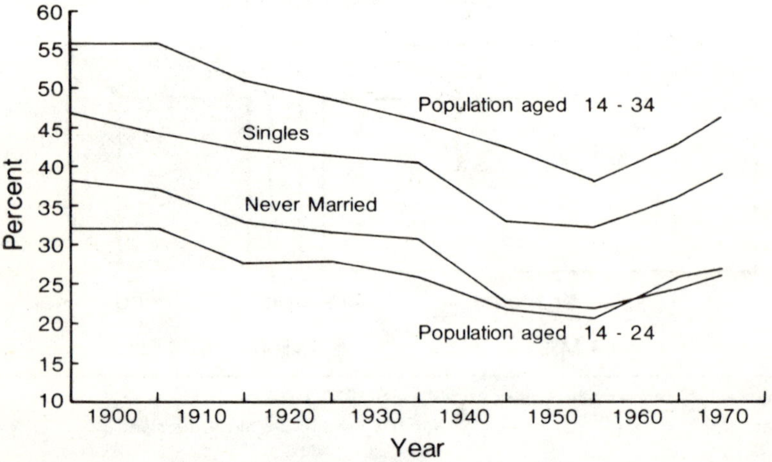

Figure 2.3 Percentage of Young and Single

The percentage of young and the percentage of singles seem to have followed similar patterns during the century.

that category, always well over half, is unmarried in any decade. And since there was a baby boom in the late forties and early fifties, it is not surprising that there was an increase in the percentage of young adults in the sixties and seventies (see Figure 2.2).

Table 2.3 confirms this speculation. The percentage of young adults, whether calculated as aged 14-24 or 14-34, has been increasing since 1960. In fact, as Figure 2.3 shows, there has been a similarity between the number of never marrieds and youth curves: all falling from 1900 and rising from 1960 on.

The increase in never marrieds between 1960 and 1979 was just under 19 million. The increase in never-married 14-24 year olds was just over 16 million. It would appear that most of the increase in never marrieds can be accounted for by the increase in the young who have not yet married.

It would seem, however, that not all of the 16-million increase in never marrieds under 24 years of age should be attributed to population. In 1960, about 72 percent of the 14-24 age bracket were unmarried. By 1979, that figure had risen to 73.7 percent (calculated from Table 2.4). If the propensity to remain single until 24 had remained at 72 percent, the increase in never-married singles would have been only 13.1 million. So the remaining 2.9 million should be attributed to a change in propensity that may have to do with outlook or lifestyle. Another 3 million, the difference between the total increase in never marrieds and the increase in those under 24, also cannot be accounted for by mere population increase. So a total of 5.9 million of the 19-million increase in the never marrieds (31 percent) must be attributed to something other than demographic factors (Table 2.5).

From a demographic viewpoint, the increase in the never-married population is for the most part the reflection of an increase in the young adult population. This increase in never marrieds is likely to be temporary, the result of the sharp increase in the birthrate in the 15 years following World War II. The declining birthrate of the 1970s may be expected to bring a reversal in the pattern of increase in young population and with it a similar pattern for never marrieds. In fact, by 1979 the percentage of 14-24 year olds and even 14-34 year olds had begun to decline.

Many Are Divorced, but There Are Not Many Divorced

The figures on divorce are confusing. On one hand, there has been a continuous increase, with spurts between 1910 and 1930, 1940 and 1950, and 1970 and 1980. The increase in the percentage divorced between 1960 and 1979 was more than 200 percent! If that rate were to continue, we should have 80 million divorced by the year 2020 and 240 million by 2040 — more than the anticipated total adult population. Such are the dangers of giving sociologists calculators.

On the other hand, the divorced remain the smallest of the 3 singles categories. In 1979 there were 50 percent more widowed than divorced in the country. Throughout the twentieth century the divorced have constituted less than 5 percent of the population. In a room containing 20 adults, only 1 is likely to be currently divorced.

Of the divorced population we do have, however, how much of the increase can be attributed to general population increase and how much to changes in mores? We calculated this for the never married by considering the change in ratio between the never married and the total of 14-24 year olds. There is no such meaningful comparison for the divorced, but we might consider the change in percentage of divorced in relation to the total population. Table 2.4 shows an increase of 3.7 million in the divorced population between 1960 and 1979 and an increase in the percentage of divorced in the country from 2.3 percent to 5.2 percent. If the percentage of total population divorced had remained at the 1960 level of 2.3 percent, the increase would have been only a little over a million. The rest of the increase, nearly 5 million, must be attributable to factors other than population. So, unlike the increase in the never married, most of the increase in the divorced population is *not* attributable to population (Tables 2.2 and 2.5). In other words, part of the increase in numbers is attributable to increase in population, but most of it is attributable to other factors that might consist in part or largely of change in attitude toward divorce.

The never married constitute more than two-thirds of the singles population and more than two-thirds of the increase in singles between 1960 and 1975 (Table 2.2; Figure 2.1). The divorced constitute a little more than one-eighth of the singles population and account for less than a quarter of the increase in numbers of singles between 1960 and 1975. But, if you are considering the increase in numbers attributable to factors other than population increase, that is, changes in lifestyle and outlook, then divorce becomes more important. For while an increase of 5.5 million never marrieds can be accounted for because of changes in mores (outlook and lifestyle), the increase in divorced for these reasons is almost as great and less dependent on population factors. It would not be surprising, therefore, to find the divorced playing a greater role in the singles movement than their overall numbers would seem to justify.

The Waning of Widowhood

Our expectation that longer life would mean an increase in widowhood is not supported by the data. In the long haul, the widowed have constituted a stable percentage of the population. From 1900 through 1979, there were never as few as 7 percent of the population widowed, and never has many as 9 percent. In 1900 there were 7.6 percent widowed; in 1979, 7.3 percent (Table 2.1).

Between 1960 and 1979, however, there was a decline in percentage widowed from 8.4 percent to 7.3 percent, even though there was an increase of 1.8 million in the total number. Using the same reasoning on widowed as we did on divorced, if the percentage of widowed had remained at 8.4 percent, as it was in 1960, the widowed population in 1979 would have been 14.2 million, which is 1.5 million greater than it actually was (Table 2.5).

Why this should be is difficult to guess. Since 1930 there has been a change in the ratio of men to women widowed from 30 percent men in 1930 (just about the same as 1900) to 15 percent in 1975. In the same period there has been a change in the ratio of women to men in the total population from 49 percent to 52 percent. So it would seem as though women are outliving men by a greater number of years, and therefore the percentage of widowed ought to be increasing. Possibly the answer here is the same as it is on the comparatively low number of divorced people compared to the high rate of divorced. Men are venturing more quickly into remarriage. However that may be, the 1979 percentage of widowed is closer to the norm, for the percentage of widowed hovered around 7.5 percent until 1960, rose above 8.5 percent by 1965, then subsided to 7.3 percent by 1979 (Table 2.4).

Demography or Mores?

The results of this demographic survey, then, indicate that population increase is responsible for about two-thirds of the increase in singles in the 1960s and 1970s; changes in outlooks, mores, or other factors account for only one-third of the increase (Table 2.5). Of the singles whose status may be attributed to outlook, more than half can be accounted for by the smallest category of the singles — the divorced. This may be why the divorced play such a strong role in changing the image of singles. It also could be a factor explaining why the divorced, as we shall see in the next chapter, continue to attract much more attention than the never married or the widowed in the popular press.

Finally, it does not appear that singles will continue to grow as a percentage of our total population. We have seen that there already has been a turndown in the percentage of 14-24 year olds between 1975 and 1979. Unless there is a radical change in past patterns, a decline in percentage of the never married should follow in the 1980s. The percentage of widowed is already declining. Further increases in the number of singles would have to depend on continued increase in the percentage of divorced. But divorce, in turn, depends for its source of replenishment on marriage, which depletes the ranks of the never married, a balancing act that is unlikely to increase the percentage of singles.

The major reason for the increase in singles was increasing population, not changing values. The stabilization of population growth in the sixties and seventies is likely to lead to a decline in the percentage and even the number of singles in the eighties and nineties.

Figures and Tables

The figures in this chapter are drawn from the tables. The tables are drawn from the United States Bureau of the Census's *Current Population Reports: Population Characteristics, Marital Status and Family Status: March 1965, Marital Status and Living Arrangements: March 1975, Population Profile of the United States: 1975,* and *Marital Status and Living Arrangements: March 1979,* as well as from the Census Bureau's *Historical Statistics of the United States: Colonial Times to 1970.* The figures include Americans aged 14 and over.

Chapter 3

CHANGES IN AWARENESS: 1900-1975

Goodbye to "Spinsters"

If there has been a distinct increase in the number of singles in the past 15 years, what would be the expected impact on society? With more singles about, the first expectation might be that there would be an increase in perception of the problems, needs, and markets involving the adolescent and the young adult. That the young are also single would be taken for granted. In fact, the transition to marriage is a normal problem confronted by people aged 14 to 24.

That there had been more singles in the past would not generally be realized. In the long period of decline in the percentage of singles (1900-1960), what would have been noticed would have been the increase in percentage of married people, and the problems, needs, and markets involved in that increase.

As for the divorced, one would expect that the tremendous percentage of increase in this category would draw attention, perhaps disproportionate attention, so that there would be a good deal written about it from 1910 on, when the increase first began to take place. But perhaps even more attention would have been paid to divorce in recent years, when the numbers involved would begin to be more noticeable in relation to the total population.

These expectations can be noted by mere observation. Obviously, there is a great deal of attention being paid to singles these days. There are singles organizations, articles about discrimination against singles in large economy sizes and in family season tickets, and much discussion about the transition to widowhood and the problems of the divorced, particularly divorced parents. But how much of this attention and concern is new? Is it really greater than it was in the past? And has the discussion matured, or is it merely another generation debating the same old question?

One means for investigating these questions is to review the titles in the *Readers' Guide to Periodical Literature* since 1900. These can be counted to get a quantitative picture of the changes that have occurred and qualitatively evaluated in order to assess the nature of change.

The advantages of this method are that the period covered is the same as that covered by the census statistics and that the *Readers' Guide* has covered popular publications, thus giving a better measure of popular rather than academic response to awareness. The disadvantages are that this approach does not take into consideration the switch in public attention from magazines to television and, of course, it does not provide quantitative statistics as reassuring as those provided by census data.

In undertaking to review the titles, a problem soon encountered was that over time the perceptions of the *Readers' Guide* editors changed, so that the topical headings presented were not entirely consistent. The most striking change was in the appearance of the concept of Singles, replacing the earlier classification of Bachelors and Spinsters. Bachelors was still the main category for single men as recently as 1965, while Spinsters was still in use in 1960. The current categories for never married are Single Men, Single Women, and Single People. In addition, two new categories appeared in the 1971-1975 period: Cohabitation and Single-Parent Families (which includes a 1975 category of Single Mothers).

The listing for Widowhood was easier, usually involving the category of Widows, with occasional reference to Widowhood and Widowers.

Divorce was a principal category in the *Readers' Guide* throughout the 75-year period. An interesting addition, beginning in the 1971-1975 period, is the category of Children of the Divorced. There were 18 articles in this category since 1950 (16 since 1970) and none before 1950. This, however, is probably a function of a change in indexing analogous to the change from Spinsters to Single Women. The articles on the subject were probably found under Divorce until the subject was perceived to be important enough to rate a subtopic of its own. It seems likely that the increase in divorce is the important factor here, since this increase led to more children being involved in divorce.

Increasing Interest in Singles

Table 3.1 indicates changes in attention paid to singles during the century. Initially we might be surprised at the great attention given to divorce as compared to the never married, especially when we realize that there have been far more of the latter to buy the magazines throughout the century. The collective editors' judgment, however, may have been reasonable. A considerable percentage of the articles on the never married were about how to get married, while a considerable percentage of the divorce articles were about how to get a divorce, or to put it from our perspective, how to become single. Thus many of the divorce articles were for the married, always a larger market than the singles.

In any event, interest in both the never married and the divorced quickened in the years 1966-1975 when compared to the previous ten years. Articles on the never married were up 178 percent; articles on the divorced increased by 119 percent (Figure 3.1). Since this was occurring in a period in which some popular magazines, such as *Look,* were being wiped out by television, there seems to be plenty of confirmation that a general awareness of singles was increasing. The percentage of widowed remained fairly constant in this period, and so did the number of articles about widowhood (an increase of 20 percent).

A longer-range glance at 5-year periods in each decade reveals that the category of never married received much more attention in the 1970s period than it had in any of the earlier

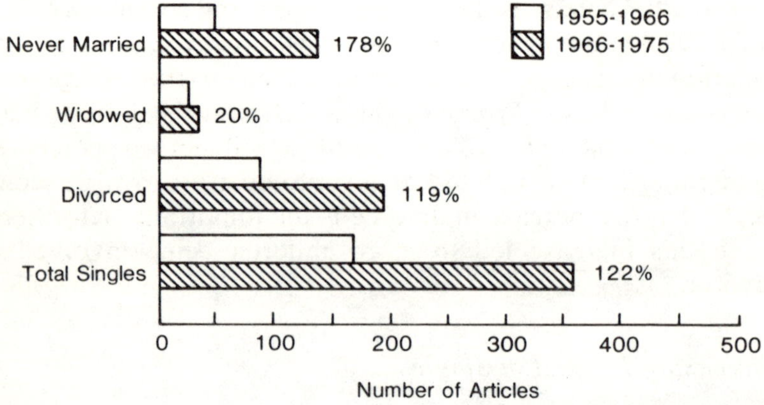

Figure 3.1 Increase in Articles About Singles: 1955-1966 Versus 1966-1975
Based on the number of magazine articles published, interest in singles has increased greatly in recent years.

periods, including those between 1900 and 1940, when the actual percentage of never married was considerably higher than it was in the 1970s. Utilizing 5-year periods, the average between 1900 and 1950 was 9 articles, as compared to an average of 23 for the 1950-1970 period, and 79 for the 1970s. Interest had more than doubled in the 2 post-World War II decades and more than tripled again in the 1970s (Table 3.1).

On widowhood, there was an average of 4 articles in the pre-World War II decade periods examined and an average of 15 in the postwar years, indicating a tripling of interest even though there was no corresponding increase in the percentage of widows and widowers.

The figures on divorce are somewhat surprising for the immediate postwar years. The number of articles devoted to divorce has not kept up with the increased percentages of divorce; the increase in articles in the 1970s was less than double the number of those appearing in any of the decades in the 1910-1940 period. Apparently as divorce became more acceptable there was less need to write about it.

Turning to the specific topics reveals that there has been a discernible change in emphasis. Generally, it appears, the perception of old maids and swinging bachelors has been dropped, to be replaced with a variety of articles on singles' lives. Perceptions of difficulties also seem to have declined, with more emphasis on ordinary coping. But there is still much concern about whether singles are happy or not (with an edge both before and after 1950 to the conclusion that they are not) and the need to "defend" single status still persists. That it is okay to be single is still not taken for granted. As for sex problems of singles, that has become an acceptable subject of popular journalism only since 1950 (Table 3.2).

Two absences are worth noting. The large increase in numbers and percentage of singles from 1960 to 1975 seems not be a major subject in itself. There were only two demographic articles, both in the seventies. And there was only one article (in the fifties) on cause: Why do people marry or remain single? These two absences are related: Since there is little awareness of demographic changes, there would hardly be much inquiry into why a greater percentage of individuals are remaining single.

Mate Finding in America

Despite the increasing interest in singles and the decline in marriage rates, there is more attention than ever paid to getting married; for example, articles on how to make yourself more attractive or how to meet potential mates. There were 34 articles of this kind from 1950 to 1975, only 9 in the 50 years preceding.

Titles about mate finding (Table 3.3) suggest that the subject and emphasis has not changed much in recent decades. The great majority of these were and are written for women.

While the singles population was still declining (1950-1960) there was already an increase in aggressive approaches to marriage, particularly among women: "My Mother Said I Should Give It a Try . . ." Before 1951 there had been no such articles except for sporadic advice on how to be approachable. And there were hardly any articles about how to meet women, a problem that many men regard as the most important of all.

(Such articles can be found, but they do not approach the subject as a problem of singles, only as a problem of the young: How do "men" meet "girls"?)

Before 1940, there were hardly any articles that were openly concerned with actively taking steps toward ensuring that one find a husband, and only occasional titles, such as "Why They Won't Marry the Modern Girl" (1921), that suggest that one might, by altering conduct or attitude, increase one's chances of being approached.

What is suggested by more recent titles is a trend toward encouraging feminine initiative ("Where to Find Men"), which is more a measure of women's growing interest in independence and equality than a change in perception of singles per se.

Making the Best of Being Single

Let us consider next the set of titles that have to do with accepting and finding happiness in the life of the single. These might be combined under some such heading as "Making the Best of It," again emphasizing the idea that singleness is not a very desirable state (Table 3.4).

There are certainly some common and repeated notes sounded in this series, but still some changes to be noted in recent years. The defenses and pleas and plaints of the unmarried, "In Defense of Spinsters" or "Why I am an Old Maid," disappear. Instead, the emphasis switches to the degree of happiness to be found in the single's status. In recent years the theme emerges that singleness is less to be defended or lamented than to be analyzed. Earlier articles on happiness include "compensations" or are phrased negatively: "Does it Hurt to Be an Old Maid?" But in the sixties the titles became less defensive: "Pleasures and Pain of the Single Life" or "When Being Single Stops Being Fun." There are more titles emphasizing the positive side of single life ("Blessings of Bachelorhood," "Happy Lot of Spinsters," "Celebrating Singleness") though bitterness and sadness appear in every period: "Necessary Melancholy . . . ," "Sorrowful Mayden . . . ," "How to Be Human Though Single," "Movin' on —

Alone." The twin themes of loneliness and unhappiness persist through the century.

Daily Life Among American Singles

Finally, there is a set of titles dealing with the concerns of daily living. These include housing, work, money, love, friendship, sex, and a little side advice to marrieds. They take problems such as greater difficulty in getting a loan as facts of life, not as problems for social reform (Table 3.5). In fact, before 1966 there does not seem to be a single article on a specific subject relating to single people that is neutral in tone. "How to Travel Alone," for instance, would be a neutral title, but "How to Travel Alone and Like It" assumes that traveling alone would normally be unpleasant unless one takes special measures. Neutral articles before the middle 1960s tend to be either very general ("Life of a Bachelor") or about other countries or cultures ("Taxing German Bachelors").

Only after the middle 1960s do you find pragmatic discussions on birth control ("Should Doctors Prescribe Contraceptives for Unmarried Ladies?"), housing ("Boys and Girls Together: Apartments for Singles Only"), financial problems ("Life Insurance for Single Women"), or institutions ("Church and the Single Person"). There is a particular increase in interest in the sexual problems of singles as separate from finding a spouse ("Sex as Athletics in the Singles Complex"). And there are the beginnings of articles for marrieds by singles ("Serving Singles — Don't Play Mix and Match").

But even in the seventies this acceptance seems fragile. There are still more articles with overtones implying defense, strenuously urging singles to perceive how well off they are, or suggesting yet newer ways of finding a person to marry. The acceptance of singlehood and marriage as normal alternative choices, no different from choosing whether to live in the city or the suburbs or whether to seek a career in business or government, is an ideal that may in time come to be accepted. But that time has not yet arrived.

The Library
Saint Francis College
Fort Wayne, Indiana 46808

Figures and Tables

Figure 3.1 was drawn from Table 3.1. The sources for the tables were *Readers' Guide to Periodical Literature,* Volumes 1-36, H. W. Wilson Company, and *Cumulative Index to Periodical Literature,* March 1959-February 1970, National Library Service, 1976.

Chapter 4

BEHIND THE TITLES: A THEMATIC REVIEW

Fourteen Themes

Reading the titles presented in the previous chapter makes you wonder about the content. We decided to make a thematic analysis of three articles from the 1970s about the life of singles, and then to compare them to three articles chosen from the 1950s. The comparison was then extended back to the 1930s and the World War I period. When we got back to the thirties and before, however, we found that articles on the single life were written exclusively by and about single women, so just one article was taken from each of these periods. It should be noted that, while the writers reflect their times, they are also unique, individual personalities, and some of their differences are attributable to this, rather than to the cultural stresses of the times.

A total of eight themes were discerned in the 1970s period, and six more themes were found in earlier periods. These themes are listed below; the first eight are those of the seventies:

(1) The normality of marriage.

(2) The variety of singles.

(3) Changes in the image of singles.

(4) Money.

(5) Loneliness.

(6) Freedom and responsibility.

(7) Attitudes toward singles.
(8) Security.
(9) Home relations.
(10) Why am I single?
(11) Sexual problems.
(12) How to fill time.
(13) Immortality problems: How is my name to live?
(14) How are women to relate to men?

The articles analyzed were picked from a variety of magazines, with an eye toward generality in the title. For example, articles about singles or spinsters in general were chosen over articles about buying a house or finding a husband. This approach is subjective and impressionistic, but does reveal the major themes and variety of subject matter.

Singles in the Seventies

Representative articles from the 1970s were: "49 Million Singles Can't All Be Right," by Susan Jacoby (1974; the author has twice been single); "For Singles, Life Isn't All 'Swinging'" (U.S. News and World Report, 1975); and "Celebrate Singleness — Marriage May Be Second Best" (Christianity Today, 1976).

In these articles the first eight themes are given substantial stress:

(1) The normality of marriage should be reconsidered. Parents ought to teach that marriage is one option and remaining single another, and that both are normal, each having advantages and disadvantages.

(2) There is a wide variety of singles. It is impossible to categorize them. Single parents with children or cohabiting couples are more like marrieds (which presumes that you can categorize marrieds), while young bachelors and old widows are very different from each other and from marrieds.

(3) There has been a tremendous change in the image of singles in the early 1970s. In the late sixties they were perceived as lonely and unfortunate; now they are seen as swinging and enviable.

(4) Singles are likely to be free and happy if they are rich. But if not, singles, particularly the young and women, are likely to have money worries that very much inhibit freedom.

(5) Singles still worry about and discuss the problem of loneliness. Susan Jacoby (1974) describes it as the "great bugaboo."

(6) There is also a great deal of emphasis on freedom apart from problems of money and loneliness. Do you "buy or rent, travel or save, change jobs, buy stocks, join clubs?" These choices are less likely to be subjects of conversation for marrieds (or singles with children, cohabiting singles, or the divorced).

(7) There is an awareness of a wide array of discrimination against singles, for example, in rent discrimination and corporate prejudice. On the other hand, there may be a corporate prejudice in favor of women perceived to be unmarried and past marriageable age.

(8) Women worry, and perhaps men do too, about safety and security. Are their apartments safe? Can they get to them safely? It can be scary to be alone every night.

The Fifties: Singles Were Second Best

Three articles were chosen from the fifties: "How to be Human Though Single," by Annie Laurie Von Tungelin (1955); "The Blessings of Bachelorhood" by Grey Villet (1959); and an article on the single life from the male viewpoint called "Feature X" (America, 1958). It should be added that in the 1950s there was a preponderance of articles about the lives of single women by single women.

Again, reviewing the basic themes:

(1) The normality of marriage is taken for granted. It is presumed that bachelorhood is temporary, that a "right girl"

will be found, that the bachelor is "prey" for presumably "wrong" girls. Single women find singleness a close second best if properly handled. The single man accepts the normality of marriage, but some people have the gift of being single.

(2) The only statement on the variety of singles is a Catholic classification that would look very odd in the 1970s: Singles could include Catholics married to non-Catholics; marrieds should include the divorced.

(3) The perception that the image of singles is changing is strong in the article by the woman. The "stigma" of being single is disappearing; it is now all right for women to work and a variety of possibilities are opened to them that had not been in the past.

(4) The only money problem perceived is higher taxes, and this is taken as a given, not as a cause or a grievance.

(5) The problem of loneliness is perceived as important by everyone. The bachelor feels that all problems boil down to loneliness. The single man feels that the need for companionship is a problem for every human. The spinster has a number of suggestions, such as keeping in touch with the young and having interests that would bring contacts. The problem of a lonely old age is also considered.

(6) The freedom motif is stressed by all: greater mobility, freedom to switch jobs, move fast, do as you please, live with fewer compromises, stay up late, and cook and dress as you wish.

(7) References to discrimination are soft-pedaled, though the single woman is aware of condescension or pity from married friends.

(8) Security is not perceived as a problem.

Then there are categories that did not appear in the articles from the seventies:

(9) The bachelor retains "home" relations, meaning he visits and takes laundry to the house of his parents.

(10) From the single man there is a set of explanations of why people are single that was absent from the seventies articles. The reasons include religion, bad luck, illness, military

service, prison, selfishness, lack of maturity, and dedication to parents.

(11) The problem of sexual frustration, absent from the seventies articles, is mentioned by the single man only to be dismissed as no different from that of marrieds who have enough children — a conclusion not likely to be found in the seventies.

(12) There is one reference by the woman to filling time, keeping busy, that had not appeared anywhere else.

(13) The mortality problem also bothers the woman: Since a single woman's name and being will not be carried by her descendants, she must do things herself that will have a lasting impact.

A Spinster in the Thirties

Back in the thirties, articles about singles were thinner, and a substantial majority were about the problems of the single woman, or spinster, as she was then known. The representative article chosen was "A Spinster I," (Anonymous, 1934). The anonymity of the author would seem strange to Annie Laurie Von Tungelin of the fifties, or to Susan Jacoby of the seventies.

(1) The view that marriage is normal is implicit, the author remarking only that it is unusual for a spinster to speak. In that perception, by the way, she is not entirely accurate. "Spinsters" spoke often throughout the century; bachelors, rarely.

(2) There is no explicit perception of a variety of singles, no examples of the problems of single men or the divorced. However, the author does write about single people as a category: Her use of "us" may mean more than unmarried women.

(3) The perception of change in image from the past is just as strong or even stronger than it was to be in later years, despite the anonymity of the article. "At present spinsterhood needs no apology. . . . The very terms of obloquy have almost faded out." The conveniences of the new small apartments eliminate the dinginess of boarding houses and render men "unneces-

sary." Yet she feels that this is not enough and that a more positive image is needed. Singles are invisible; they are not there as a market or a political force—a loss all around: "Just to see an advertisement addressed to us alone would be something." Her problem with identifying "us" may have arisen from lack of a name: "Old maid" she considers outlawed, "maiden lady" outdated (as it must have been, because it does not appear in the later decades), and "spinster" bookish.

(4) She is aware that her inheritance plus her talents in real estate give her an economic position that carries privileges. She considers that she is writing about "a more fortunate class" with enough wealth to be independent.

(5) Loneliness is a problem, but not the central problem. Along the way she mentions childlessness as no more a problem that it is for childless couples, and, as others were to do 20 years later, she refers to and dismisses the possibility of loneliness in old age as being more of a problem for singles than for marrieds.

(6) The freedom theme is as prevalent as it is to be in later years: fredom to eat, sleep, read, celebrate, wear, travel, and spend as one pleases. There is also considerable attention to a freedom to think that is shared by single women and unhappily married wives. But "generally no one thinks less than the contented wife."

(7) These contented wives provided one difficulty in relations with others, since they are hostile and envious toward spinsters. Structurally, too, society is organized in couples, and hostesses have problems finding a vis-à-vis for her. She admits that she herself misses a host at her parties, and that she invites bachelors for balance. However, she has only scorn for professions of pity, whereas 20 years later Von Tungelin (1955) professes amusement.

(8) Security, a problem of the seventies, is not discussed either in the fifties or the thirties.

(9) Home relations are mentioned in two ways. First, she says that her parents had not trained her to be single, only to marry. Second, she had not perceived herself as a spinster,

since she lived at home, until the deaths of both her parents when she was 30.

(10) While she thinks no explanation for not marrying is needed, she gives one: She did not fall in love. She thinks she bears no secret scar, but that her mother was disappointed. The statement is mild, but still there is no comparable statement from the single women of the fifties or seventies.

(11) On sexual inhibition she speaks strongly: Sexual starvation is nonsense. "The world has gone mad on sex." There are doctors "who, if called in by a spinster, would diagnose a broken leg as sex starvation." The women of the fifties and seventies do not mention the subject.

(12) There is no reference to filling time.

(13) The immortality problem is not perceived as such, but there is an open desire for career, position, and prestige, though the author is careful to assert in other places that she is a person of no great importance or education.

(14) The only subject raised here that did not appear in the fifties or seventies is a problem of relating to men. Women associate too often only with women, they cannot talk to men; but she does better than many married women because of business and committee relationships. The problem of opposite-sex relationships existed, of course, in the fifties and seventies, but the problem was not so much how to talk to the opposite sex as how to meet and relate to them without creating problems of jealousy, gossip, or well-meaning intervention from the marrieds.

An Old Maid During World War I

The spinster from two decades further back — the World War I period — is different in many respects from those of later periods. The article is called "Why I Am an Old Maid" (Milton, 1915). The author refers to herself as Marge Milton, but indicates that she is using a pseudonym. She is 45, from Springfield, Illinois.

There is an underlying aura of melancholy about her article. It is the most moving of the articles by women and when she says, toward the end, "I am almost always happy," one is filled with sadness for the evocation.

Reviewing the themes:

(1) Normality of marriage is absolutely taken for granted. The article was written to explain an abnormality, to promote understanding in the reader.

(2) There is no sense of other singles, except that the fate of the bachelor is something other and better. But the focus is solely on the never-married woman.

(3) There is no sense that any change is taking place. The term "old maid" is seen as cruel, but no other is proposed. Yet, economically and educationally, Marge Milton was not inferior to the women who wrote in later periods.

(4) She was an assistant professor at one period and had family money. But she does not perceive that this gives her any advantage.

(5) Loneliness suffuses the article. A marriage proposal that did not come off was never forgotten, always a cause of sorrow. Yet loneliness is not directly addressed as it is by the other women.

(6) Freedom is alluded to, but not valued.

(7) The whole article is a plea for kindness and understanding. Ms. Milton is neither amused by nor scornful of pity. Especially she does not want to be thought odd, while almost acknowledging that she is.

(8) The problem of security is again absent.

(9) Home relations are poignant, first with a disappointed mother, then a sympathetic father needing care, then happy siblings and their children.

(10) Why she is single is the title of the article. The two men who asked, she did not love — the man she loved did not ask. She vowed she would not marry except for love, but the vow seems retrospective.

(11) There is no mention of allusion to sexual inhibition or problems of any kind.

(12) The problem of filling time seems implicit, even though she does interesting, useful work.

(13) There is no immortality problem. She sees her career as useful, she is not a drag on society, but there is nothing positive to be found in her view of her own life.

(14) She is able to have male friends and to relate constructively to them, seems to sense no problems about them as the 1930s spinster does, but is never permitted to tell the man she loved that she loved him. Twenty years later, she still cannot quite write it.

Focusing on never-married women for the earlier periods is not to assume that unmarried men, the widowed, and the divorced did not have similar problems, only that they did not often reach print. It could be that expectations were different for others, so that only for unmarried women could never having a spouse or children overwhelm all other problems.

How the Themes Have Changed

Looking sectionally at our themes, there are some suggested changes in awareness.

(1) the normality of marriage was being challenged in the seventies; in the earlier periods it was not.

(2) Little perception of the variety of people classified as singles — all of those who are not married — appears before the seventies. Before that, bachelors, spinsters, divorced, and widowed are rarely linked in any relationship.

(3) The perception of change of image of at least subcategories of singles, such as single women, was as strong in the fifties and thirties as it was in the seventies, but it was not evident in the sample chosen for the World War I period.

(4) In all periods, the singles focused on were middle-class and not poor. It would appear that singleness, like alienation, is a problem one has time for only when basic subsistence problems are in hand.

(5) The problem of loneliness has been continuous and important for singles all through the century. It was explicitly perceived in the thirties, fifties, and seventies, though less stressed and focused on in the thirties. It was the all-important

implicit problem for Marge Milton in 1915, though she did not identify it as such.

(6) Freedom was perceived as the greatest advantage of singleness in the thirties, fifties, and seventies but little valued by the 1915 writer.

(7) The theme of discrimination and social pressure against singles appears throughout the century, but the stresses vary greatly. In 1915 the focus was on individual callousness toward singles; in the 1930s it was on the difficulties marrieds have in coping with singles; in the 1950s the focus was on condescension of the marrieds; and in the 1970s it was on structural discrimination.

(8) Security seems to be a problem only since the seventies. Before that, there was not the least hint of the idea that it was unsafe to be single.

(9) Home relations seem to become more important the farther back you go. They were absent in the 1970s, at a laundry level in the 1950s, basic in terms of training and socialization in the 1930s, and of poignant importance in 1915.

(10) Explanations for singleness grow in intensity as you go back. They were absent in the seventies, academic in the fifties, downplayed but perhaps rationalized in the thirties, and of crucial importance in the 1915 article.

(11) Problems of sexual inhibition or frustration were not mentioned in the seventies, academically discussed in the fifties, passionately discussed in the thirties, and, again, unmentioned in the 1915 article. Turning that around, and making a speculative, contextual judgment, it appears that sexual inhibition existed in 1915 but was suffused by the more overwhelming problem of loneliness; in the 1930s it was possible to discuss the subject even if the conclusion was that it did not exist; the 1950s discussion, by a man, was more honest and objective; the 1970s absence does not indicate a return to World War I, but an assimilation of the problem into proportion in a more sexually explicit society.

(12) The idea of filling time occurs irregularly; it does not appear to be an important problem for anyone. There was just a

sense in the articles from the 1950s and 1915 that if you did not keep busy, bad feelings would set in. But this relates, perhaps, to general recurrent or even underlying loneliness.

(13) The immortality problem was perceived only in the thirties and fifties. It could be that in an organizational period it has become a general problem, or that our perceptions of family and land have been sufficiently weakened so that it has become no one's problem. It could be that in 1915 it was buried by more overwhelming problems.

(14) The problem of opposite-sex communications was implicitly strong in 1915, explicitly mentioned in 1930, and then seemed to fade out. It seems to follow the pattern of sex relations, but is less intensive. In the 1970s an article by a woman entitled "I Can Sleep with Any Man I Like" might have had a better chance of getting published than an article entitled "I Can Talk to Any Man I Like."

Were the Seventies Different?

The singles of the seventies seemed to take themselves for granted rather more easily than had the singles of earlier periods, even though they constituted a smaller minority than did the singles of the four decades preceding World War II. The most important factor, perhaps, is the explicit identity of singles. Even though they had higher numbers in earlier periods, they did not perceive themselves as a category, so there was little possibility of association and even less of sensitizing the majority to the discriminations that were taking place or to the possibilities of a significant new market.

There are disadvantages, as our deviance theorists have taught us, in the process of labeling. Individual singles of high ability may have lost something, in that the success they may have had anyway may be perceived as coming only because of some kind of compensatory affirmative action. It was not important that James Buchanan was single or that Franklin Roosevelt was handicapped. Today they might be identified as the first single president and the first handicapped president, as

John Kennedy was identified as the first Catholic to hold that office. At a less exalted level, the single who achieves promotion may be perceived to have attained a higher position because he or she is divorced or has never married, that is, because of irrelevant advantages rather than despite irrelevant handicaps.

The singles of the seventies were also different from those of earlier decades in that they were the first to perceive of themselves as normal. That perception is still not widely accepted, even among singles, but it scarcely existed at all in earlier decades.

This change, in turn, made it possible for singles to react more constructively to discrimination. Discrimination had long been perceived, but it always had been an individual problem. One had to learn to accept and cope with it. In the seventies singles were beginning to seek changes, at least to the extent of making proposals that would bring greater social equality.

The disappearance of "home" as the place where one's parents live is another novelty of the seventies. It is true there was one article in the seventies period, listed in the titles but not examined here, that indicated that singles can go home again. But they can go home because it is no longer necessary to prove anything by living away from home. If you get along with your widowed mother and you live in the same town, there is perhaps no reason that you should maintain two households. It is an economic and social choice, no longer a question of psychic independence.

The disappearance of sexual inhibition or frustration themes in the seventies is encouraging. It does not mean that singles do not suffer from sexual frustration — marrieds do too, after all — but that society now permits solutions that would have been impossible in the earlier decades. The social battle is being won; now all the individual has to do is overcome his or her personal legacy of guilt, religion, and fear of inadequacy.

Most refreshing of all is the disappearance of the litany of explanations for singlehood by singles themselves. The writers of the articles we reviewed, at least, no longer felt it necessary to explain how they happened to be past 30 and still single. Whether this acceptance is general among singles, not to mention marrieds, is a question we shall investigate in Part IV.

There is no question that there was a change in the seventies, but there are continuities too. The image that things are changing for singles goes back at least to the thirties. The writers of articles about singles continue to be middle-class in outlook, as, no doubt, are their readers. The advantage of freedom has been perceived by singles throughout the century. It has been considered the number-one advantage of singlehood. And the disadvantage of loneliness, for all the developments of the seventies, continues to constitute as much of a problem as it did in each of the preceding decades. But these stereotypes of singles, like the stereotypes of marriage, will need further investigation.

It does appear, despite these continuities, that singles made considerable progress in the sixties and seventies. Previously unperceived problems have surfaced and been discussed, and some have been resolved to the extent that it is now possible for singles to get on to questions of life. They can discuss loneliness as a confrontable if not resolvable problem, rather than accept it as an inevitable burden. And they can discuss more mundane problems, such as whether to buy a house or a condominium, without first having to argue that they are not sexually inhibited, or insist on how happy they are, or explain how it is that they happen to be single at all.

PART III

Single and Married Lifestyles

Chapter 5

SINGLES AND THEIR PARENTS

Stringers and Swingers

Two images of the single are very common. On one hand, there is the person who is tied to his or her mother's apron strings. On the other, there is the swinger.

There is the man who never could sever the relationship with his mother or whose mother would never let any other woman into his life. There is the woman who never left home, whose parents shielded and protected her until she became too old to marry, or who selfishly kept her at home to look after them in their old age.

In a totally different world is the swinger. As the lascivious bachelor who resisted marriage, his history goes back as far as that of the prim spinster. But in more recent years his image has been polished by the development of such things as the condominium, the stereo, and the pornographic home movie. Moreover, his life has been enriched by the development of a feminine counterpart, the liberated woman who leaves home, supports herself independently, and does God Knows What in her leisure time, if not actually on company time.

These images, while contradictory, are not necessarily incompatible. We have seen that there are a very large number of singles, and that they hardly form a single community. There could be both "stringers" and swingers in great numbers, and their paths need never cross. But will these stereotypes play in Dayton? We didn't think they would.

We devote this chapter to a consideration of the relations between respondents and their parents in order to assess the validity of the silver cord stereotype. Chapter 7 will be concerned with the sex lives of singles as compared to marrieds, and we will attempt to decide whether they are indeed more likely to be swingers. In between, in Chapter 6, we went to take a look at the everyday lives of singles, when they are neither stringing nor swinging. What else do they do after work? What do they do on weekends? In what ways do the everyday lives of singles differ from those of marrieds?

No doubt in many ways the lifestyles of singles are different from those of the married, since family needs may create demands on the time and desires of married people more frequently than they do the singles. On the other hand, marrieds, if they are not both working, can split their tasks, while the single must both work and maintain a home. So it is not certain that singles really have more leisure time to pursue fun and, even if they do, whether that fun necessarily takes the form of greater pursuit of sexual activities.

Remembrance of Things Past

The suspicion that parental relationships may have something to do with marriage choices goes a long way back in the mythology of marital relationships. The most general association is that the parents (or the mother in the case of the male) have been too possessive or protective. Thus males who do not marry and often those who get divorced are perceived as "mama's boys." Women who have never married are often perceived as having father fixations or as being victims of an overprotective family.

This image can also apply to a person who sees the parent of the same sex as having presented an inimitable model of devotion or commitment. At an Interaction meeting, one never-married woman in her thirties remembered her mother as "the most committed woman in the world" to her father. "I would like to be like her," she added, "and never look at anybody else, but just be committed to that one person."

Studies of relationships between singles and their parents are still in the exploratory stage, with each study raising as many questions as it answers. Wallin (1954: 20) found that the happier a man perceived his parents' marriage, the more favorable his attitude toward marriage tended to be. Rawlings (1966) explored a number of parent-child relationships, but found significant correlations in only two areas: fathers' work schedules and parental disgrace. The single person was more likely than the married to have had a father who had an unusual work schedule, one that differed from those of other fathers in the neighborhood, or was more likely to have had a parent perceived of as being disgraced because of drug abuse, prison record, infidelity, or because a father was considered a poor provider or a mother a poor homemaker.

Spreitzer and Riley (1974) found that among men who never married, "very poor" relations with mothers were far more characteristic than "good" or even "poor" relations (a ratio of three to one). For women who never married the ratio was about two to one. "Very poor" relations with fathers were likely to be found in twice as many men who never married as compared to those who had poor or good relations. But they found a very different situation concerning relations between girls and fathers. Twice the percentage of never-married women had "good" relations with their fathers as had "poor" relations.

Except for Spreitzer and Riley's finding on the relations between girls and fathers, these findings do not support the apron strings image. All other findings indicate that, far from being bound by the affection or possessiveness of the family, singles may have been turned off by what they perceive to be repelling aspects of their family situations. They do not seem to have been deterred from marriage by family bonds, but by the lack of them.

This possibility is further supported by some of the negative findings in the Rawlings (1966) study. She found, for instance, no significant relation between marital status and perceptions of parental affection or cooperation. Nor did it seem to make much difference whether families were perceived as democratic or authoritarian, whether parents were perceived as fair or unfair, or whether families were rich or poor. She felt, out of the results of her study, that future research should be directed toward finding out more about the inner psychic relationships within a family.

Following Rawlings's suggestions, we decided to try to find out whether psychic family relations had anything to do with civil status.[1] We tried to find out whether childhood perceptions of family relationships affected marital decisions, or whether present relations with parents might still be a factor. We also tried to distinguish between memories of how parents related to each other and how the parents related to the child.

WARM AND COLD HOUSEHOLDS

With so many remembering warm parental relations, we were not surprised that there was not a significant difference between the married and single segments. About 27 percent of the marrieds regarded their parents as cold or conflicting as compared to 31 percent of the singles (Table 5.1). The breakdown into subcategories, however, indicates a possible contradiction. The percentage of divorced growing up in cold households seemed high (42 percent), but the remarried, who were for the most part formerly divorced, were low (18 percent). If the divorced and remarried were taken together, 32 percent of them come from households with cold-conflicting families, a figure similar to the other categories (Figure 5.1). On the other hand, the findings from the singles organization, Interaction, supports the idea that the singles, especially the divorced, may come from homes in which parental relations were not warm and loving; they reveal higher percentages of never marrieds (37 percent) and divorced (49 percent) remembering cold parental relations.

These findings do not substantiate the apron strings theory. They would, at first glance, suggest that the divorced were less likely to remember having warm parents and more likely to remember having cold parents. But the contradictory memories of the remarried, most of whom had been divorced, cast doubt on the validity of this inference. If anything, the findings suggest that what one remembers about one's past is strongly influenced by one's present situation.

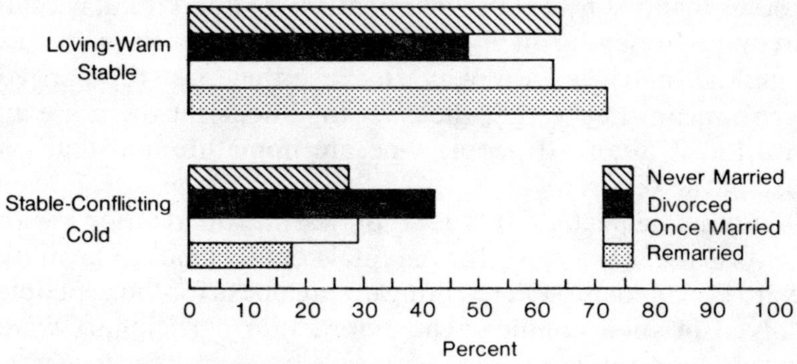

Figure 5.1 Parental Relations to Each Other

Does our present situation affect our memories? The divorced are least likely to recall their parents as being loving, while the remarried, who most likely had been divorced themselves, are most likely to have such memories.

Earlier it was noted that singles are disturbed by psychoanalytic explanations that relate their singleness to their parents. The apron strings explanation is disturbing to singles for another reason, for it implies that one cannot cut a mother's apron string because one is immature, unwilling to take responsibility. Asked about this, the singles in the Interaction group were forceful in their assertion that singles are as responsible as marrieds.

"Most singles I know have enormous responsibility," remarked a divorced woman in her 40s. "Me for one. I have a child that I am raising. I have a house that I have to keep. And I'm holding down a job. And I'm doing them all with what I consider to be a pretty darn good job of it." She added that she knows "an awful lot of single women who are doing the same thing, and single men who are."

But was this also true of people who had never taken on the responsibility of marriage in the first place? "I even know some never marrieds who have adopted children," said a divorced woman. "You might find some marrieds that are irresponsible," added a divorced man. "Mainly," suggested another man, "because they depend on one or the other of two people that are in the relationship and they are not responsible to themselves. Most singles are very responsible to themselves."

But one divorced man in his thirties remarked, "There are divorces that occur because of immaturity. I don't think we can stereotype by saying all divorces are okay. This is the same [as saying] all marriages are okay. Because they are still married doesn't mean they've got their act together. But there are an awful lot of divorced people who are immature and that's a cause of the divorce."

Another aspect of this lack of warmth in relations with parents is the stereotype that parental conflict leads to hostility toward the opposite sex, resulting in singleness for those people involved in such conflict. The Interaction participants were divided about this.

"Baloney," snapped one divorced man. "That's way out of proportion. Both parties, females and males, need each other." But an older divorced man, who had long been married, was not so sure. "It's all according to the kind of experience you've had from a kid on with the opposite sex," he mused. "If you've had trouble with 'em from the time you were a child, you'll have a hostility toward them."

THE NEED FOR OPENNESS

If emotional relationship with parents did not seem to be a decisive criterion in assessing differences between singles and marrieds, what about openness of communication? Would singles and marrieds have different memories about how they communicated with their parents, or how their parents communicated with each other?

At first glance, it appeared that memories of communication also could not be identified as a factor that distinguished singles from marrieds (Table 5.2). It did not seem to matter whether respondents remembered both parents as being open, or only the father, or only the mother, or neither. The percentages for singles and marrieds seemed to be about the same.

But when Table 5.2 is broken into subcategories, it becomes apparent that the situation of the divorced is different. They were much more likely than the other categories to recall neither parent being open toward them. Further, they were

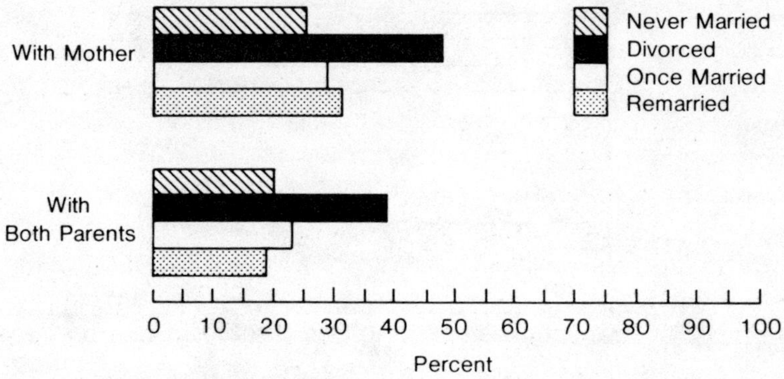

Figure 5.2 Closed Communications with Parents
The divorced really stand out in terms of remembering closed communications with parents.

much more likely than any other category to have felt closed off from communication with their mothers, perhaps the parent most frequently available (Table 5.2; Figure 5.2). These results were confirmed by similar findings from Interaction, a large group of mostly divorced singles. Bearing in mind that these results must be taken as tentative, since once again the remarried do not reflect the memories of the divorced, it looks as though lack of openness between parent and child may be reflected in the child's socialization and possibly affect his or her ability to communicate with others. This would seem to be a subject worth exploring further, particularly since our data would seem to contradict Rawlings's finding on the importance of fathers' work schedules.

In any case, it is clear that the apron strings hypothesis is not supported here either. If anything, it is possible that divorced singles may owe their status, at least in part, to never having had any apron strings. That is to say, if your mother did not openly communicate with you and allow you to freely communicate with her, this may have negative effects in your marital relations and could even be a factor precipitating divorce.

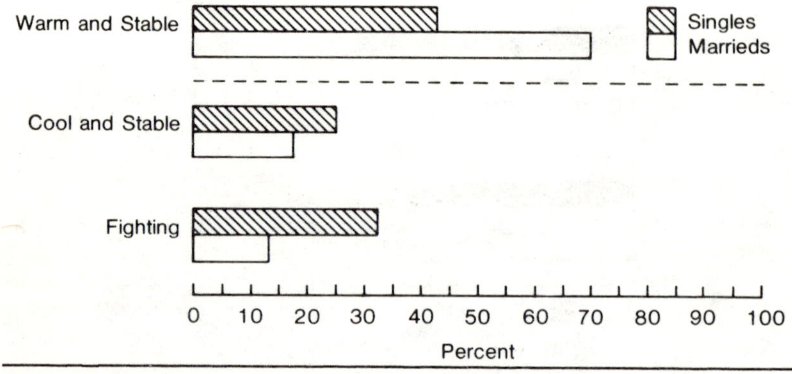

Figure 5.3 Current Relations with Parents

There is no doubt that marrieds are more likely to have better current relations with their parents than singles.

Current Relations with Relatives

PARENT FIGHTERS

So far we have been discussing memories — respondents were asked to recall how things had been. Differences in responses between the divorced and the remarried lead us to wonder how much memory is affected by the current situation. Now that respondents have reached adulthood, what are their current relations with their parents like? Whereas the results of questions about the past lend themselves to different interpretations, the results on the present situation seem to be clear and decisive. Married people are much more likely than single people to have warm and stable current relations with their parents. Single people are more likely to have cool but stable current relations with their parents, and are much more likely to fight a great deal with their parents (Figure 5.3; Table 5.3). Indeed, 70 percent of the marrieds in our sample felt they had warm relationships with their parents, while fewer than half of the singles felt that to be true. On the other hand, almost a third of the singles said they often fight with their parents, while this was true of only about one-eighth of the marrieds. Responses from the Interaction group closely supported these results from the overall study.

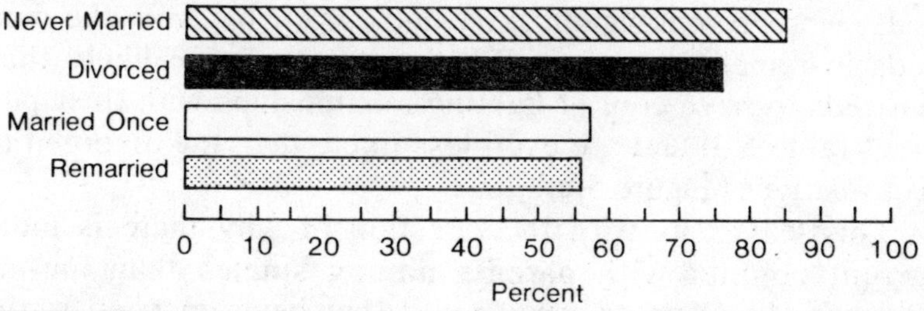

Figure 5.4 Shall We(I) Visit the Folks this Week? No!
Better put the extra chops in the refrigerator, Mom. It looks like your single kids won't stop over this week either. Visiting the relatives is for the marrieds.

Nor did it make much difference this time when the categories were further divided. Never marrieds and the divorced are much less likely to have warm, stable relations with their parents than either of the married categories, and both singles categories are more than twice as likely to fight with their parents as the married categories (Table 5.3).

VISITING THE FOLKS

Did the perceptions of relationship reflect in behavior? Fortunately, we were able to check this, because we asked about leisure activity for other purposes and discovered that singles are much less likely than marrieds to visit their relatives (see Table 6.3). More than 40 percent of the marrieds placed visiting relatives among their first 3 choices for a social outing. Less than 20 percent of the singles made a similar choice.

It is not possible to tell from these figures how much connection there is between the atmosphere we experience in our homes as children and our adult relationships with our parents. It may be that the single status itself interferes with parental relationships, regardless of what the socialization process might have been. One reason this appears to be so is that the remarrieds have much warmer relationships with and are less likely to fight with their parents than the divorced, even though most of the remarrieds were formerly divorced (Table 5.3). Another reason for suspecting that current fights are about current problems, rather than history, is that the never marrieds, who are not significantly distinguishable from the marrieds in remembrances of things past, are more likely than marrieds to have cool or fighting relationships with their parents (Table 5.3) and are even less likely than the divorced to visit relatives (Figure 5.4).

This leaves us with the question of why there is more current conflict with parents among singles than among marrieds. In Chapter 1 we noted that being married is the acceptable, approved status. This results, as Stein (1976: 39) indicates, in parents applying the greatest pressure to marry. Thus the conflict reported by the never marrieds may be a reflection of this parental pressure to marry. This may also be true for the divorced, since their single status may bring demands on the parents for child care and support. Be that as it may, it also appears that people do marry and settle down and that, when they do, it is reflected in warmer relations with parents and a considerable increase in social interaction with relatives.

No Strings Attached

This exploration of the comparative perceptions of singles and marrieds reinforces the results of previous research: The apron strings stereotype has not been substantiated by the data. You may meet a 50-year-old mama's boy, but if you do, the odds are that he will be married. It is probable, however, that you will not think of him as a mama's boy, because you will never ask: "Why do you suppose he didn't remain single?" or "Why do you suppose he never divorced?" Nor are we likely to say, "She would have remained happily single but she felt she had obligations to her family to marry."

No, if family is a factor in marital choice, it is more likely that closed relationships affected the choice to remain single. However, the different responses of the divorced and the remarried are puzzling. It is possible that the remarrieds have a more favorable view of marriage, and hence of their parents, than the divorced. It is also possible that a higher percentage of the remarried chose to remarry because they had a favorable

Profile: Family Background

	Parental Relations		*Parental Openness*	
	Warm/Loving	*Cold/Conflicting*	*Both Open*	*Neither Open*
Gender	little difference	male	little difference	male
Civil status	remarried	divorced	married once	divorced
Age	50+	25-29	50+	18-24 or 50+
Education	college degree	some college	college degree	high school or college degree
Political identity	liberal	neutral	liberal	conservative or neutral
Religious affiliation	Protestant or Catholic	other[a]	Catholic or Protestant	Catholic or other

a. In this and all other tables that refer to religious affiliation, "other" refers to any religion other than Catholic or Protestant.

view of marriage coming out of their memories of parental relationships. Further study of the divorced and the remarried will be necessary in order to answer this question.

It does appear, however, that there may be a relationship betwen family socialization and divorce. Children who felt communications blocked with parents, particularly their mothers, may continue to have communications problems in marriage. This impression is reinforced by their continued perception of either hostile or cool relations with their parents today and their reluctance, as compared to marrieds, to visit relatives. The hypothesis that a parental communications block is an important factor in future divorce is also worth further study.

Profile: Family Background

Adding various other independent variables to our glance at the respondents' parental relations and emotions gives us a summary picture of those individuals most likely to have grown up in households of warm or loving parental relations, as well as those who had parents who were open with their emotions.

If you remember being raised in a household of warm, loving, and open parental relations, then typically you would be an older (50+), remarried male or female with a university education. Also, you are more likely to be a political liberal of the Protestant or Catholic religion. No clear profile emerges for children of communicationally closed parents, but if you were raised in a household where the parental relations were cold or conflicting, then you are more likely to be a youngish (25-29), divorced male with some college education, politically neutral, and neither Protestant or Catholic.

NOTE

1. We find it strange that singleness is usually defined as a marital status. The use of the term "civil status" allows for singleness to stand on its own rather than in its relationship to marriage. Besides, as a marital status, the term "single" seems contradictory.

Chapter 6

THE USE OF LEISURE TIME

Who Has Time for a Nice Time?

TWO VIEWS OF THE SINGLE'S WEEKEND

Many a Sunday evening, the married man (and even more so the married woman!) may wonder if he has time to be married. He has taken the children to the zoo in the afternoon, after church in the morning, and Saturday he cleaned out the garage. Now it is time to prepare for tomorrow's work, and during the coming week there will be three evenings out on family affairs: Parent-Teachers' night, soccer coaching, and dinner at his mother-in-law's. About 11 p.m. he starts to read and by 11:10 he is asleep.

He thinks about his single friends in their condominiums. They haven't been cleaning garages, going to church or to the zoo, much less escorting children to art classes or worrying about what they're doing at college. No, they've been reading, listening to their stereos, snacking when hungry, bicycling along the river, probably stopping at the art gallery, playing poker, adventuring. When they come to work tomorrow, they'll be refreshed and full of stories of the weekend.

When he asks them about this, however, his single friends seem to indicate that his vision is somewhat romanticized. When they are working during the week, nothing is getting done at home, and so they have had to clean house, make beds, and do the laundry. Where he can just go to church or the zoo as he pleases, they have to make a production of it, calling someone up, facing rejections, working too hard at having fun. And there's nothing more dreary than going to the art gallery alone

— what is the point of going if you can't share experiences with someone?

"I'm going to college full time," exclaimed one divorced woman in the Interaction group. "I'm supposed to be going to discos every night? I couldn't."

Married people with children may have more responsibilities, but they also can share the tasks.

Each of these images of time has a certain amount of plausibility. Is there any way to sort out who has more time for fun? One way, we thought, might be to focus on the use of time for leisure rather than worrying about who has the worst of the chores. So we asked, in several different ways, how much time people gave to leisure, and what they did with it.

SINGLES GO A'ROAMING

We should bear in mind that social outings may not be the center of our lives, whether for reasons of time, budget, or inclination. Almost half of the singles (48 percent went out socially no more than once a week, while among marrieds that figure rose to more than three-quarters (76 percent). But it is also clear from these questions that singles do go out socially more frequently than married people (Figure 6.1; Table 6.1). Almost twice the percentage of marrieds as singles said they went out less than once a week/hardly ever. On the other hand, more than 3 times as many singles as marrieds said they went out 3 times a week or more.

We would not have been surprised to find that breaking down our categories would give us different results. If marrieds were kept home by children, so would be the divorced, even more so since they had no other partner to baby sit. But, as it turns out, the divorced are almost as venturesome as the never marrieds, except for the 25-29 year olds, who are probably most affected by the baby-sitting problems. For instance, well over two-fifths of both never marrieds and divorced go out at least twice a week.

No matter which way you look at it, singles do go "a'roaming" far more than marrieds. One explanation for this may be

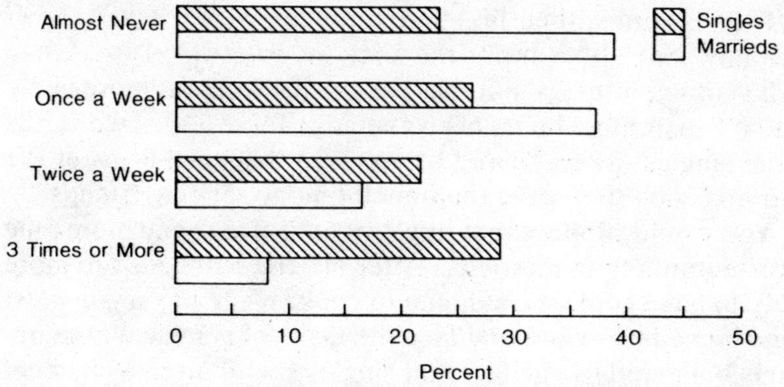

Figure 6.1 How Often Do You Go Out?
It's clear that singles are more likely to go out than marrieds.

that the singles segment of the sample was significantly younger than the married segment. Of those who do go out more than twice a week, two-thirds are under 30, and it is the younger divorced and never married (18-24) who go out the most (Table 6.2).

Where Shall We Go?

When people do go out, where do they go? We suggested a number of choices, and asked respondents to indicate their order of preference. We also asked them about their leisure activities during the work day, and since leisure activities may be performed at home, we included some of those. This time we asked how much time was spent on each type of activity.

SOCIALIZING WITH FRIENDS

In this age of impersonality, where personal relationships have supposedly been eroded by urbanization, organizational moving, and television, it appears that among all respondents visiting with friends is still the most popular social activity. Going to restaurants, also a social activity that usually involves friends or family, was a close second (Table 6.3).

An identical 55 percent of singles and marrieds listed visiting friends among their first 3 preferences. When asked, however, how much time during the week they were likely to give to such visiting, it turned out that the singles were far more likely to give two or more hours of an evening (Table 6.4). Two-thirds of the singles, as compared to no more than two-fifths of the marrieds, said they gave that much time to visiting friends.

You would suppose that singles would also spend more time at restaurants than marrieds. After all, the marrieds are more likely to have someone at home to cook, while the single must come home from work and face the task. This logical assumption is bolstered by the fact that singles spend up to 63 percent of each food dollar eating out; this is 3 times what the marrieds spend (Newsweek, 1978: 77). But among respondents in the sample, marrieds were more likely to choose restaurants for socialization than singles (58 percent versus 44 percent). It may be that singles actually do go to restaurants more than marrieds, but do not interpret everyday eating out as a social occasion, whereas for the married, especially for the spouse who does the cooking, eating out is always a social event.

Another kind of socializing involves visiting relatives. This has been discussed already in Chapter 5, where we indicated that marrieds are much more likely than singles to mention visiting relatives as a preferred activity. In fact, the difference in preference (42 percent versus 16 percent) is the most marked of any activity between the segments (Figure 6.2).

Another kind of socializing preferred by marrieds is membership in a social club. Though a less popular activity than visiting relatives for both segments, visiting social clubs appears to be more of a family activity. For some reason it proved to be particularly popular among the remarrieds, who were likely to be found at a social club more than twice as often as a single (Table 6.4).

If, however, the club is a nightclub, then you are more likely to find singles than marrieds present (Figure 6.2). In fact, nightclubs are twice as popular among singles as among marrieds. If you are staid and married, you may think of a restaurant as a frequent social pleasure and a nightclub as a very exceptional place to visit. But among singles in Dayton, which

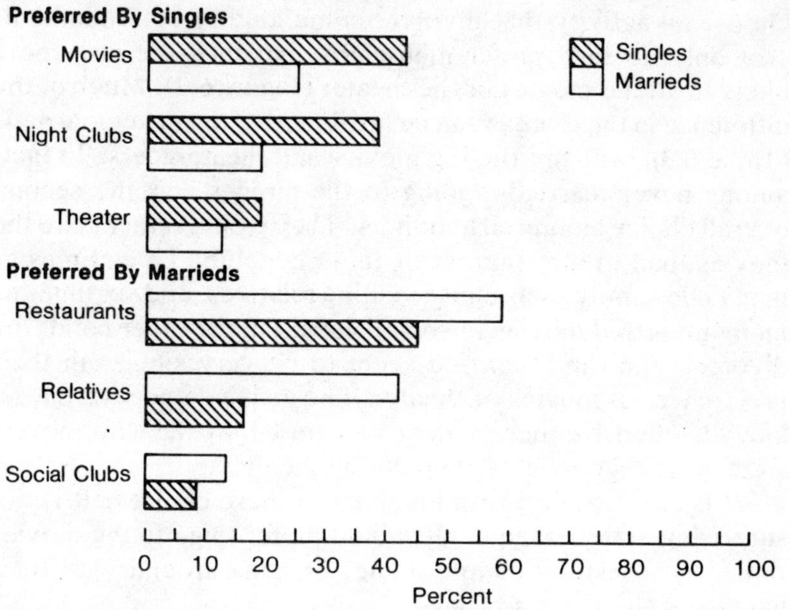

Figure 6.2 Social Outings

It would seem that marrieds tend to have a preference for activities that require social interaction.

is not usually regarded as a swinging place, nightclubs are almost as popular among singles as are restaurants (38 percent versus 44 percent). And nightclubs do not seem to be especially the province of the young never marrieds. In fact, nightclubs prove to be a little more popular among the divorced (41 percent versus 37 percent). The reason behind the wide difference in the popularity of nightclubs between the two marital segments may be summed up by a comment from the owner of a singles' bar: "For city dwellers, the bar scene fills an immense vacuum. Let's face it, people don't meet at church anymore" (Newsweek, 1973: 54), and so a regular part of their budget is set aside for drinking and socializing (Brooks, 1981: 68).

ENTERTAINMENT

The nightclub differs from other forms of socializing in that it also provides entertainment. You converse with your friends, but you also watch some kind of performance.

It does appear that singles are more likely than marrieds to choose an activity that involves some kind of entertainment. Not only do they prefer nightclubs, but they are also more likely to attend movies or the theater (Figure 6.2). Much of the difference in these areas can be attributed to the never marrieds (Table 6.3), who are the big movie- and theatergoers. In fact, among never marrieds, going to the movies was the second overall choice among all activities. They would rather go to the movies than to a restaurant or to a nightclub. Three times as many chose movies as chose visiting relatives, and six times as many preferred movies to social clubs. On the other hand, the divorced and the remarried seem to be very similar in their preference for movies or theater. The married once were least likely to choose either. With all categories, by the way, movies were more than twice as popular as the theater.

It is easy to see youth involved in these choices. It is not surprising that young people would prefer to go to the movies rather than visit aunts and uncles or hang around with their parents at the German Club.

It seems likely, then, that the preference of singles for entertainment is more a preference of youth. This is confirmed by a look at home entertainment: television (Table 6.4). Here we find that more than two-thirds of the never married and married watch television two hours or more a day. The only category that falls below this figure is the divorced. Having no partner, it may take them longer to finish their evening chores. They may also, as our Interaction respondents indicated, be taking courses at the local university to finish interrupted degree work; and, as noted, they go out more, seeking adult companionship. In any event, it appears that singles have a greater taste for entertainment than marrieds.

Incidentally, it seemed to us that our respondents spent an incredible amount of time watching television. After all, by the time you have finished eating and washing up, how much time is there in an evening? Maybe 3 or 4 hours? Well, not only did an average of well over 60 percent of the respondents estimate that they watched television at least 2 hours a night, but about

40 percent of them figured they averaged 4 hours. Of course, part of this "watching" occurs while the respondents eat and do household chores.

GETTING INVOLVED

One other area of socializing that seems to fall into a different category are those activities that require an active role by the participant. Such activities include sports or hobbies and community service.

The majority in all categories thought they spent 2 hours or more on a workday or evening on hobbies or sports (Table 6.4). Almost three-fourths of the never marrieds thought they spent this much time, and more than two-thirds of the divorced, whereas both married categories were under 60 percent. Here the singles seem to prefer activities that involve something more than just sitting and talking. This could be a consequence of youthful energy or, possibly, singles on the whole want a little insurance in their social activities; since they may not know their partners well, or may be on a first or second date, activities can ease the introductory strain.

The majority of all categories perform no community service (Table 6.4), but among those that do there is not much to choose between singles and marrieds. The never married appear to be the most community-oriented and the divorced the least, but the differences among the categories are not striking.

What Shapes the Choices?

We have already seen that the divorced seem to be under more time constraints than others. Very few (6 percent) can give 4 hours of an evening to sports or hobbies and they spend less time watching television than the others. They also spend less time than any of the others on community service. Having full responsibility for work, home management, and care of children could certainly account for these differences.

Another factor could be a greater need of singles to find companionship. The singles spend more time visiting with friends, but they also spend more time in activities that provide a protective buffer: nightclubs, movies, theater, sports. They could have a greater need for socialization, but, as we noted, also a greater need for protection via activity while finding their way into new relationships. In addition, the divorced may find staying home a more lonely situation since they were previously accustomed to an adult companion.

It could be also that the divorced, in a time of extreme vulnerability, are forced to seek out new friends because they feel deserted by their married friends. Several members of Interaction commented on this with considerable warmth.

"How about your friends?" asked one divorced woman in her 30s. "I had a lot of what I thought were close married friends right in my neighborhood. We were partying back and forth. I've been divorced for two and a half years. I've never been invited over, they never call up. I run into them once in a while and that hurts, when you feel they were friends of yours and when you're divorced they don't want to hear from you."

This comment precipitated several more, indicating that the divorced perceived that in one way or another their new status threatened their old friends. "The insecurity lies in the people that don't invite you to their homes," commented one younger woman. "Because if people are secure in themselves, they'll invite you."

"If you think back on the married parties you went to," added another of the younger women, "the men are in one room and the women are in the other room. So what is the threat if they invite a single woman? Because the men are in one room discussing sports . . ." "Maybe that's where they're afraid you'll be, in there with the sports," a man suggested. "It's the image of the leopard woman in the commercials," another woman added. Married women, she thought, "believe single women become the creatures in the negligees."

But an older man believed married women were also afraid of him. They were afraid, he said, "that I would show the men that I was having such a good time, that they would get divorced!"

On the other hand, as a divorced woman from Interaction pointed out, single women, unless invited, may be excluded from activities for which an escort would seem to be appropriate. "I'm not that aggressive," she said, apologetically. "You know, I still cannot call a man. I'm back in some years ago when men called women."

We have not yet explored income in relation to going out because the income factor is not clear from these data. On the one hand, visiting friends is an inexpensive activity that seems to be preferred by singles. On the other, theaters and nightclubs are expensive, and they are also preferred by singles. Marrieds also spend lots of time visiting friends and much more than singles visiting relatives, also an inexpensive activity. But they prefer restaurants, which can be expensive. Another factor is the possibility of difference between preference and performance. You may prefer to go to the theater, but your pocketbook may only take you to the movies.

As for the marrieds, sometimes their choices may be restricted less by income or need than by the other partner. One woman in the sample, who said her 25-year marriage has been mostly happy, explained how different social preferences can affect choices. "As my husband is antisocial," she said, "it makes it difficult because I like people, like to go places, eat out occasionally (he refuses), so therefore I have to do these things alone or stay home. This is the unhappiest part of my marriage. There were nine children in my family, my husband was an only child, which might have some bearing on his being antisocial."

Work, Education, and Income

Choices of leisure are also likely to be affected by the kind of work one does, since this related to class and class influences leisure preferences; by education, which affects ones tastes; and by income, which determines the extent to which those tastes can be gratified.

WORK

One interesting finding about work among respondents in the sample was that never marrieds were more likely to be blue-collar workers as compared to the divorced or married categories (Table 6.5). We thought this might have been a function of age, since the never marrieds were younger than the other categories, but the finding held at any age below 50. Clearly, the never-married person is more likely to be a blue-collar worker; a blue-collar worker is more likely never to have married.

One interesting area of self-classification is that of homemaker. Typically, you would expect a nonworking married woman to so describe herself, but rarely a single woman, who would be working to support herself and her family. And this proved to be the case, for only 5 percent of the singles described themselves as homemakers, compared to 24 percent of the marrieds. Still, if nearly all the singles did not see themselves as homemakers because they had other work, you would expect the marrieds who did not have other work to so describe themselves. If all the marrieds were in situations in which one partner was working and the other was maintaining the home, there should have been close to 50 percent of the marrieds describing themselves as homemakers. That only 24 percent described themselves so suggests that either half the families in the sample had two working members or that the term homemaker has come to be perceived as something to be disparaged, rather than as something to be proud of (as it would have been to the spinsters writing in the 1930s or World War I years).

EDUCATION

Since the never marrieds were much more likely to be factory workers, it might be supposed that they would also turn out to be the category with the least education. But that was hardly the case. Education and white-collar work did not appear to be too closely related (Figure 6.3). For example, almost half of the never marrieds had white-collar work, with a quarter (26 percent) having college degrees, whereas two-fifths of the remarrieds had white-collar jobs, even though only a seventh (14 percent) had college degrees.

Once again it appeared as though age might be a factor. The younger never marrieds were, perhaps, beginning their occupa-

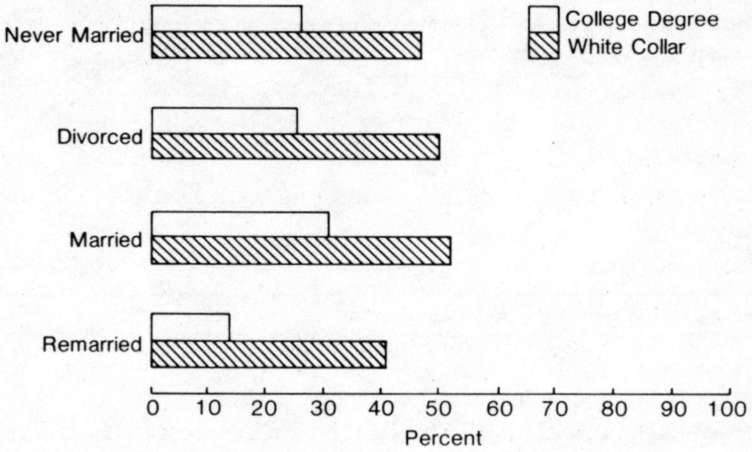

Figure 6.3 White-Collar Work and College Education
The remarrieds, who are older, are somewhat less likely to have college degrees or white-collar jobs.

tional careers, and had not yet reached white-collar positions. But once again, checked out at almost any age, there does not seem to be a great difference in education between singles and marrieds. Above the age of 40 singles are more likely than marrieds to have college degrees. Over all, the marrieds have a very slight advantage in percentage graduating, but a higher percentage of the singles have had some college education. It does not appear that differences in education can explain either differences in leisure preferences nor the greater percentage of never marrieds engaged in blue-collar work.

INCOME

We have seen that stereotypes are confused about income, since they sometimes portray the single as an affluent bachelor, and sometimes as poor compared to the married because he has only one income. From what we have already seen of the job structure, the affluent bachelor image has begun to fade. It is likely to be wiped out when we turn our attention to income. Even in white-collar occupations, far more marrieds have in-

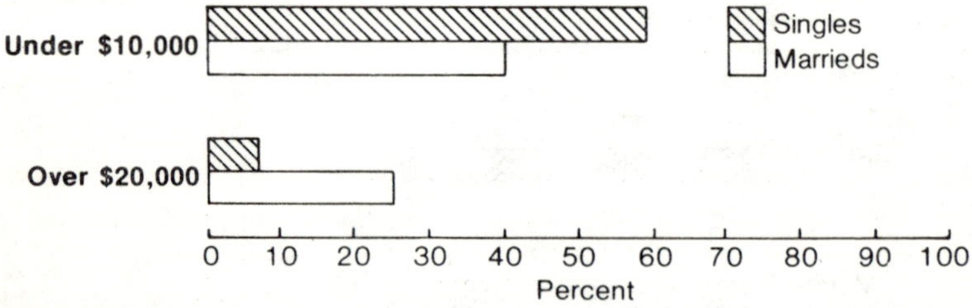

Figure 6.4 Incomes in the 30-50 Age Bracket

Income differences between marrieds and singles cannot be accounted for by differences in age.

comes at the upper levels than do the singles despite a similarity in educational attainments. Part of this income difference is attributable to dual incomes for the marrieds. Thus more than twice the percentage of remarried as compared to singles report making $20,000 or more per year (18 percent versus 8 percent) although they are less likely to hold college degrees (14 percent versus 26 percent) or white-collar positions (41 percent versus 48 percent). Nor do slight advantages in numbers with college degrees and white-collar occupations among the married once explain their 3:1 advantage in $20,000 incomes (23 percent versus 8 percent; Table 6.7).

Once again we thought that part or all of this discrepancy might be attributable to the younger age of the singles category, so we reexamined the data, this time limiting our comparison to the singles and marrieds in the 30-50 age bracket, and once again the pattern did not change. Over three-fifths of the singles reported incomes under $10,000, compared to two-fifths of the marrieds. On the upper end of the scale, 26 percent of the marrieds reported making more than $20,000, as compared to only 7 percent of the singles (Figure 6.4; Table 6.4).

On the whole we can say that a considerably higher percentage of singles perceive themselves to be poor, while a considerably higher percentage of marrieds perceive their income to be at least comfortable. Certainly these figures do not support the stereotype that singles, despite their preferences for movies, theaters, and nightclubs, can be called rich. By almost any comparison to marrieds, they appear to be relatively poor.

Only one person among those in the sample commented on the absence of money, and she was a never-married single. Asked if there was any way in which she would like to change her life, she replied, "Just for one day I'd like to be a person who was able to just spend money — to buy all those things for family and friends that you've always wanted to."

An older never-married man from the Interaction group suggested that lack of income can contribute to remaining single in the first place. "I would say probably the main reason (I didn't marry) was that I was unemployed at the age when most people get married. Then, after that, it was probably moving around a lot."

If singles are not rich, at least, as one divorced member of Interaction suggested, they can be credited with contributing to the gross national product. "What happens to the economy," he asked, "if all the singles wind up getting married? You go back to one-car families." But as it is, "they're splitting up, she's buying another car, he's buying another car; they're buying another house. . . . Divorces are boosting the economy."

DISCRIMINATION?

So it appears that marrieds are more likely to have white-collar positions and higher incomes than singles regardless of age and education (Figures 6.3 and 6.4; Tables 6.5 through 6.8). There are a number of factors involved in these figures, but it does seem possible that employment discrimination against singles, strongly suggested 25 years ago by William Whyte (1957), may still persist. Given the comparable educations of singles and marrieds, why do singles not have proportionate work and income? Sex and race discrimination could play a part, since a higher percentage of singles are women and minority groups have a higher percentage of singles than whites (Newsweek, 1978). Could it be that, in hiring men, corporations are still considering wives, and that a man over 30 who does not have a wife has a harder time getting a job appropriate to his age and education?

Profile: Most and Least Likely to Go Out

	Most	*Least*
Gender	male	female
Civil status	never married	married once
Age	18-24	50+
Education	high school	less than high school
Political identity	liberal	conservative
Religious affiliation	none	Protestant

Work and Leisure

What is the relationship between work and leisure? We can see that a higher percentage of singles, particularly never marrieds, are blue-collar workers, but we also see that age is not a factor. Are we dealing with a large number of working men whose leisure activities consist of dropping by the bar and hobnobbing with their chums? That does not relate too well to the preference of singles for the theater, which has not been a center of working-class leisure since the days of the groundlings.

Are we dealing with a number of college dropouts with poor self-images who do not feel able to take on the responsibility of white-collar work? Certainly a higher percentage of singles failed to finish college, but that can be turned around. You can just as well say a higher percentage of singles have experienced college. We can talk about college dropouts and graduate school dropouts, for that matter, but how college attendance is valued depends on perception. How the marrieds and singles perceive themselves is what matters, and we shall be looking further at their self-perceptions in the next five chapters.

One other possibility is that for some singles it may be that leisure time is more important than working time, and that blue-collar work serves them better because they do not have to worry about it when they are not doing it. We may get some further insight into this in our chapters on sex, happiness (which includes having fun), and perceptions of the future ("Five Years from Now").

All we can say for the present is that there is no reason to perceive that singles choose work that is different from that chosen by marrieds. There may be some reason to believe that singles are discriminated against in being chosen for jobs. And it does not appear that income has much effect on leisure since the poorer categories — the poor singles — choose forms of leisure (nightclubs, films, theater) that may be somewhat more expensive than those chosen by marrieds.

Profile: The Roamers

Who is most likely to go out? A young (under 24), never-married person, most likely a male with a high school education, a liberal political orientation, and no church affiliation.

Who is most likely to stay home? An older (over 50), once-married female, who is conservative, Protestant, and who never graduated from high school.

Chapter 7

SEX IN THE SINGLE'S WORLD

No Matter What, It's Wrong

Now we come to a sensitive point. What do singles do with their sexual energies? No matter what, it is unacceptable.

Do they bed every person of the opposite sex they can? Then they are lecherous.

Do they take cold baths? How Victorian!

Are they voyeurs? Buy adult books, go to X-rated movies? Ludicrous! Embarrassing! Sad!

Do they masturbate? Ugh, a dirty habit.

Do they repress their desires? That's unhealthy. It's bound to come out somehow.

Are they queer? Contemptible! Pitiful!

If none of the above, then they must be sexless, neuter, paraeunuchs.

Well, what should a single do, then? Marry, that's what. Society has traditionally seen premarital intercourse as something bad, something that will bring about unwanted marriage or produce illegitimate children, with the likelihood of divorce and economic dependency in the event of the unwanted marriage, along with various guilt and anxiety feelings (Nye, 1967: 245). These attitudes and feelings have deep roots in our society. There is a general taboo against sex, going back to St. Paul and carried through Augustine through Roman Catholic natural theology. It is a line that many branches of Protestantism fully adopted. The only kind of sexual relations (rather reluctantly) accepted were those of lawful marriage, for purposes of procreation only, and preferably without passion or orgasm. There has been strong acceptance of marriage as the final outcome of courtship and as the only legitimate introduction to sexual expression (Libby, 1978: 168). This viewpoint has been and still is widely upheld by law. In many states, for instance, nonmarital cohabitation is still held to be a crime, complete with fine and jail sentence (Macklin, 1978: 197).

The ideal, though powerful, has been violated throughout the centuries. But in the twentieth century, and particularly in the past two decades, sexual mores have been challenged as never before by the dissemination of information about sex, sexual techniques, and means of birth control. The women's movement, with its challenge to the double standard, has contributed to the change. The movement has led to such obvious consequences as the erosion of the *in loco parentis* of colleges, and even such seemingly irrelevant developments as the return of married women to work has made available more privacy for young never marrieds in their own homes (Duberman, 1977; Macklin, 1978; Hunt, 1974). While old laws and moral barriers die hard, there does seem to be a more permissive and supportive attitude toward sex outside of marriage within our society. In a Gallup Poll, less than half the sample (48 percent) thought that premarital sex was wrong. This is a decline of 20 percent from a mere 4 years earlier, and this change of belief was found in all segments of the sample (Murstein, 1978: 273).

The literature in the field reflects these changes in attitudes; there has been a sharp increase in premarital sexual experience, a substantial majority of young women under 25 have had sexual experience, and there appears to be an increase in nonmarital cohabitation (Hunt, 1974; Zelnik and Kantner, 1977; Spreitzer and Riley, 1974; Macklin, 1978).

The literature also indicates that greater permissiveness is the trend among the marrieds. Kinsey in 1948 indicated that half of all married men had engaged in extramarital sex by the age of 45; 20 years later, Gebhard would add 10 percent to this figure on men while reducing the age of occurrence by 10 years. Similar increases were found for wives. Believing that the trend has continued, since there is no reason not to, Ramey (1978: 267) notes that less than half of the people in nuclear families are monogamous. This brief examination indicates that there appears to be more overt writing about sex for singles and, correspondingly, a decline in signs of sexual suppression. But it is difficult to draw conclusions on sexuality due to inconsistencies in research efforts. The Kinsey studies consisted mostly of non-randomly selected volunteers who were young, college-educated, and middle-class. Hunt questioned people after they had participated in small group discussions and had only a 20 percent rate on return. The *Redbook* study used volunteers from the magazine's readership (Gagnon and Greenblat, 1978: 296-301), as did Hite from *Ms* and *Penthouse*. In addition, there is very little comparative data available (Macklin, 1978: 203).

But how do these changes affect singles? Do they meet sexual needs, not through romantic love, but by "swinging" with numerous partners in casual sexual encounters that involve no commitment on either side? Is the single more likely to be a swinger? (The term is also used to describe extramarital switchers, since the aim seems to be the same.) If so, does this kind of lifestyle provide greater sexual satisfaction than staid monogamy? It would not be surprising to find that singles have had more sexual partners than marrieds, since sexual partners are not exclusively reserved for them. But whether swinging, with its implication of selfishness, is the sexual lifestyle of most singles is a question that needs investigation.

We have left the campus and visited the American heartland. And we have questioned singles and marrieds alike. We have, furthermore, posed the hypothesis that the changes in American life are general, and that singles are not much different from marrieds.

It appears that we were wrong. Singles are more likely to be swingers. Compared to marrieds, they have more partners but get less satisfaction. Significant differences were found in all aspects of sexual activity investigated.

Swing Your Partner

HOW MANY PARTNERS?

To delicate older-generation sensitivities, it seems a little uncouth to ask perfect strangers, however anonymously, about the quantitative aspects of intimate and personal relationships. "How many sexual partners have you had?" "How many times a week do you have sexual relations?" A reasonable reply might be "none of your business" or crumpling up the questionnaire and chucking it in the wastebasket.

Such a response might have been all the more appropriate when you consider how the computer affects the delicacy of the question:

> 67. With how many sexual partner(s) have you had sexual intercourse?
> ______ 1) None
> ______ 2) 1
> ______ 3) 2 or 3
> ______ 4) 4 to 6
> ______ 5) 7 to 10
> ______ 6) 11 to 20
> ______ 7) more than 20

But seven-eighths of our patient and cooperative respondents, having reached question 67, answered with no more apparent hesitation than they had expressed in deciding whether they preferred movies to theater. (Let me see, I go to the movies more, but I'd really prefer the theater if I could afford it. Let me see, it would be seven partners if you count Cedric. But was he really a sexual partner?)

Also, it should be added, there was a significant difference in interpretation between the authors. One author originally consolidated the figures from the question as follows: 0-3, 4-10, 11 or more. The other author responded, "Wait a minute. To me, the most important difference is between one and two!" Incredulous, but patient and tolerant, the first author shrugged and revised the table to 0-1, 2-3, 4-10, 11 or more (Table 7.1). Even in quantitative analysis interpretation depends on perception, and that perception would depend on one's own experience. This being the situation, any figure chosen to represent swingers would bring about a debate.

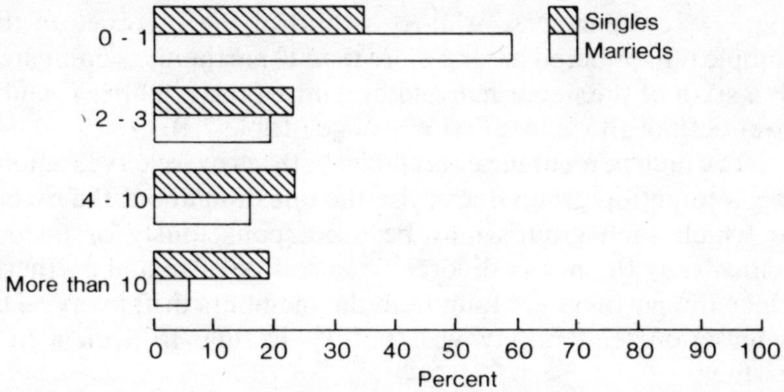

Figure 7.1 How Many Partners?
The more sexual partners a person has had, the more likely he or she is to be single.

In any event, no matter where you begin counting, swingers are more likely to be single than married (Figure 7.1). A total of 50 percent more singles than marrieds remembered having 4 or more partners. By a ratio of 3 to 1, they remembered having more than 10. However, if we take 3 partners as a cutoff, and one author thinks that is a pretty low number, the majority of singles are not swingers. More than half have had fewer than 4 partners and more than a third have had 1 partner or none. Interestingly, despite the common perception of a more promiscuous society, more than three-quarters of the marrieds report having fewer than 4 partners and more than half report having no more than 1.

At the upper end of the scale, there were some indications of freestyle (or catch-as-catch-can) swinging among singles. Of those who had more than 10 partners, well over half (61 percent) indicated they had had more than 20 partners (Table 7.1). The supplementary Interaction study, focusing on singles who seek social companionship, showed even a higher percentage of singles — 37 percent — having had sexual relations with more than 10 partners and 9 percent having had more than 40 partners. But most of the Interaction respondents are divorced and the findings show that the divorced are more likely to have more sexual partners. Almost a third of the divorced in the sample remembered having more than 10 partners, as compared to a sixth of the never married, a tenth of the remarried, and a twentieth of those in a first marriage (Table 7.1).

The high percentage of divorced with active sex lives among the Interaction group does raise the question about the extent to which such groups may be used, consciously or unconsciously, by the newly divorced as a source of sexual partners. Once the partners are found, do the members drift away? The Interaction leaders say yes, until it is time to seek a new partner.

WHY SO MANY?

The participants of Interaction had a great deal to say about this. For one thing, they suggested that the activity begins with the recognition that divorce is coming. After some discussion among divorced members about the relationship between divorce and sex, one younger woman remarked, "I think a lot of it is cheating."

"Cheating?"

"Men find other women and women find other men."

"It seems to me," said the discussion moderator, "that's the second step. There must be a first step as to why they're seeking other people."

"That's more a symptom than a cause," another young woman agreed. "I think when one person in a marriage seeks somebody outside, the marriage is already in trouble."

"Right."

"If you're not getting any attention at home."

"If you're starving, you've got to go to another restaurant to get something to eat."

All these comments came from women.

Turning their attention to the activity of the divorced, a divorced man and woman presented the following duet, the man beginning: "I see the divorced people, as a whole, in a situation in which they want no strings, they treat sex on a very casual basis . . . "

"Right. And not on a personal basis."

"Not on a real deep personal basis."

"Right."

"And therefore they can hold that on a level where they don't put any . . . "

"human . . . "

"human holds on the opposite person's . . . "

"feelings. They don't put *anything*."

A younger woman interposed to suggest that casual sex required some defining. "Now to me," she added, "after say six or seven times over a span of six months or more with the same partner, that's not casual sex."

"Once a month, or you forget," a man added.

An older man suggested a searching process is going on. "A lot of times if you were satisfied with your sex life when you were married, you look for the same thing."

"And that's hard to do," asked the moderator, "because it took years to build up?"

A woman in her forties saw the activity as tapering off after a time. "When you are going through a divorce, one of the stages is affirming your manhood or your womanhood, and that does involve sexual activity. But then it tapers off as you realize how unsatisfactory one-night stands, or whatever you want to call them, are. Then moderation, definitely, and selectivity sets in. So it's skewed to the first several months, or whatever, of a divorce, and then it changes as you grow as a human being."

Although no mention of loneliness was made by the Interaction discussants, this condition would seem to be a factor in the sexual activity of the divorced. This implication is seen in the examination of loneliness in the next chapter. More of the divorced would express this feeling than any other. Smith (1979: 18) confirms this conjecture when he notes that the main reason given by the divorced for their sexual behavior is loneliness. Other items mentioned were strong sex drives, that sex is a natural activity, a need to reaffirm sexual attractiveness, fear, retaliation, a necessity to dull the pain, and boredom.

Adding the variables of gender and age to the comparison brought about a more complete picture of the segment of the sample having had many partners: the swinger. As might be expected in a society that employs a double standard for sexual behavior, more males are likely to be swingers in regard to number of sexual partners (Table 7.2). Thus, four-fifths of the females had fewer than 4 partners, as compared to three-fifths of the males. But 16 percent of the males in the total sample had experienced 10 or more sexual partners, as compared to 6 percent of the females. Adding age to this description reveals that swinging may be influenced by acceptance of changing mores. Twice as many under 30 remembered having more than 10 partners, compared to those who were over 40 (Table 7.3).

This first glance at swingers has revealed it to be a rather limited behavior pattern among marrieds or singles. Certainly it appears that there are swingers to be found in middle America, and it would appear that they are more likely to be single than married. Still, from the testimony of the Interaction group, it may be that such activity, for many, is short-term and not a regular way of life. Generally swinging appears to be less extensive than Kinsey or Gebhard believed it to be. And while some people with past histories of swinging are to be found among the marrieds, we cannot tell whether this lifestyle continues, or represents a period from past life as a single. One thing is clear, however, even though a swinging life exists or has existed for a few married people, the older tradition of no premarital intercourse, or intercourse limited only to a person subsequently married, continues to persist. Two-thirds of the once married indicated that they have had only one sexual partner in their lifetime. Utilizing the subcategories, the swinger is most likely to be a young (18-29), divorced male.

GREENER GRASS

If swinging is limited in scope of participation by both singles and marrieds, then the stereotype may be more a factor of perceptions shaped by such literary influences as Playboy and pornographic films. If this is so, then the sample is likely to believe that the grass is greener, that is, that others are more sexually involved than they are. As a means of checking this idea, we asked how people perceived others in the same category regarding number of sexual partners. Respondents in the sample tended to guess that others had had more sexual partners than they had (Table 7.4; compare Table 7.1).

Though more than 40 percent of the never married had had only 1 sexual partner or none at all, only 14 percent believed this was true of others. It was not just a case of the young believing the boasts of their peers, because the once marrieds were no different. Two-thirds of them said that they had had only 1 partner, but only a quarter of them believed this to be true of others. The never marrieds and the marrieds, at every level of activity, and even the swingers believed that others of their own kind had had more partners than there actually were represented by the sample.

Only the divorced were likely to perceive themselves as being more active than others. It would appear that the divorced find it difficult to believe that others of their own kind have had as many partners as they have actually had.

The Interaction group was similar in their beliefs about the grass being greener, that is, they also believed that others of the same civil status had more partners. Thus the stereotype may indeed be a media creation.

SEX WITHOUT LOVE

Our finding of a limited number of swingers contradicts the conclusion that there has been a general shift in attitudes toward sexual experimentation without love (for example, see Hunt, 1974). Another confirmation of the belief that the swinging stereotype is, perhaps, more of a media creation comes with two questions concerning the circumstances of acceptable sexual behavior.

Attempting to assess the relationship betwen sex and love, we asked the singles if they would engage in sexual relations to avoid losing a partner. There was not much difference between the answers of the never married and the divorced (Table 7.5). Singles, by a three-to-one majority, said no, they would not engage in sexual relations just to keep the affections of a particular person. The Interaction group gave the same answer even more strongly, by a four-to-one majority. "You're in deep trouble if you do that," said a divorced woman from the Interaction group.

Well then, did singles require love before urging or agreeing to sexual relations? Here the singles proved to be much more evenly divided, again without much difference between never marrieds and divorced. Half said that love was not a necessity in sexual relations. Actually, the only category to indicate a majority of this necessity was the never-married female. In contrast to divorced women, they were far more likely (69 percent versus 44 percent) to believe that love is a necessary prerequisite to having sex. It may be recalled that a large percentage of the divorced had recalled having a larger number of sex partners. Thus it would appear that as one becomes more sexually experienced, the need to rationalize sexual encounters with terms such as love or marriage becomes less necessary. The fact that a large majority (76 percent) of single males or females would not be intimate in order to keep a date, but only half require love — and those mostly never-married females — indicates that having sex implies strong feelings of affection but not necessarily a strong commitment.

Again the Interaction answers closely reinforced the answers of the singles in the sample. "I have had sex with women whom I didn't necessarily like," said one divorced man in his 30s. "I really enjoyed that part of it. It's an activity, sometimes, that's separate from all other dimensions."

"It's like any other activity," said another. "It's like tennis. Sex is sex. This business about casualness is a bunch of baloney. I mean the fondling is good when it's going on, right? I mean at the moment it's good, or else it's bad, right?"

But a divorced woman in the same age bracket responded: "I think it's easier for men to live that way than women. I think the majority of women see themselves as being somebody's mother or their sister." But then she added: "I think we have to have more compassion for the results of our situation. What if we have a baby? Is the kid going to be illegitimate? If we've got six boyfriends, who do we know the father is?"

To which another woman responded: "Oh, but not with the contraception and information that's available to women today! It's an individual thing."

After seeing the results, we wondered if "love" had been too strong a word. What would the response have been if we had substituted the word "affection?" This bothered the members of the Interaction group too, and they kept worrying about the word.

"How would you define love?"

"An emotional attachment," said a younger divorced woman. "That you really care for people."

"You have to have a deep desire to please the person," said an older man.

"How about 'like'?" suggested another young woman. "You like a person, you enjoy being with him. You don't have to be in love with him."

In reality, swinging contradicts the ideal that romantic love should be exclusive and possessive (Reiss, 1972: 243), that is, that there should be strong, affectionate feelings accompanying sexual relations.

Thus, it seems that there is considerable willingness among singles to engage in sexual relations without marriage. Those who are willing, however, want some positive feelings to be involved. Most of them say they will not have sexual relations alone as the price of a relationship. This leads to a modification by Macklin (1978) of Hunt's conclusion. She notes that affection is generally believed desirable. Reiss (1972) refers to this situation as "permissiveness with affection." This is the general belief that premarital intercourse is acceptable for both women and men under such conditions as a stable relationship with love, engagement, or strong affection present (Moneymaker and Montanino, 1978: 31). And Sagarin goes so far as to say that America has completely accepted the "one-to-one," young adult, heterosexual, consensual, affectional relationship (Moneymaker and Montanino, 1978: 35).

Several Times a Week

Number of partners is one gross measure of swinging, but another of interest in college dormitories and probably among Type A personalities — those oriented to things that are faster, bigger, and better — is the frequency of sexual relations. The computer-shaped question on this subject seemed even more indelicate:

> 66. During the last six months, how often have you had sexual intercourse?
> ______ 1) Never or almost never
> ______ 2) Once or twice a month
> ______ 3) Once or twice a week
> ______ 4) Several times a week
> ______ 5) Daily or more often

Again, seven-eighths of our respondents were gracious enough to answer the question. Having seen the results of the question on number of partners, we expected a similar pattern. But, as it turned out, we got quite a different answer when we turned our attention from number to frequency (Figure 7.2). Marrieds were more likely to have sexual relations twice a week or more. Singles, once a week or less. If singles had more variety, marrieds had a greater frequency.

This time, however, a breakdown into subcategories revealed something else: a very different pattern between never marrieds and divorced. It is clearly the never marrieds who are most likely to go without on any given night, while the divorced are more likely to experience sexual relations on an every-other-night basis than even the married (Table 7.6). This is not to say that if you are divorced you are likely to be engaging in sexual relations frequently. On the contrary, the divorced are more likely than the married to have very little current sexual

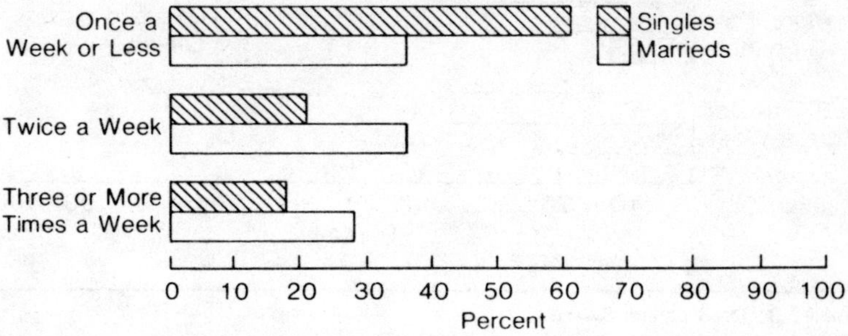

Figure 7.2 How Often?

It would appear that there is a correlation between marriage and frequency of sexual relations.

activity: 42 percent of the divorced indicated a frequency of once per week or less as compared to 36 percent of the married. A comparison with the Interaction sample indicated that even those divorced persons who were actively seeking social contacts were even less likely to be experiencing sexual relations frequently. About a third (36 percent) of the Interaction sample divorced indicated that they were having sex once a week or less while more than half (55 percent) indicated that they were having sexual relations no more often than twice a month, and a good many (26 percent) not at all. This is, perhaps, not surprising, since the divorced, not having the reserved partner of the married, have sex on a more opportunistic and irregular basis. On the other hand, swingers have more frequency and more of the divorced are swingers (Table 7.7; Figure 7.3). Thus, among the divorced there are likely to be those with more frequency and those who are cut off from sexual relations.

The problem of sexual inactivists may not be solvable by remarriage. The divorced are more likely to have an active sexual life than the remarried (36 percent versus 25 percent), while sexual inactivity is about equally likely for each category (42 percent versus 43 percent). It should be borne in mind, however, that the divorced category was somewhat younger than the remarried category and the younger tended to have sex more frequently.

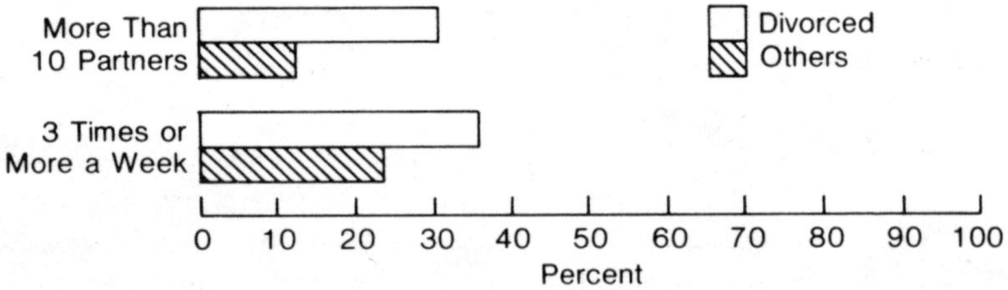

Figure 7.3 Divorce and Swing

Whether you count sexual partners or sexual frequency, the most active are more likely to be divorced than not.

The gender and age variables also show similar variations between number of sexual partners and sexual frequency. Thus, twice as many males as females had more than 10 sexual partners, but the frequency figure shows only a slightly higher percentage of males (27 percent) to females (21 percent) reporting a frequency of 3 or more times per week (Table 7.8). Not surprisingly, the oldest age category (50+) have the fewest reporting a high frequency range. But it is surprising that the youngest category (18-24) would also have fewer reporting this frequency range, since this category was second only to the 25-29 year olds in the number of those who are swingers (Tables 7.9 and 7.3).

This glance at frequency of sexual relations indicates that there may be a relationship between the number of sexual partners and frequency of intercourse among the singles, but such is not the situation among the marrieds. The person most likely to be among those that have the highest frequency would be a middle-aged (25-49), divorced male — the very person who is high among those with many sexual partners. But the category next most likely to be having sexual intercourse on an every-other-night basis is the once married — a category with few participants among the swingers.

In a poll conducted by *Playboy* magazine (Hunt, 1974), one of the reasons given by men for marriage was a steady sex life.

If twice a week is a steady sex life, it would appear that this goal is best obtained by marriage. If swinging is what is wanted, divorce should be considered. If sex is considered objectionable, it is best never to marry.

Love and Satisfaction

The questions about love may provide some qualitative information about the sex lives of singles. But the question of satisfaction with sex life still remains. If singles, and especially the divorced, are likely to have a more active or adventurous sex life, while marrieds are likely to be more steady, which is the more desirable status? Is the single life more exciting? Is marriage more satisfying? Or is the quest of some singles a sign of doubt or anxiety? Or, on the other hand, is marriage a sexual bore?

There is evidence that marriage provides greater sexual satisfaction. A *Playboy* study indicated that married men are more satisfied with love than single men (Hunt, 1974: 12). *Redbook's* "startling new report" indicates that number of partners is not a valid index of satisfying sexual relationships (Tavris, 1978b: 193).

Our answers support these findings. Though singles are more likely to be swingers, marrieds are clearly more satisfied with their sex lives. Only 6 percent of the marrieds were shown to be swingers, but four-fifths of them were sexually satisfied (Figure 7.4; Table 7.10), whereas a fifth of the singles were swingers but only half were sexually satisfied.

The breakdown into the various subcategories of the sample reinforces the conclusion that there is little relationship between sexual satisfaction and the number of partners. The divorced and the never married were among those with higher numbers having more partners, but that was not the situation for sexual satisfaction. The divorced, who were most likely to be swingers, were also the most likely to be among the dissatisfied. The males were more likely to be swingers, but less likely to be sexually satisfied (Table 7.11). From the standpoint

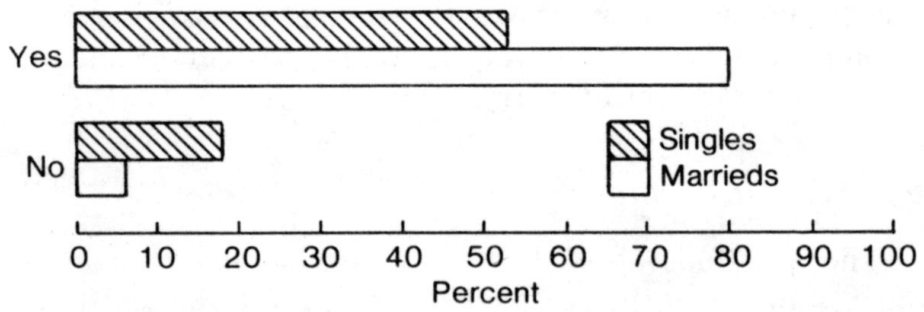

Figure 7.4 Are You Satisfied?
Marrieds are much more likely to be satisfied.

of age, the youngest categories (18-29) were among those having more than 10 sexual partners but they were also among those most likely to be dissatisfied (Tables 7.12 and 7.3).

A younger divorced man commented on this discrepancy with a rather effective mixing of metaphors:

> The physical sexual activity is not the issue, and I think that is not what most people look for when they engage in that kind of sexual activity. You know, it's like when you go to the carwash, I assume, not to sit there and watch the water run down, you go to get the car washed. But people are certain to want an intellectual and emotional fabric to weave with this partner, and apparently they tend not to find it, and it's that emotional satisfaction of compassion and tenderness and feeling of togetherness that they look for, and not the fact that they can get laid.

The idea that swinging may be lacking in those items considered important for sexual satisfaction is summarized in a study made by Hetherington et al. (1977). They noted that pleasure in having diverse sexual experiences was a factor for men in their first year following divorce. But by the end of that period, "they want longer lasting, more meaningful relationships." Similar was the situation for divorced women: "For them, casual sex brought on feelings of desparation, depression, and low self-esteem." In sum, for both divorced men and women,

> the formation of lasting intimate relations involving deep concern and a willingness to make sacrifices for the partner as well as a strong attachment and desire to be near the other person, was a strong factor in happiness, self-esteem, and feelings of confidence in sexual relations [Hetherington et al., 1977].

If sexual satisfaction is not the result of swinging, why do people engage in swinging? In addition to the items mentioned earlier in the Smith (1979) study, Interaction respondents indicated that sex provided them with a number of positive feelings, and that this was especially true for the divorced, who have a need to overcome a sense of rejection. Sex provides them with feelings of being attractive, acceptable, and worthwhile, and so gives them feelings of personal power. These feelings, in turn, add to their self-esteem and provide them with a sense of self. For the divorced, sex was also a "used-to-it" habit which, "like an itch, wants to be scratched."

Murstein (1978: 125-127) also notes that this game of catch-as-catch-can requires less time consumption, is less emotionally demanding than an affair, and is also less expensive. It is a means of eliminating sexual boredom via variety, and in this manner one can learn a lot about sex. Sexual satisfaction however, may not be an outcome of swinging since the increased possibility of venereal disease, the constant search for a new partner, and the lack of emotional closeness may prevent sexual enjoyment or even the ability to perform adequately. All in all, it appears that while swinging may be fun, it also may lead to dissatisfaction. Whether it is one or the other depends on the basic reasons for the numerous partners. Fisher (1972: 155-156) believes that the divorced tend toward much sexual activity because of their unhappiness and need for bridging the gap between themselves and others; what is really being sought is an enduring intimate relationship. The findings of

Hetherington et al. (1977) and in later chapters in regard to loneliness, happiness, and future marital desires would seem to confirm this conclusion.

In sum, the divorced are the most likely to be dissatisfied and the most likely to be swingers. If they tire of swinging and the dissatisfaction grows too great, remarriage seems to be a reasonable solution. The remarried proved to be even more likely than the married to be satisfied with their sexual lives, and none at all responded that they were very dissatisfied (Table 7.10).

The Swinger Image

It appears that there is some justification for the swinger image among singles. If a person swings from one partner to another, he or she is most likely to be divorced. On the other hand, any given single is unlikely to be a swinger. Swingers are in the minority in any category, even that of the divorced. And if the person has ever married, the chances are that his or her sex life is inactive, and that he or she has had fewer than four partners in his or her lifetime.

Married people are more likely than singles to report having sexual relations with a person they love, and they are more likely to be satisfied with their sex lives. But a given single person is also likely to be satisfied with his or her sex life, and is probably not having sexual relations with a person for whom he or she does not feel some affection.

If a Joe Namath swinger image applies to anyone, it would be to the divorced. Joe himself, being never married, is likely to have had few sex partners in his lifetime, and sexual relations once a week or not at all — at least, that would be the probability if he lived in Dayton and were not a former football star and television personality.

Profile: The Sexually Satisfied

Significant findings from this study show that if you are a typically sexually satisfied person then you are also married or remarried, less likely to change moods frequently or to be bored, and more likely to be satisfied with your day, to see your friends as less happy than yourself, and to see yourself as a happy person. You are more likely to go out often socially, to spend more time with your spouse, and to spend less time watching television. You are also more likely to come from a home where both parents were open in their emotions. Finally, the figures show that your sexual satisfaction may be related to sexual intercourse frequency but not necessarily to the number of sexual partners you have had.

Comparing those who are the most and least sexually satisfied and those who have had the most and fewest partners will clarify the relationship somewhat between these two factors. Overall, more females note being sexually satisfied than males, though the males have had intercourse with more sexual partners. A divorced person is most likely to have had the most sexual partners — though the divorced are less likely than the married to be sexually satisfied. Considering age categories, the 25-29 year old is more likely to have had the most sexual partners and to be among those that are more likely to be sexually satisfied. Thus it would appear that the relationship between sexual satisfaction and the number of sexual partners is negligible.

Those most likely to be satisfied are remarried females between the ages of 25 and 39, while the least satisfied are most likely to be younger (18-24), never-married males. On the other hand, the most satisfied male would be married and in the 25-39 age range, and the least satisfied female would be an older (40 or above), divorced female. These findings tie in with the Kinsey findings (1948), which concluded that males reach their sexual prime at a relatively early age, whereas females do not reach this point until their late thirties. Thus the least likely persons to be achieving their sexual needs would be the young, never-married male and the older, divorced female, which is what our findings also reveal.

A final comparison of the most and least sexually satisfied in our study indicates that the sexually satisfied would be found among all the education categories, with little difference as to

Profile: Sexual Behavior

	Number of Partners		Frequency		Satisfaction	
	Least	*Most*	*Least*	*Most*	*Least*	*Most*
Gender	female	male	female	male	male	female
Civil status	married once	divorced	never married	divorced	never married	remarried
Age	50+	25-29	50+	25-29 or 40-49	18-24	30-39
Education	less than high school or high school	less than high school	high school	college degree	some college or degree	little difference
Political identity	conservative	neutral	conservative	neutral	liberal or neutral	liberal or neutral
Religious affiliation	Protestant	none	none	Catholic	other or none	Catholic

numbers among them. Regarding religion, the most satisfied are more likely to be Catholic, and politically they are likely to be liberal or neutral. The least satisfied are more likely to have some college education or a college degree, are likely to be neither Catholic nor Protestant, and are likely to be politically liberal or neutral. In sexual matters, political conservatives are not included among the extremes of either satisfaction or dissatisfaction. In other words, conservatives are conservative.

PART IV

Single and Married Outlooks

Chapter 8

LONELINESS: THE GREAT BUGABOO

Are Singles Deviant?

Much of the sociology of the sixties and seventies has to do with perceptions of deviance. One category after another has been perceived to have suffered from discrimination, discrimination often unperceived by either the perpetrators or the victims. In calling attention to the discrimination, defenders of these categories have, of necessity, called attention to the categories themselves. The risk is always that in calling attention to the category one may provide a target for discrimination, even as one provides a means for recognition and change.

For example, the handicapped have gained access to more buildings and probably more jobs, but future mayors like John Collins of Boston or presidents like Franklin Delano Roosevelt will be labeled as handicapped, not as men who happen to be in wheel chairs. There is now a category called "handicapped" that we can help or discriminate against. We have seen that the spinsters of earlier decades had no perception of themselves as singles. And the census data, to this day, classifies as "singles" only those that have never married. The divorced and widowed were also perceived as categories, but, along with the never married, their common civil status went unnoticed.

Thus singles, by identifying themselves as such, are providing awareness and organizational structures that aid in reducing the perception of their being deviant and thereby help redress social inequities. But they are also creating a category that can be identified, classified, and targeted for conscious or unconscious discrimination.

Throughout the century, singles have been perceived as deviant by the marrieds. They have been opposing powerful norms that have defined marriage as the most desirable status for adults. But the problem of this deviance varied according to the category. The problem of the never married was the same as that of any other problem of psychotherapy: The victim must first recognize that there is a problem. Once that was acknowledged, he or she was ready to take steps toward entering normal society, to rise above the selfishness of living for oneself or the integrity of refusing to journey to the Catskills to meet somebody. The divorced, on the other hand, had followed the norms and tried marriage. The problem was the failure to reconcile, and so the divorced person had suffered or caused irreparable damage. The widowed were an acceptable deviant problem, since they were experiencing what now would be called a normal stage of development.

Those who are now challenging this concept of deviance, who insist that many singles are choosing an alternative within the norm, are themselves challenging the norm by attempting to redefine it. Thus, whether they challenge the concept or accept themselves as deviant, singles are swimming against a tide, taking on an extra social burden that may have psychological and physical consequences. The burden is likely to be carried by the divorced as well as the never married, since breaking a marriage adds yet another set of psychological problems, carrying possibilities of grief, guilt, and burdens of added responsibility (Bell, 1966: 705-710).

On the other hand, from the viewpoint of many of the married as well as advocates of singlehood, the absence of family responsibilities can lead to a carefree existence, a happier situation in which singles have more fun. For example, in Chapter 6 we saw that singles do seem to spend more time at leisure activities. Chapter 7, however, showed that greater activity does not necessarily lead to greater satisfaction. Could it be that both of the above viewpoints will follow the patterns previously indicated? Do singles, having to challenge norms in one way or another, pay a cost in negative psychological consequences, yet, because of their greater freedom, experience a more exciting and fun-filled life? Or is our original hypothesis fundamentally correct? Would an investigation of everyday life show that singles do not differ much from marrieds, that compared to marrieds they neither suffer greater emotional problems nor have more fun? Would it turn out that singles are neither happier nor unhappier than marrieds?

To investigate these possibilities, we attempted to ask questions that would throw some light on feelings of loneliness, which was described in Chapter 4 as "the great bugaboo" of singles. But we were not certain that what people said about loneliness would be conclusive, either because the literature of the seventies had persuaded the singles to understate their feelings or because the marrieds, having made a compact against loneliness, might be unwilling to recognize it. So we also asked some questions about health, to see whether answers about stress, drugs, alcohol, or contemplation of suicide would either contradict or reinforce answers about feelings. Although loneliness is a psychological state, its links to physical ailments and to suicide have been shown (Rubin, 1979: 85). Finally, we wondered whether these feelings and conditions would be reflected in perceptions of happiness. This chapter deals with loneliness, Chapters 9 and 10 deal with health, and Chapter 11 discusses happiness and fun.

Lonely Acts

LONELINESS VERSUS ALONENESS

> Her loneliness — My God, had this always been so? — had been largely caused by her sense that she was supposed to have a man, supposed to have someone, or else be the pathetic woman in the rain, staring into a lighted house [French, 1978: 434].

The significance of any act depends on perception and interpretation. Thus *Newsweek* (1973) observes that a new, "less blatant" version of the old singles club has come into existence. These clubs are usually built around some sort of special interest that offers the singles something beyond one another.

Blatant? "Singles are lonely. The existence of singles clubs and their popularity proves that." Does it? Is getting together in a bar, a club, or a church, for that matter, automatically a sign of loneliness? Is it blatant unless your purpose is to go bowling or to succor the distressed? Or is it simply a sign of health and sensibility?

One member of Interaction, a divorced man in his 40s, was particularly critical about the pursuit of loneliness by sociologists. "Don't consistently introduce loneliness and singles," he said. "Talk to singles ad individuals. I do something because I feel that way and I want to do it and not because I'm trying to offset loneliness. If I want to talk to Mary or not talk to Mary, or talk to Jane or not talk to Jane, I do it not because I'm offsetting loneliness but because the individual is interesting to me or I want to communicate with the individual and I resent being put into this slot that says, 'Goddamit, the only reason you're talking to Jane is you're offsetting loneliness,' and that's bullshit."

This criticism has its point. Certainly there are many stereotypes that line the activities of singles with loneliness. But there has been enough evidence in past findings to justify a comparative study of loneliness, especially when it is found that the most commonly expressed idea among respondents regarding the word "single" was that of being "lonely." The swinging single is pictured as going to singles bars not to celebrate freedom but with the hope of meeting someone, anyone, even if it is only for the evening, even if it means a casual assignation. After all, "it's better to be surrounded by people you don't want to talk to . . . than to drink alone in your apartment" (Newsweek, 1973: 54). Are we "so afraid of loneliness that we flee from solitude, fearing emptiness?" Was Margaret Mead correct when she suggested that the "reason we cluster together with such determination is because 'nowhere in childhood or youth is there any training or any practice in self-sufficient isolation'?" "Who wants to be free when it means being alone?" (O'Brien, 1973: 39-40, 62).

But are we really so inept at isolation? Does being alone mean being lonely? Of course, if you go into a singles bar you are going to find a large group of single people, some of whom may be feeling lonely. But we have already seen that on any given night most singles are not at a singles bar, or for that matter at church or alone at the theater. They are likely to be home, some drinking, to be sure, but also watching television, or working in the cellar making a lowboy, or baking kugel, or reading Herodotus. Possibly the person home alone is married, baby sitting for a spouse. Or even if both spouses are home, they may be engaged in separate activities in the same or different rooms. Thus it is painful to be lonely but it can be pleasant and valuable to be alone. According to Robert Weiss, loneliness is a result of two different social needs: a sense of attachment (an intimate relationship) and a sense of community (a network of friends who share our interests and concerns; Rubin, 1979: 85). Loneliness, then, is not necessarily a question of whether one does things with someone, but of whether there is someone to turn to, to call, to touch, when these needs are to be fulfilled. That is, "you are lonely when you feel there is nobody upon whom you can rely to augment you, especially in conditions of stress or threat" (Lear, 1980: 202).

> I don't understand myself. I don't love him. I don't even like him. I want no part of him, really. But sometimes I get so lonely for him. . . . Now I get an empty, scared feeling that nobody would care whether I lived or died [Lear, 1980: 204].

JOINING AND EATING

In an attempt to understand the significance of loneliness, we chose three kinds of acts: joining organizations, eating alone, and entering an empty room. Joining has already been mentioned as an activity that is associated with loneliness. Eating is a daily ritual that we may engage in alone or with others. Often we look for someone to have lunch with and sometimes we are disappointed when no one is available. On the other hand, sometimes we want to brown bag alone and work through a problem, in which case we may be disappointed when someone seeks to join us. Entering an empty room is an experience more likely for singles, so we wondered whether singles and marrieds would respond differently.

As it turns out (Table 8.1), most people think that they join social clubs for some other purpose than to assuage loneliness. Only 21 percent of the singles and 16 percent of the marrieds in our sample acknowledged loneliness as a reason. So joining may be a sign of loneliness for some, but not for most, though it figured more in the considerations of the singles.

As for eating alone (dining alone, we phrased it, which may have eliminated the image of a grab-and-run breakfast or a brown bag), that experience seems to have had a more significant impact (Table 8.1). A considerably higher percentage of singles and marrieds thought that dining alone was a lonely experience. But once again the percentage of singles was somewhat higher (46 percent versus 34 percent).

As one divorced woman in her 40s explained: "I have no trouble now, but when I was first divorced, that was very difficult to do. It was even difficult for me to go into a restaurant at night with another woman. And now I would go in by myself and not think about it. But that took a while. I have finally learned to speak up and tell them I do not want that table by the kitchen door because I'm a single woman, I want that one over there, the best one in the house!"

This metamorphosis from withdrawal to assertiveness was described by another younger divorced woman with reference to going to the movies: "A lot of times there'd be a movie or something. I wouldn't go alone. One night I did. I said, 'You know, that's really stupid. I've been wanting to see this movie, it's not that far to go, why shouldn't I go? You go with somebody to a movie, you sit there, you don't talk anyway.' So I went to the movie, and I ran into several couples that I knew, and one of the couples said they were going out for pizza and a beer after the movie and I had the best time, just the three of us, and I thought, 'Well, that was really dumb that I hesitated to go alone.'"

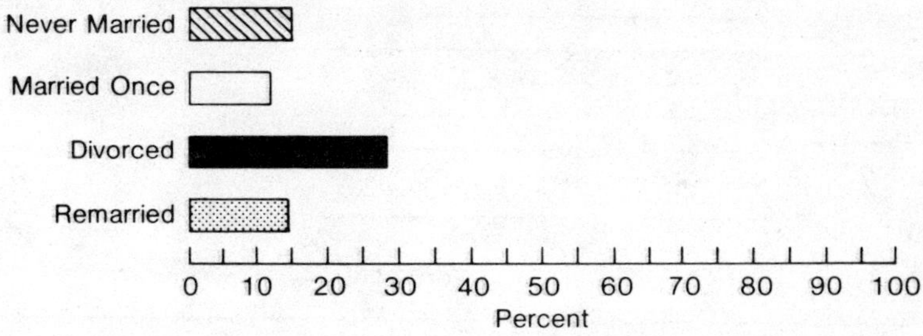

Figure 8.1 Apprehensive About Entering an Empty Room
The divorced certainly stand out clearly on this seemingly innocuous question.

THE EMPTY ROOM

37. Are you apprehensive upon entering an empty room?
______ 1) Yes
______ 2) No

An empty room? This seemed like a strange question. Why apprehensive? At first glance the findings seemed similar to those on joining social clubs. A low percentage of both categories associated the act with loneliness, but once again it was the singles (18 percent versus 13 percent) who were more apt to do so. But this time, when subcategories were considered, it turned out that the divorced were considerably more affected than the other categories. By a two-to-one ratio, the divorced reported feeling apprehensive about entering an empty room (Figure 8.1).

As one divorced person put it, being alone is difficult when newly divorced. It accentuates one's vulnerability. The empty room compounds feelings of loneliness.

The Interaction group was no help in explaining this one:

> Question: How do you feel about just walking into an empty room?
> Woman: Sometimes it's great!
> Man: Fantastic!

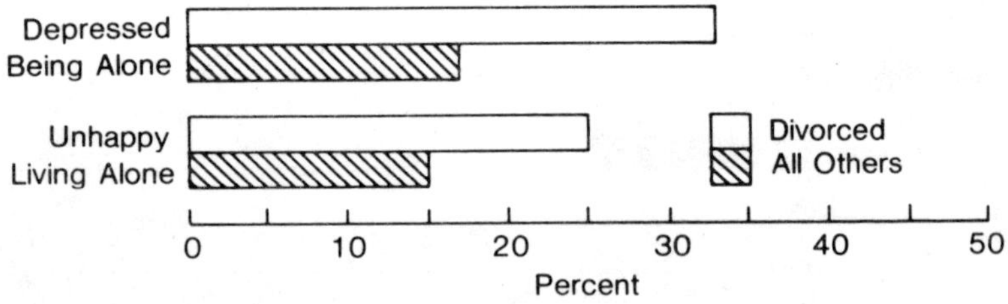

Figure 8.2 Lonely Being Alone
Being alone may not mean loneliness, but it is more likely to for the divorced.

Being Alone

The loneliness of the divorced, suggested by the empty room, became manifest in the answers to a pair of questions about simply being alone (Figure 8.2). The divorced, by almost a two-to-one percentage compared to other categories, said they were depressed being alone. Not surprisingly, then, a considerably higher percentage of divorced compared to others said they were unhappy living alone. These are people who have made the switch from having a constant adult companion. As a remarried female noted, "When I was single, I missed being close."

In terms of acts or just being, it would appear that the divorced are more likely to feel lonely than are the never married. The divorced, compared to all other categories, are more likely to feel lonely upon entering an empty room, just being alone, or living alone (Figure 8.2). The never married scored high only on dining alone (Table 8.1), the activity most likely to be perceived as lonely by all categories, since it is a social activity that is expected to be done in twos. On the other hand, the never married, compared to all other categories, were least likely to perceive living alone as a lonely experience. What may be involved here are changes in perceptions over time. The never married may not be lonely because they have not experienced marriage, and therefore have not experienced the implications of loneliness. Two-thirds of them still live at home or with roommates of either sex. Others may be looking forward to breaking free.

It was a never married who actually lived alone who could have spoken for all singles in expressing her feelings about loneliness and independence at the same time:

> I hesitate to go place[s] alone — the empty, lonely evenings do me away. I hate not being able to just sit and talk to someone. But at times when I look back on my growth since college I think — Hey, I'm making it on my own — knowing that I can support myself and do for myself without *totally* depending on someone is a treat.

Still, loneliness does not seem to be an all-consuming bugaboo, even to the divorced. Only dining alone was perceived as a lonely experience for nearly half of the singles, with the never marrieds somewhat more likely to be affected by that experience than the divorced. On any of the other questions, at least two-thirds of the divorced and four-fifths of the never marrieds did not perceive loneliness implications.

Sharing

One of the common assumptions about singles is that they are deprived of emotional attachment — "That central, intimate tie that in our society is most commonly provided by marriage" (Lear, 1980: 202). The married person, at the end of the day, can let off steam, share problems, discuss the distressing and delightful events of the day with a spouse. But the single, though he or she may have friends, does not know any one person intimately enough for sharing: "After the divorce, what I needed most was someone to share things, problems with and conversations with adults." In a *Playboy* (Hunt, 1974) survey on reasons to marry, just two were rated "very important" by clear majorities of men: "Having another person to share one's life" (74 percent) and "having someone to share important life experiences with" (62 percent). Formerly, this need could be assuaged by being a part of a network of friends or a community of common interests. We have become a nation of migrants, however, moving away from the extended family, from friends, from community, to our own nuclear nests.

Without such attachments, the loneliness of emotional isolation is more pronounced (Lear, 1980: 202, 204).

This idea of the importance of sharing was reiterated in our study in a response to a question about marriage. Asked what the greatest advantage of being married is, marrieds and singles alike most frequently replied in terms of sharing feelings: "companionship and someone to share decisions with"; "companionship"; "love and companionship"; "someone to share both the good and the bad of life"; "the opportunity to converse with someone every day"; "having someone to share your life with"; "being able to share your life with someone you love"; "togetherness is very important to me"; "love is caring and having children and sharing things, and doing things together." The word that turned up most frequently in these responses was "companionship." Apparently, these situations can also be met by a majority of singles.

In an effort to get at this feeling of sharing, respondents were asked in two different ways how often they felt there was no one with whom to share happy and sad moments and how often they felt they had no one with whom to discuss problems. The majority of singles and marrieds alike felt that they did have someone with whom to share (Table 8.2)

Among the minority who felt deprived, singles were more likely to feel the absence of someone with whom to share. And, once again, more of the divorced were likely to feel this absence than any of the other categories (Figure 8.3). Apparently both singles and marrieds felt the absence of discussion more than sharing happiness and sadness, but here the gap between the categories was much narrower (Table 8.2).

The never marrieds, when separated from the divorced, do not appear to be especially lonely. They are somewhat more likely than the married to feel an absence of sharing (18 percent versus 9 percent) or of discussion (26 percent versus 18 percent). But they are as likely as the remarried to have someone to talk to (74 percent versus 75 percent). The divorced, on the other hand, were twice as likely as any other category to have no one with whom to discuss problems (49 percent) and were far more likely than marrieds to have no one with whom to share happy and sad moments (25 percent versus 9 percent).

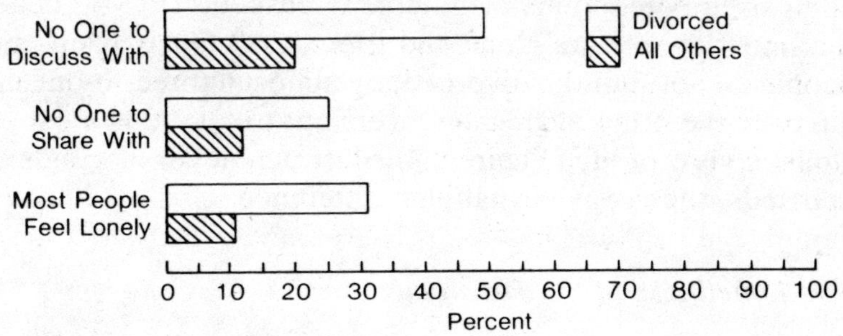

Figure 8.3 Lonely Feelings: Often/Mostly True

No matter how you approach it, loneliness appears to be the great bugaboo for the divorced.

From the supplementary comments in the sample, there were two that mentioned loneliness directly: "As a single person I am very lonely," and "I'm generally lonely, unless I go to visit friends/relatives. I just enjoy being around people who care and listen to me." One of the women who so commented had never married, the other was divorced. By contrast, a remarried woman declared that at least she had found what she had been looking for: "With my present partner I feel emotional caring and that as a whole he accepts me."

Surprisingly, belonging to a social organization does not appear to affect these feelings of being alone since the Interaction responses to these questions were similar to those of the singles in the general sample. One divorced woman said, "The only time I am really lonely is if I have something really fantastic or really bad to share. Every day I'm not lonely."

A divorced man noted how the situation affects the feelings. "Last night my daughter had a Christmas play and I had to sit by myself in that lousy audience, and I didn't have anybody to share that with, and I was disgustingly out of it."

It could be, also, that divorce begins with the loss of companionship. "I was married for 24 years and we just grew apart," a woman from Interaction recalled. "We're still friends, but our lives took different directions — different interests — and we just finally drifted apart."

One more check on feelings of loneliness was made by comparing perceptions of others. We asked: Do you believe that most people are alone and friendless? Once again, most people do not, but the divorced, by almost a three-to-one margin over the other aggregates, were apt to take this most pessimistic view of life (Figure 8.3). Between never marrieds and marrieds, there was virtually no difference.

The Loneliness of the Divorced

In terms of self-perception, at any rate, most people, married or single, do not seem to see themselves as suffering from loneliness. But the divorced seem to be susceptible to loneliness far more than any of the other categories in several ways. They are the most likely to be distressed by everyday situations, the most likely to feel cut off from people, the most likely to take an existential view of the human situation.

This came as something of a surprise. When we saw that singles were more lonely than marrieds, we expected that the difference would be manifested in the never marrieds. After all, the divorced were likely to have children, to maintain relations with a former spouse, to develop relations with new friends, to retain old friends from marriage, perhaps even to maintain relations with favored relatives from the previous marriage. Not only that, but, as we have seen, they go out more often, especially to nightclubs. They may be tired and harassed, but lonely?

On the other hand, the divorced have the obligations they had in marriage if they have custody of children. That may be why they respond especially to absence of adult companionship for purposes of discussion. Or they may miss the whole scene, experience a really empty nest. As one older divorced woman put it: "I had a house full for so many, many years, that wasn't [just] my kids, it was neighbor kids, teenagers, and I enjoyed that tremendously. Now the house is quiet. And you know, it's taken me a while, but I'm getting used to it."

In any event, visiting nightclubs and bars does not appear to be an answer to loneliness. It appears that a good many of the divorced in our sample are like the people interviewed in studies mentioned earlier. They are not going to nightclubs with friends to enjoy a good time, they are going alone in search of — to use the word they use most themselves — companionship.

> I'd really looked forward to being on my own again . . . now the days seem endless. Do you know how long it takes to eat dinner if there's nobody else at the table? Ten minutes. It's not that I miss Tony, I just miss having another warm body in the house. I mean, even if you're fighting all the time, there's a connection [Maynard, 1974: 99].

Profile: The Lonely Person

Again, a picture of the lonely person can be developed from those findings considered significant.

If you are a lonely person, you are less likely to see yourself as being a happy person most of the time, more likely to have mood changes often, more likely to be often bored, less likely to be satisfied with your day, and more likely to see single and married friends as happier than yourself. Also, if you are lonely, you are more likely to come from a home where neither parent displayed emotions, and your current relations with them are more likely to be cool or frequently antagonistic.

Perhaps your loneliness is indicated by the fact that you are less likely to go out often but also less likely to spend time with your spouse, and if very lonely, less time with your friends. In fact, if you are very lonely, you also spend less time on such leisure activities as hobbies and sports.

Apparently your loneliness affects your health somewhat, since you have a slightly higher overall illness score than that of the least lonely person, and, if you are among the very lonely, you seemingly deal with this loneliness by being the most likely person to get drunk. Perhaps this is why you are also more likely to think about suicide often. Finally, you are likely to have sexual relations less frequently, but all the same report sexual satisfaction. This finding again supports our conclusion of the previous chapter regarding the relationship between sexual frequency and satisfaction.

Profile: Loneliness Feelings, Based on Six Loneliness Items

	Dining Out		*Depressed*		*Enter Empty Room*		*Join Social Organizations*		*Unhappy*		*Deviant*	
	Most	*Least*	*Most*	*Least*	*Most*	*Least*	*Most*	*Least*	*Most*	*Least*	*Most*	*Least*
Gender	female	male	little difference		female	male	little difference		little difference		little difference	
Civil status	never married	re-married	divorced	married once	divorced	married once	never married	re-married	divorced	never married	re-married	divorced
Age	18-24	50+	18-24	40+	18-29	50+	18-24	25-39	50+	18-24	50+	24-29
Education	high school	college degree	less than high school	college degree	less than high school	college degree	less than high school or college degree	high school	less than high school	some college	less than high school	some college or degree
Political identity	conser-vative	liberal	neutral	liberal	little difference		liberal	conser-vative	neutral	liberal	little difference	
Religious affiliation	Catholic	other	Protestant	Catholic	Protestant	other	Catholic	other	little difference		Protestant	Catholic

Our portraits of the most and least lonely are taken from a composite of the following six items:

Would you dine out alone?
Are you depressed when alone?
Do you feel apprehensive when entering an empty room?
Have you ever joined a social organization to find companionship?
Do you equate living alone with unhappiness?
Is there something deviant about a person who chooses to live alone?

The most lonely person is likely to be a 40-49-year-old divorced female with less than a high school education, a Catholic or Protestant, who is politically neutral or conservative.

Our least lonely person is most likely a 30-39-year-old married or never-married male with some college education or a college degree, a political liberal who is neither Protestant nor Catholic.

Profile: Those Most and Least Likely to Feel Lonely

	Most	*Least*
Gender	female	male
Civil status	divorced	little difference among categories
Age	40-49	30-39
Education	less than high school	some college or degree
Political identity	conservative or neutral	liberal
Religious affiliation	Protestant or Catholic	other

Chapter 9

IN SICKNESS AND IN HEALTH

Is Singlehood Dangerous to Your Health?

We have seen that most of our respondents did not perceive themselves to be lonely. Even a majority of the divorced, the category most likely to be lonely, did not give responses indicating loneliness on any given question.

It is possible, though, that respondents tend to err on the side of optimism. A married person is not supposed to feel lonely, so if negative feelings exist, they must come from something else. It would almost be disloyal to one's spouse, whom one has pledged to have and to hold, to admit loneliness. Therefore, we approached the problem from a different standpoint, asking a number of questions about health, substance use, and death in order to see if such feelings were being expressed in these terms and if the differences between singles and marrieds expressed on the subject of loneliness would also be expressed in other ways.

The literature on the subject of health is exceedingly rich and varied. It is not surprising, then, that studies have come to a wide variety of conclusions. Generally, the married are perceived to be healthier than singles (Pearlin and Johnson, 1977). This may be due, as our prior chapter implies, to the unfulfilled sharing needs of singles — no one with whom even to have an argument, a lack of support, exclusion from various relationships — especially during holiday times. Greater stress may also be a factor of having to take total responsibility, of having to make all decisions. Finally, there is the stress of appearing alone in situations in which norms call for a partner. Thus, marriage has been found to be a protection against psychological stress (Braito and Anderson, 1978; Pearlin and Johnson, 1977; Somers, 1979). For example, single men have been found to be more socially maladjusted, more subject to depression, or more likely to suffer nervous breakdowns than married men. Similarly, single women over 30 were found to be more maladjusted, depressed, neurotic, and passive than their married counterparts (Gilder, 1974; Braito and Anderson, 1978; Libby, 1978). Such is the health of men and women that marriage is seen as a much better deal for the health of men than for that of women, which is another way of saying that singleness is a better deal for women than for men. According to Bernard (1979), "on almost any index you can name — mental health or whatever — married men are the best off." For example, Gove's (1979: 90) summary of various studies on psychiatric treatment found lower rates of treatment for married men than for married women, whereas there were higher rates for men than for women among the unmarried, and Bird (1972) found that single women over 30 were healthier than single men over 30. In sum, the stress of being single can result in illnesses — both physical and psychosomatic — and in such emotional and psychological responses as fear, anxiety, and depression.

Other studies continue the idea that marriage is more rewarding for men than for women. For example, married women were found to be the category most under stress, more plagued by anxiety and depression than never-married women, and three times as likely to display phobic symptoms (Braito and Anderson, 1978). Never-married women, on the other hand, were found to be above average in "personal and social adjustment" (Libby, 1978).

A reason for this difference, according to Bernard (1979), is the selectivity factor in marriage. She notes that our societal norms demand hypergamous marriages; that is, a husband must be "above" his wife in terms of age, height, education, occupation, and so on. The result is that men at the bottom of the scale in resources lose out in the marriage market, and, similarly, women at the top of the scale lose out because of their high qualities (Kain, 1981: 2).

Adding the subcategories reveals, perhaps not surprisingly, that divorce and separation were found to cause the greatest psychological stress to the individual (Somers, 1979; Gove, 1979). Libby (1978) found, for example, that never-married women were less depressed than divorced or separated women but, contrary to this general idea and our own findings, never-married men were more depressed than divorced or separated men. Generally, however, never marrieds fare better than the divorced or separated (Braito and Anderson, 1978).

Even though the results of these studies are greatly condensed and sometimes seemingly contradictory, a pattern emerges. Singles are more likely to have health problems than marrieds, but single women are less likely to have them than are married women. Finally, the divorced are more likely to be under psychological stress than everyone else and, if the prevailing pattern holds, this would be more likely for men than for women. In sum, the message that emerges from this medley of physical and mental health problems is one that is different from those we have encountered so far and one that is contrary to the stereotype of the swinging bachelor and the lonely spinster: Singlehood is good for women but bad for men.

We shall follow the pattern of the preceding chapters, looking first to see if there are differences in the health of singles and marrieds, then looking at the subcategories. Finally, in Chapter 10 we shall compare the responses of men and women.

Physical Symptoms

It is impossible to sort out physical and mental symptoms. In a given individual high blood pressure may come for purely physical reasons, although some doctors would argue that most physical ailments have mental causes. It is not our purpose to try to sort out these areas of contention. We simply included three physical symptoms that are often associated with mental stress: frequent headaches, stomach ulcers, and high blood pressure.

The results were decisive and surprising. In every case, marrieds were more likely to suffer from these physical prob-

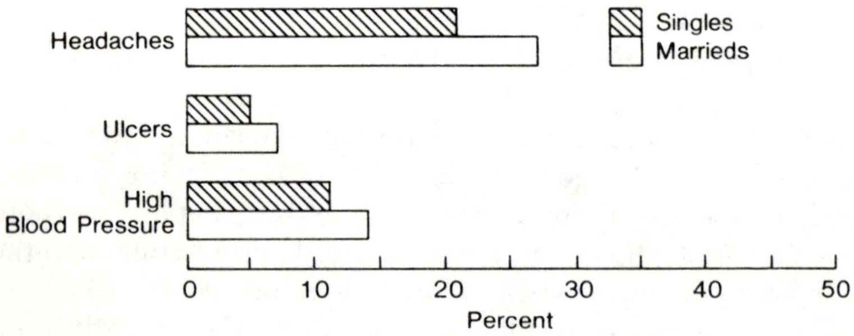

Figure 9.1 Physical Symptoms

A major surprise: Marrieds are more likely than singles to suffer stress-related physical symptoms.

lems than were singles (Figure 9.1). The breakdown into the subcategories, however, reveals that it may not be a question of singles versus marrieds, since the divorced were most likely to have ulcers and the remarried high blood pressure (with age a possible factor here, since they are the oldest category). But, all the same, if physical symptoms are a measure of mental anguish, our married respondents proved to be more susceptible than the singles (Table 9.1).

This may be due to a couple of seemingly contradictory ideas. Married people, as compared to single people, have more responsibilities and thus more difficulties in taking time off from work when feeling ill or in leaving an unhappy job situation (Verbrugge, 1979: 269). The result may be increased hypertension, which results in such stress-related illnesses as high blood pressure and stomach ulcers. Similar is the situation for the divorced, who may have to work and take care of children. On the other hand, married people can count on some home care and attention. That is, marrieds may be more aware of their illnesses and deal with them because their mates "nurse" them or encourage them to visit a doctor when they feel ill. Another factor here may be the greater number of activities engaged in by the singles. As we saw in Chapter 5, singles go out more and engage in more physical activities, thus releasing feelings that may otherwise lead to hypertension and related physical illnesses.

Mental Health

In order to understand the mental health problems of singles and marrieds, we asked a battery of questions designed to focus on three aspects of psychological stress: anxiety, guilt, and depression. Trying to get at anxiety and guilt, we asked about insomnia, nightmares, irrational fears, and crying spells. We also asked about feelings of worthlessness, despondency, and lack of interest in sex. Then we fed back questions about loneliness feelings, to see if they would be answered differently in this context (Table 9.1).

The responses indicate that more singles suffer from behavioral symptoms, such as nightmares or crying spells, than marrieds, but the difference is negligible. On the other hand, the responses on the direct symptoms are decisive: More singles worry, more are likely to feel guilty, despondent, worthless, or lonely (Figure 9.2; Table 9.1), and the loneliness question brought a more decisive contrast than it had when asked directly. A popular explanation for these responses is that married people are happier and so less stressed than singles (Berbrugge, 1979: 267). The happiness factor can be involved in these figures on mental health feelings in two ways. As our study and others reveal (Chapter 11), more marrieds believe they are happy most of the time and so the popular explanation is borne out. But the explanation also implies that married people are supposed to be happy, since they supposedly have their sharing needs fulfilled, and so such feelings as anxiety, guilt, and depression may be repressed or denied. The results are the stress-related physical illnesses noted above. On the other hand, singles are solely responsible for their financial needs, are all alone in the decision-making process, and, as we noted in Chapter 8, are more likely to have no one with whom to share happy or sad moments or with whom to discuss problems. Perhaps, then, the surprise is that more singles did not

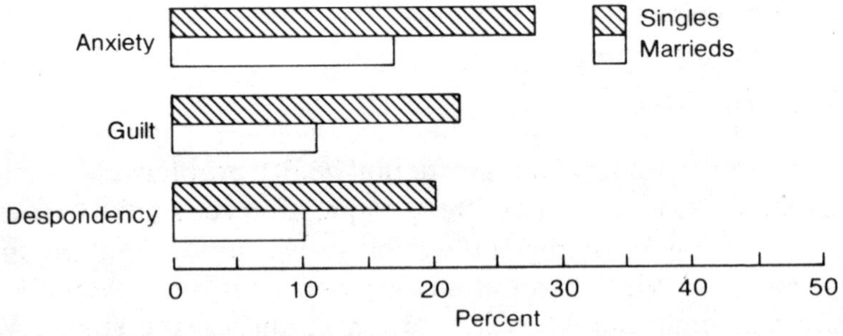

Figure 9.2 Signs of Psychological Stress
Singles, however, are clearly more likely to experience psychological stress symptoms.

express these feelings, rather than that more singles than marrieds did.

THE DESPONDENT DIVORCED AND THE SLEEPLESS REMARRIED

Once again, the breakdowns into subcategories immediately highlight the divorced. They are without doubt more subject to guilt and despondency feelings than the other categories. The question on sex seems to highlight this factor. We have seen that the divorced are both more likely than other categories to seek sexual partners and less likely to be sexually satisfied. As it turns out, they are also the least likely of all categories to be interested in sex. It seems, then, that their sexual dissatisfaction leads to a lack of interest in sex despite what appears to be a greater effort to find partners. One wonders, then, if the effort is being made because it is what one is "supposed" to do according to the stereotypes, and, as Fisher (1972) claims, as a means of dealing with loneliness. Or perhaps it is a means of reinforcing one's ego after the negative experience of the predivorce period: "To prove to myself that I am an attractive person and not what my husband said, I had several sexual encounters right away." Other measures also show the divorced to be subject to despondency (Figure 9.3). Turning to the never marrieds, we see that they are also more subject to

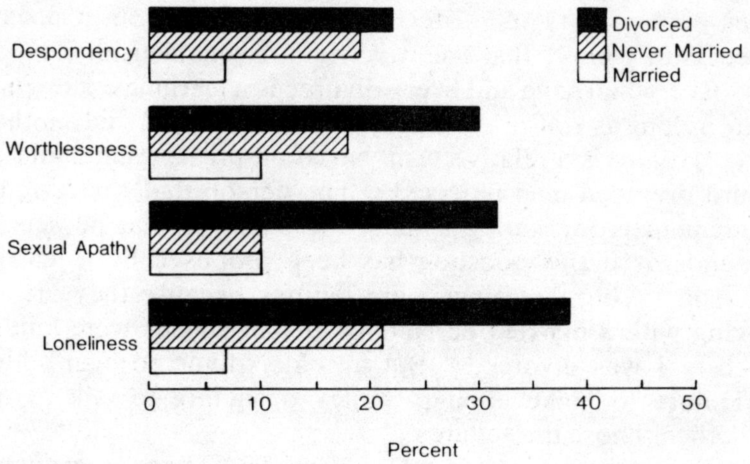

Figure 9.3 The Despair of the Divorced

Once again, the divorced are most likely to experience negative feelings.

guilt and despondency than marrieds in every category except for their interest in sex.

The picture on anxiety, however, is less decisive. The divorced have the least number troubled by lack of sleep, whereas the remarried, who are as likely to worry as the divorced, prove to be far more troubled by insomnia than any of the other categories. Oddly enough, it is the never married who are the most likely to suffer from worry and anxiety. This comes as a surprise because the stereotypes indicate a happy, swinging, nonresponsible existence for this category.

ARE SINGLES FAILURES?

We discussed with the Interaction group this pattern of guilt, despondency, and, particularly, worthlessness among singles and we wondered if it added up to a perception of failure. The response was extremely lively, but the divorced men seemed most stung by the question.

"I'm sure," said one, that "everyone who has been divorced will say, 'yes, the marriage failed.' However . . . that doesn't imply one is a failure in one's professional life, in one's ties with parents and sisters and aunts and so on, it doesn't necessarily imply that one was a failure scholastically."

Every marriage and every divorce is a learning experience, and as long as you're learning, you're not failing," said another.

"Failure is a relative term based on present standards," a third divorced man reflected. "The person that's making the judgment is measuring against the standard that he sets. It sounds as if this question has been proposed by a married person saying that singles are failures because they are not living with a married person. I felt that singles were failures before I was divorced." But an older divorced man added, "Failure to make enough money or failure to talk to one another. Those *are* failures."

The conversation turned to marrieds. "Those married people out there who have been married to one person, period," laughed one of the younger divorced men, "they're only a winner once. But the guy that's been married and divorced six times, why he's won the hand of six different women! He's a hell of a winner."

A divorced woman, the first to express a view on the subject, added: "There are a lot of marrieds that stayed together who are more miserable than the people who got divorced."

The Use of Drugs

ALCOHOLISM

In considering what singles do with their leisure time (Chapter 6), we have already encountered the image of the lonely single drinking at the bar or drinking at the nightclub in hope of human encounter. One comment on this by a single was that drinking at a bar was better than drinking alone at home.

Supporting this image, the divorced have been found to be more likely to die of cirrhosis than any other category, especially the divorced male (Gove, 1973: 54-55). Drinking also has been found to be mentioned as a major cause of marital separation, so it is also a consequence (Hunt, 1974: 27-28). Certainly,

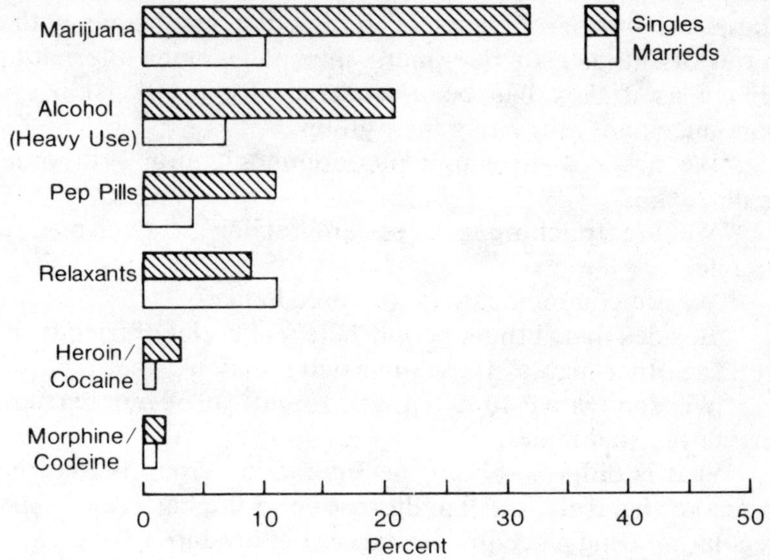

Figure 9.4 The Use of Drugs
Singles are more likely to use drugs in every category, except relaxants.

in Dayton, singles are three times as likely as marrieds to be drunk at least once a week (Figure 9.4). Unlike some of the prior findings, the distinction on this point between never marrieds and divorced is slight, and the main distinction is between singles and marrieds (Table 9.2).

The Interaction group noted that the family situation of the married household serves to restrain drinking and drunkenness. "I was reluctant to drink in front of my children," a divorced man remarked, "but now I can have those drinks after work to 'unwind' and to join the 'crowd' at the local bar." One study indicates that this lack of a "censor" may be a factor in somewhat greater use of alcohol and other drugs (Hughes and Gove, 1981).

The Interaction group, which in so many ways reinforced the results of the general study, differed very sharply here. The singles in this group do not often get drunk. Their collective percentages, in fact, are a bit under those of the married in the sample (5 percent compared to 7 percent). Informed of these statistics, the participants of Interaction responded with a series of enthusiastic one-liners, men and women alternating, almost as if they had been rehearsed for a television spot announcement promoting their group:

"We are not drowning our communication" (divorced male).

"We are touching and we are feeling" (never-married female).

"We are communicating" (divorced male).

"Besides that, I think people here make a lot of friends that you see other nights" (never-married female).

"We don't have to get drunk to get rid of our barriers" (never-married male).

What is different about the Interaction group is that they promote themselves as an alternative to the bar scene. Their regular meeting place is a Unitarian Fellowship, where, things being as they are, drinks are not served. This strongly suggests that heavy or frequent drinking is either a response to loneliness or despondency, or at least a part of the setting: One drinks in a bar even though one's purpose in going there is to meet people. In that case, the establishment of social organizations for singles such as Interaction could have a very significant effect in reducing alcoholism among singles.

PILLS, POT, AND SHOTS

Less attention has been paid to drugs other than alcohol in relation to singles. Generally these are perceived as especially associated with the young. But the answers of our respondents indicate that singles are three times more likely than marrieds to smoke marijuana frequently, or to use heroin or cocaine, or to take pep pills such as amphetamine or dexedrine. However, except for marijuana, there was little use of these drugs by any category; fewer than 10 percent of either category use heroin, cocaine, morphine, pep pills, or psychedelics (Table 9.2; Figure 9.4). But, to reiterate, those who do are more likely to be singles. Marrieds, on the other hand, show a slight preference for relaxants, such as tranquilizers or sleeping pills. Singles are more likely to smoke marijuana than to get drunk, and much more likely to do either than to take any other kind of drug (Figure 9.4).

A breakdown into subcategories indicates that the divorced, who, as noted, are more likely to sleep well, are also less likely than anyone to use sleeping pills but more likely to use tranquilizers — an item that ties in with their responses on the stress symptoms. The never married are more likely than any other catetory to smoke marijuana, while the remarried, though not approaching either of the singles subcategories, are more than twice as likely as the once married to smoke marijuana (Table 9.2). There is not much difference among the subcategories in the use of psychedelics such as LSD.

Attempting to combine the findings on drinking and drugs leads to difficulties. As the findings on the use of stimulants and relaxants imply, there may be a considerable difference in reasons for getting stoned and getting sloshed, and so the meaning of these figures are difficult to interpret. While one can be fairly dubious about effects of drugs — getting drunk, use of heroin, cocaine, morphine, codeine, or psychedelics — the results are clear: Singles are more likely to be involved, although, except in the case of alcohol and marijuana, not very frequently. Marrieds are likely to engage in more frequent use only in the case of relaxants, and even there they are surpassed by the divorced in the case of tranquilizers. On the whole, the results from the respondents on use of drugs correlates with the results on psychological stress, except that this time the difference between the divorced and the never married does not stand out.

Death and the Single

Given the information we now have on health, the final question we might ask is about mortality. Singles, after all, do seem to suffer less from physical ailments even if they are under more stress. Do they survive as well as marrieds? Do they live as long? Does the greater stress they encounter make them more likely to take their own lives?

Once again, studies already conducted on the subject seem to indicate that single men are more vulnerable than married men. They die younger and are more likely to commit suicide (Bird, 1972: 171; Gove, 1973: 65). But somewhat surprisingly, given the trend of the literature on the subject, single women are also more likely to commit suicide than are married women (Somers, 1979: 1818; Brody, 1979: C-1). Particularly hard hit are the widowed, who are ten times more likely to die in the year following the death of a spouse than other persons of the same age and sex whose spouses survives (Brody, 1979: C-4; Gove, 1973: 51). This vulnerability to death was observed in the nineteenth century by Durkheim, who remarked that the bond attaching the single man "to life relaxes because that which ties him to society is itself slack." He also observed, however, that while marriage reduced suicide among men, it increased it among women (Gilder, 1974: 32; Bernard, 1979: 5).

Since our respondents were all living, we were not able to establish anything about their mortality. But we did ask them if they had contemplated suicide. Among those who said they had often contemplated suicide or had actually planned it, the divorced were by far the most prominent (Figure 9.5). The divorced of the Interaction group thought about it far less than the regular sample but had the same numbers planning suicide. When it came to actually attempting suicide, however, the remarrieds had the highest percentage (7 percent) and the never marrieds were second (4 percent; Table 9.3). It would appear that when it comes to suicide, the divorced think about it as a means of solving their stress problems, whereas the oldest subcategory, the remarried, take more direct action.

An interesting aside to this result is provided by the divorced of the Interaction group: Those who had been divorced more than once had a much higher percentage attempting suicide than those in their first divorce or the never married. Memory and current outlook could play a role here. After all, at one time all respondents had been never married, and if they are currently feeling good, they might not remember that years ago they had often contemplated suicide. Attempting suicide, on

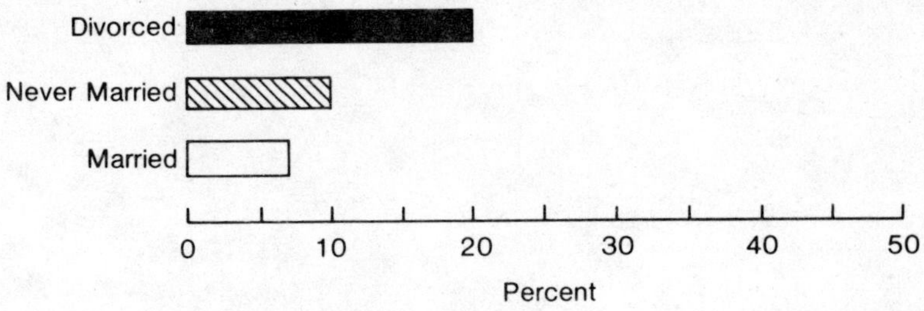

Figure 9.5 Frequent Contemplation of Suicide
The divorced are more likely to be preoccupied with thoughts about suicide.

the other hand, is something most would remember (though not necessarily report). In short, the situation may affect memory.

This examination of the health of singles versus marrieds supports prior findings that marriage is good for one's health. Nonetheless, there were some surprises, the main one being the greater propensity of marrieds over singles to suffer from stress-related physical illnesses. Perhaps, as noted, this is due to their suppressing "bad" feelings, for not to do so would be a denial of the happiness of their marriage, and to their greater awareness of such illnesses because of more attention from a mate.

Another surprise, in a sense, was the marrieds' greater use of relaxants. This finding would seemingly support our belief that marrieds may suffer more from feelings of mental stress than they admit. In another sense, the greater use of relaxants by the marrieds versus marijuana and drinking by the singles indicates that members of both categories suffer from feelings of mental stress, but that they have different means of coping with those feelings.

Chapter 10

IS MARRIAGE GOOD FOR MEN, BAD FOR WOMEN?

We noted in the beginning of Chapter 9 that the consensus of scholarly opinion (see Braito and Anderson, 1978; Fields, 1980; Libby, 1978; Bernard, 1979; Gove, 1979) indicates that marriage is better for men than for women. We wondered, therefore, whether our findings on health would vary if sex as well as civil status were considered.

Stress for All

This kind of breakdown for illness and stress (Table 10.1) produced some startling results. It would appear that, in terms of physical illness, divorce is indeed good for women and bad for men. Divorced women are less likely to report suffering headaches and high blood pressure than are the married, while the data suggest that remarriage can result in an increase in these complaints, and in ulcers as well. Meanwhile, divorced men are more likely to report an increase in high blood pressure and ulcers, while remarriage for them would seem to lead to a reduction in all three physical symptoms, including an absence of ulcers.

The more direct questions on stress, however, indicate that divorce is likely to increase stress for both sexes, in some cases dramatically (Figure 10.1). Divorced men and women alike are more likely than marrieds to report suffering from irrational fears, nightmares, anxiety, guilt, despondency, loneliness, feel-

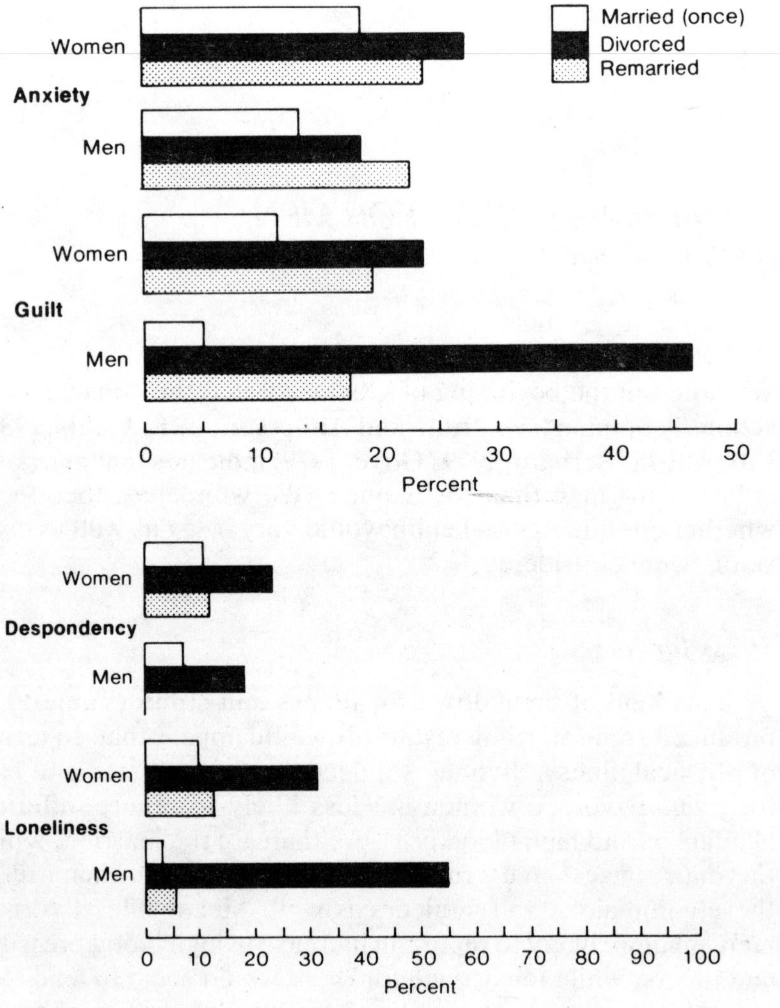

Figure 10.1 The Stress of Divorce

It would appear that remarriage often reduces the stress felt by the divorced.

ings of worthlessness, and sexual apathy. For men, the increase in likelihood of experiencing guilt and loneliness is particularly striking, and some men report crying spells, which had not been reported at all by the once married. Insomnia was the only symptom that decreased for both divorced men and women.

Remarried women are less likely than the divorced to report any of the stress characteristics except insomnia, which, for some reason, is much higher for them than for people of either sex in any other category. Remarried men also are less likely than divorced men to report direct stress in all areas except insomnia and anxiety. The drops in loneliness, guilt feelings, and sexual apathy are considerable.

Turning to the other singles category, never-married women cry more often than women in any other category and are most likely to worry. Never-married men are more likely than men in any other category to experience insomnia, worry, and despondency.

As a whole, it is difficult to conclude that singleness is particularly less stressful for either sex (Figure 10.2). Single women are more likely than married to report stress in every category except insomnia. They are more likely to experience loneliness, nightmares, crying spells, irrational fears, and sexual apathy. Single men are more likely than married to experience all the stresses except irrational fears and nightmares (and those were nearly even), much more likely to report guilt, despondency, loneliness, and worthlessness. When it comes to stress, it appears to be civil status rather than gender that is the major factor.

EQUAL RIGHTS TO DRUGS

Looking at the use of drugs by sexes, it would appear that this is one area in which equal rights are being attained. There are drugs for everyone. Men are much more likely to get drunk than women, and somewhat more likely to smoke marijuana than women, but that applies only to singles. Women, on the other hand, are more likely to use amphetamines (Table 10.2).

A closer look at drinking patterns shows that while men are likely to get drunk more often than women, the MDR (marriage-divorce-remarriage) patterns are similar. That is, the divorced of both sexes are more likely to get drunk than they were before acquiring this status; this subsides after remarriage, though it is still higher than it was at first marriage (Figure 10.3). In fact, the stress of divorce may be emphasized by the

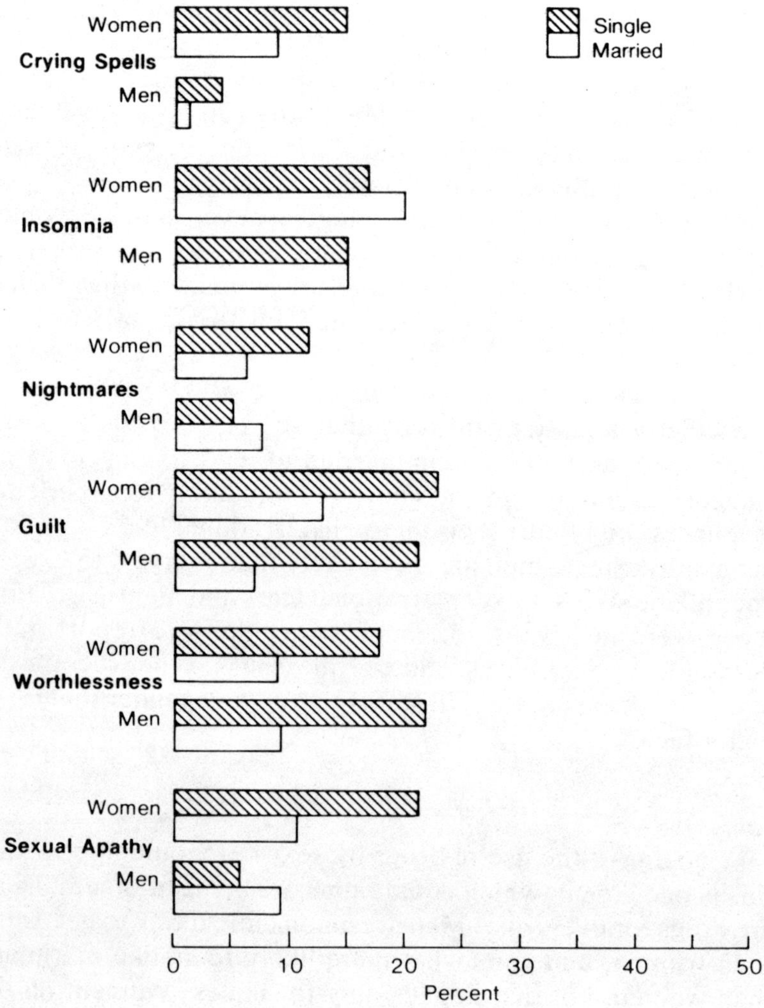

Figure 10.2 Good for Men, Bad for Women?
It would appear that marriage may be good for women too.

fact that divorced women are more likely to report getting drunk than married men.

Since our never-married sample was young, we thought we might have a mixing of the culture pattern of the young, but it turned out that the never marrieds under 30 were less likely to

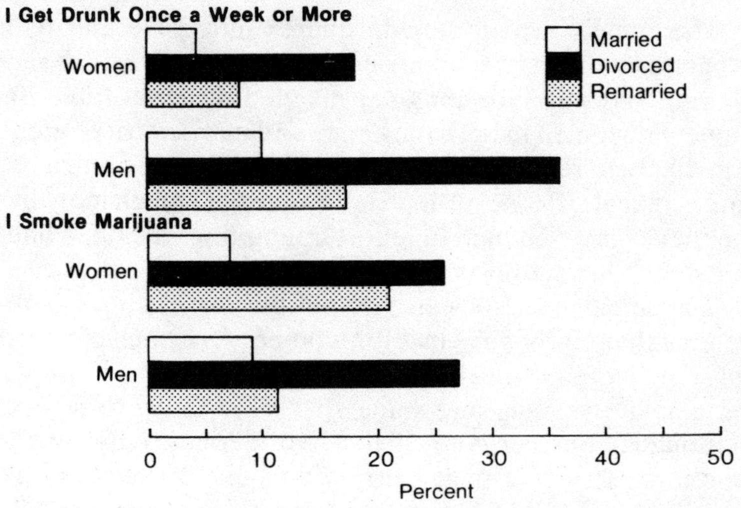

Figure 10.3 MDR Patterns for Heavy Drinking and Smoking Pot

The divorced are the most likely for either sex, though men are more likely to drink or smoke than women.

report themselves often getting drunk than were the never marrieds over 30.

As for marijuana, we find double-digit use reported by both sexes in all categories except the once married. The use of this drug by males over females is not as great here. In fact, in the marijuana MDR pattern it all but disappears, with the most striking feature being that remarried women are much more likely to smoke than remarried men. This may be due to the fact that, as we have seen, remarriage is not as good for them as it is for men.

Women are more likely than men to use amphetamines whether single or married. The heaviest users, at 15 percent, are divorced women. Heavier psychoactive drugs are not used as much by people in any category, but single men are three times as likely to try them as any other category. Use of relaxants is fairly evenly distributed by sex as by marital category.

In sum, it appears that singles are more involved with the taking of drugs and that men are somewhat more likely to be involved than women (Table 10.2).

DEATH AS AN ALTERNATIVE

The breakdown of suicide figures into male and female categories indicates that married men are more likely to report thinking about suicide than are married women (Table 10.3). However, women in both the single and married categories are more likely to report attempting suicide. The breakdown of the singles reveals that never-married women are much more likely than never-married men to report attempting suicide, a finding that somewhat supports the old spinster-bachelor image.

The suicide statistics also do not provide clear support for the idea that marriage is bad for women. One such clue is that single women are much more likely than married women to contemplate suicide, and somewhat more likely to report attempting it. Furthermore, if married men are more likely to contemplate suicide than married women, the idea that marriage is a better deal for men than for women is not supported.

MARRIAGE AS AN ALTERNATIVE

Taken as a whole, the various statistics on stress do not support the notion that marriage is bad for women. Except for physical symptoms, married women seem generally to be under less stress than single women. Single women are somewhat more likely to get drunk and use drugs than married women, and more likely to contemplate or attempt suicide. There is some indication that marriage may be better for men than for women. But even here the picture is somewhat mixed, with single women more likely to show signs of stress than single men in such diverse areas as experiencing nightmares, feeling lonely, incidence of sexual apathy, or attempting suicide (Tables 10.1 and 10.3). In any event, if we can establish that singlehood provides more stress for both sexes, there does not seem to be much point in trying to develop a score sheet to establish, between the sexes, who has the best of marriage and who the best of singlehood.

It should be remembered, however, that on all health items save one only a minority of either the singles or the marrieds, and often a small proportion, reported these symptoms regardless of gender or civil status. The one exception was that a majority of both sexes among the singles reported contemplating suicide. But even quite healthy persons, at some moment of despair, may contemplate suicide. It could be argued that the ability to consider suicide in a range of alternatives is an indication of health. After all, the most famous soliloquy in English literature ("To be or not to be . . . "), widely memorized by high school students with the tacit approval of sober and austere boards of education, is precisely on this subject.

Divorced Men and Women

THE DIVORCED MAN: CANDIDATE FOR DISASTER

Having established that for singles and marrieds in general there is not a decisive difference between the sexes, we thought we would take a closer look at the divorced man as a subject of stress. Our belief that he might be in greater trouble than the others is based on findings from previous studies (see Pearlin and Johnson, 1977; Chiriboga, 1978; Hunt, 1974), on our own observations earlier in this chapter on the divorced compared to other categories, and on considering the fact that the divorced male is usually the person who leaves the family setting and faces the trauma of divorce alone.

A comparison of the divorced man to others (Figure 10.4) indicates that he does indeed seem to experience more stress in certain areas. We compared the divorced male and female in areas in which there seemed to be a considerable difference in their stress responses, and then compared the divorced male in these same areas to other male counterparts: the never married, who also live a single life, and the remarried, who provide an alternative model for the divorced man.

This comparison indicates that divorced men are nine times more likely than divorced women to report high blood pressure, four times more likely to report ulcers, twice as likely to feel lonely or guilty, and twice as likely to get drunk. Women, on the other hand, are more likely to worry, use amphetamines, or attempt suicide, and are twice as likely to report sexual apathy.

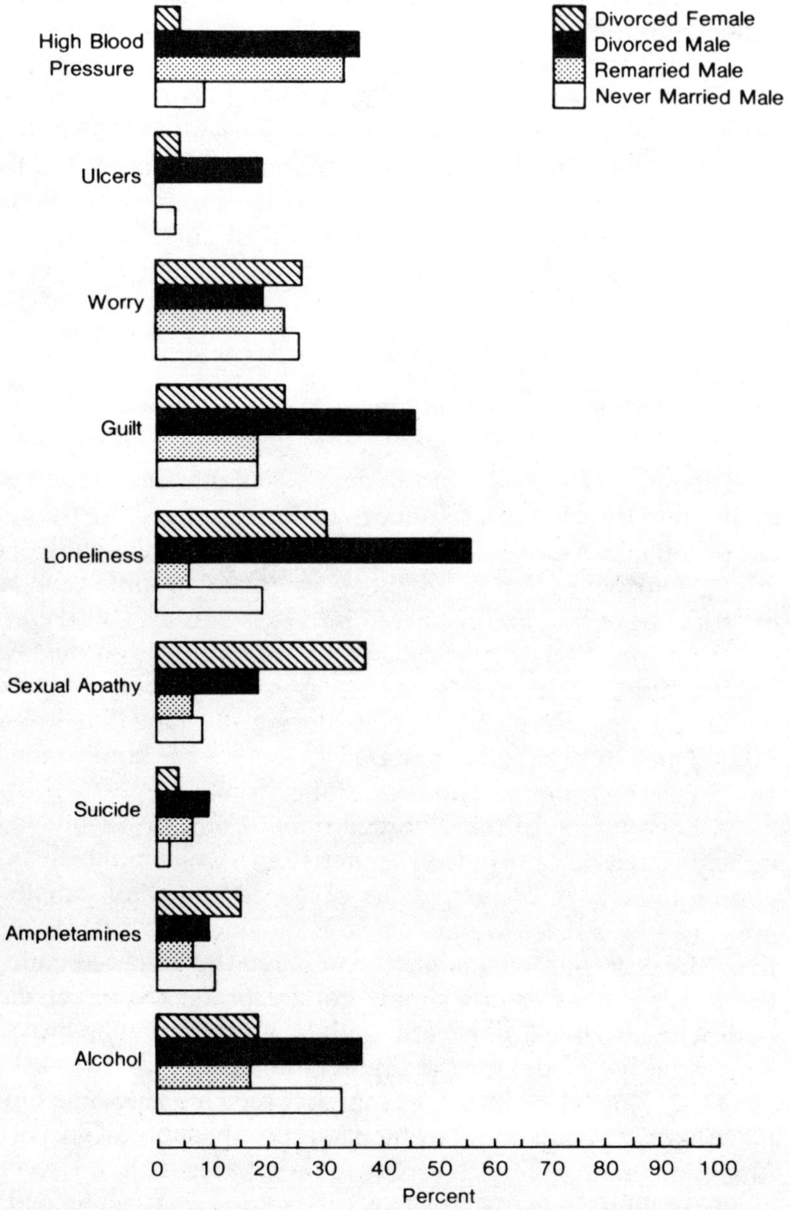

Figure 10.4 The Divorced Man: Candidate for Disaster?

The divorced man rates higher than other men in seven of these nine categories, and higher than divorced women in six categories. Yet he is the least likely of any category to worry!

Compared to his male counterparts, the divorced man is much more likely to suffer from loneliness and guilt and more likely, though on a lower scale, to report ulcers, sexual apathy, and attempted suicide. He is much more likely than the remarried man to get drunk and somewhat more likely to suffer from high blood pressure or to use amphetamines. He is much more likely than the never married to suffer from high blood pressure and somewhat more likely to get drunk, though both score high in this activity. He is slightly less likely than the never married to use amphetamines and, amazingly, considering the rest of these statistics, less likely than any of the other male categories (as well as less likely than the divorced woman) to worry! Why are there so many signs of stress in the divorced male? Perhaps because he must make the greatest adjustment in regard to former status: He is the one who must leave the familiar, the comfort of his home, neighborhood, children, and friends; he is the one who is most alone. The propensity of divorced men to remarry also means that a random sample of divorced men is likely to contain a high percentage of the recently divorced, and the recently divorced are the most likely to reflect stress (Hetherington et al., 1977).

It is hardly surprising, then, that divorced men are quick to remarry. When they do they are likely to find relief in many areas, although with two families to support their blood pressures are likely to remain high and they are more likely to worry than before.

WOMEN AND CHILDREN

Even though divorced men show the greatest signs of stress, still you would expect that divorced women would be affected by the heavier burden of responsibility for children. And certainly divorced women are more likely than any other women to report guilt, despondency, and loneliness. But in the area of stress one would most expect to be related to children — constant worry and anxiety — divorced women are outscored by never-married women (32 percent versus 26 percent; Table 10.1; Figure 10.1). This may be due to the greater coping skills developed by the formerly married as parent, homemaker, and provider, or to relief from a conflict-dominated situation.

When the Interaction group was asked if children are a cause of stress, it was not surprising that only divorced women answered. But their perceptions of stress seemed balanced by perceptions that their relationships with their children were really pretty good.

"Well, just the fact that you don't have any time to yourself. They're there every night, you gotta cook dinner for them, you gotta know where they're going. I can't just come and go or stay away for a couple of days if I feel like it, because I have teenagers at home."

"Particularly the friends I'm thinking of are women with teenage boys. They seem to have more problems than some of my other friends."

"My ex-husband and I have a very good working relationship over the kids. They go from one place to the other as they choose without restraints on them, so we've never had any arguments about this is my weekend or your weekend, we let the kids choose, whoever's got the most interesting weekend, that's where the kids go, but I think that's probably an unusual working situation and it really relieves the strain on either of us as concerns the kids."

"I find that my children are much stronger now, I think they're different people than they would have been had we not gotten a divorce. But during the first months of separation and divorce, the stress level was very high."

There was also some feeling that the fear of handling teenagers causes some women to defer the question of divorce until "the kids are about to leave. Only then do you ask yourself, is this the way I want to live the rest of my life, and is this who I want to live it with?"

As other studies have shown, divorce is usually difficult for everyone involved (see Hetherington et al., 1977). This may be due to the various sources of pain encountered by those making the transition from marriage through divorce. Pickhardt (1981: 26-27) notes that there is pain due to the losses built into this major life change: the loss of understanding in moving from the known into the unknown; the loss of the valued familiar in giving up valued relationships, activities, and objects; the loss of power in dealing with your wants and needs; the loss of acceptance by old married friends; the loss of confidence in dealing with the new situation; and the loss of identity with the loss of old activities, possessions, and social supports. It is little wonder that Hetherington et al. (1977) conclude: "We did not encounter a victimless divorce."

Profile: Sickness and Health

Returning to the original question, it would appear that singlehood, if not dangerous, is at least more risky than marriage. Singles are more likely to report stress, more likely to use drugs, and more likely to contemplate suicide. Single men are more likely to show stress than their married counterparts. Single men are likely to show somewhat more stress than single women; the divorced are more likely to feel stress than the never married; and divorced men appear to be under the greatest stress, the most likely candidates for disaster.

In discussing illness we utilized a number of elements, including physical and stress-related illnesses, drugs, which included alcohol, and activities related to suicide. This summary of significant findings will use a total score of both physical and stress symptoms, getting drunk (as a means of dealing with the category of drugs), and the significant findings in regard to suicide. Drugs other than alcohol were not included because there were not enough persons involved to produce meaningful findings.

It is to be expected that there would be some significant findings in the areas of health discussed in this section similar to those we saw regarding sexual satisfaction. It would seem logical that good health would be a prerequisite for sexual satisfaction.

The most likely person to suffer from physical illness is the 40-49-year-old remarried female who had not completed high school, and who is a Protestant and a political conservative. The least likely person to suffer from headaches, ulcers, or high blood pressure is the younger (18-29), married-once male with some college education, who lacks religious affiliation and is a political liberal.

Profile: Illness

	Combined Physical		Combined Stress		Drugs – Relaxants		Drugs– All Others		Drunk		Suicide		
	Most	Least	Most	Least	Most	Least	Most	Least	Most	Least	Least Never	Most Planned	Most Attempted
Gender	female	male	female	male	female	male	male	female	male	female	female	female	little difference
Civil status	re-married	married once	divorced	married once	little difference		not married	married once	divorced	married once	married once	divorced	re-married
Age	40-49	18-29	30-39	50+	40-49	18-29	18-24	50+	18-24	50+	50+	18-24	18-24
Education	high school	some college	high school	high school or degree	high school	college degree	high school	college degree	high school	some college	high school	little difference	less than high school
Political identity	conser-vative	liberal	neutral	conser-vative	neutral	conser-vative	liberal	conser-vative or liberal	liberal	neutral	conser-vative	conser-vative	neutral
Religious affiliation	Protestant	none	little difference		Protestant	other	none	Catholic	none	Protestant	Catholic	little difference	other

The stress-related illnesses reveal the beleaguered divorced again. Despite some high percentages in feelings of loneliness and guilt, the most likely candidate for the overall stress title is the 30-39-year-old divorced female, rather than the divorced male, at either end of the educational range, a political neutral with no particular religious distinction. The person suffering least from stress is the older (50+), married male with a high school education, also a political neutral with no particular religious distinction.

Moving over to the drunk category, we were not surprised to find that the person most likely to be drunk is the young (18-24), divorced male, while his opposite — the older (50+), married female — is the least likely to get drunk. The most likely drunk also has a limited education (did not finish high school), notes no religious affiliation, and is a political liberal. The least likely drunk has some college education, is a Protestant, and is politically neutral.

The final item in our illness summary deals with suicide. The person most likely to have contemplated suicide is the young (18-24), divorced female with little education, of no religious distinction, and a political conservative. The one most likely to have made the attempt is the young (18-24) remarried of either gender who also has little education, is a Protestant or of another religion other than Catholic, and is a political neutral. The person least likely to have had suicidal thoughts is the older (50+) married-once female with a high school education or less, who is a Catholic and a political conservative.

Chapter 11

THE PURSUIT OF HAPPINESS

In the chapters on health we have been focusing on the negatives of life: stress, alienation, drunkenness, suicide. We observed, in passing, that most of our statistics represent minorities. Most people are not alienated in any particular area, nor do they get drunk weekly, and the vast majority of singles and marrieds do not attempt suicide. That is comforting, possibly, but still it leaves a residue of bleakness.

In this chapter, therefore, we examine a positive side of life: happiness. When relations with parents, visits with friends, sexual encounters, and amphetamines are sorted out, how is life in the greater urban metropolis? What is important to happiness? Are people happy in general? Are marrieds happier than singles? And will it turn out, once again, that the divorced are the least likely to be happy? Not to keep you in suspense, the answer to each of the last three questions is a qualified "yes."

What Is Important?

To begin with, we wondered whether singles and marrieds would have different priorities in sorting out their feelings about happiness. So we asked our respondents what really is important to them for happiness. After discussing the matter with our friends and students, these were the aspects of life we decided to ask about:

health
marriage

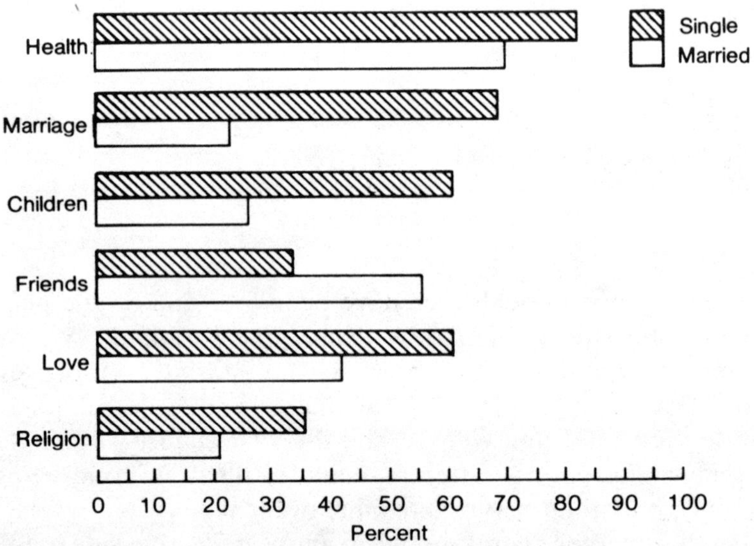

Figure 11.1 What Is Important to Happiness?

Only friends are more likely to be more important to singles than to marrieds for happiness.

children
friends
love
sex
personal growth
success
religion
contribution to society

DIFFERENCES BETWEEN SINGLES AND MARRIEDS

In six of these areas there proved to be a double-digit percentage difference between singles and marrieds (Table 11.1). But only one of these areas, friends, was more important to singles than to marrieds. Marriage and children were considerably more important to marrieds, which is to be expected, but so were love, health, and religion (Figure 11.1).

The response to the importance of friends to happiness among singles is not surprising, since we have already seen that visiting friends is one of their major activities and that friendship networks constitute a major source of social support (Adams, 1976; Starr and Carns, 1972), as well as being a major need in dealing with loneliness (Weiss, in Rubin, 1979). That love should be so much more important to marrieds is a matter of interest and concern. Is it that the young have become more cynical? Is it that the divorced are experiencing a "sour grapes" reaction? Is it that marrieds are experiencing a deeper love, or only that they judge that they ought to? Is it that some people do not marry because love is not important to their happiness? Or is it that love becomes more important to happiness once one is in love? The responses to the items on marriage and children imply that it is the latter. That is, people judge only items in their current milieu in dealing with happiness.

In the case of health, youth may be a factor. The never marrieds and divorced, being younger categories, may include some that may take health for granted. This suspicion is confirmed when it is noted that health was selected as very important to happiness by 72 percent of the youngest category (18-24) versus 92 percent of the oldest category (50+). In any event, health is highly valued by all categories: It was reported as more important than any other area by respondents in all categories.

Religion is the only area that fewer than 10 percent of the people in any category thought important. Religion is also one of two areas (the other is children) in which there is more than a 10 percent difference between the two categories of singles. Also, religion is one of the three items (along with contributions to society and success) that less than one-third of the sample thought important to happiness. This may reflect a growing secularism in America, or it may mean that religion is important for reasons other than happiness. The breakdown into subcategories reveals that only 9 percent of the divorced, compared to 25 percent of the never marrieds and 37 percent of the marrieds, reported religion as being important. This low rank-

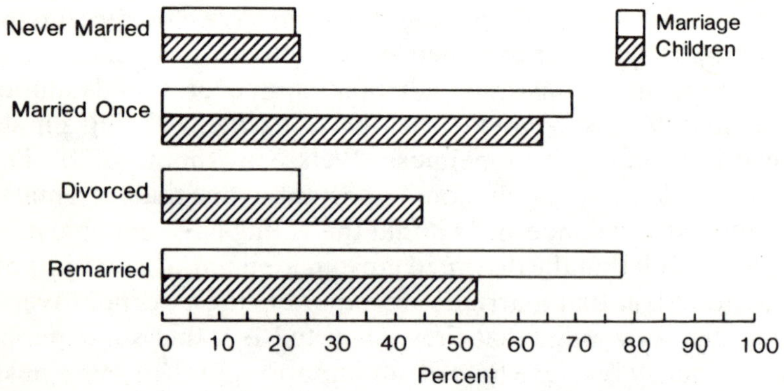

Figure 11.2 Marriage and Children: Importance to Happiness
After divorce, marriage becomes more important to marrieds than ever.

ing of religion by the divorced may be a reflection of their status, that is, the divorced are people who lack religious orientation. It could also be that the divorce experience affects their faith, or that they feel that most churches are still set up only for families.

> Toughest of all is going to church alone with her two teenage daughters. Like the neighborhood cookout or the Saturday-night dinner party, most churches still function on conventional togetherness [Brooks, 1981: 31].

The value of children to happiness involved the widest disagreement among the four categories. It is one of two areas between the singles, and the only one between the marrieds, in which there is a 10 percent difference. Relatively few of the never married consider children to be important to happiness. This may explain the declining birthrate or it may be a reflection of the question asked, since never marrieds do not usually have children and may have been thinking of current factors in their lives in answering this question. But children are of less importance to the divorced than to the remarried and, again, less important to the remarried than they are to the married (Figure

11.2). Since most of the remarried had been divorced, it would be interesting to know what happens here. Is it that marriage rekindles a concern about children, or that the divorced are distracted somewhat from children by other problems, including that of seeking another mate? Perhaps it is a function of age: This oldest category — the remarrieds — are more likely to have children.

Most of the comments on children from respondents came from the once marrieds:

"I enjoyed raising my children, watching them grow into maturity. I would not change places with anyone."

"Very happily married, no serious problems, 5 great children."

The greatest advantage to marriage: "Having children and being a family." "Love in caring and having children."

As for the low ranking of marriage by singles, there is something puzzling here that is not revealed in the figures. In another question, which is to be discussed further in Chapter 12, 90 percent of the singles thought that they would marry sometime in the future. Thus it would appear that the judgments about the importance of marriage, like those about children, were based on the present. As some Interaction people noted, substituting the term "a meaningful relationship" for the term "marriage" would have brought a higher importance ranking. It also could be that marriage is seen as necessary or desirable for reasons other than happiness. Marriage may be perceived as necessary for security, for companionship, for children, or simply as a social norm that in the long run is too powerful to be challenged.

PRIORITIES FOR HAPPINESS

A profile for happiness can be drawn by considering what is important to more than half of the respondents in each category (Figure 11.3). For the majority of singles, health, friends, and personal growth are important. The majority of the marrieds also include health but do not include friends or personal growth, substituting marriage, children, and love. An addi-

Area	Marrieds	Singles	
		Never Married	Divorced
Health	✓	✓	✓
Marriage	✓		
Children	✓		
Friends		✓	✓
Love	✓		
Sex			✓
Personal Growth		✓	✓
Success			
Religion			
Contribution to Society			

Figure 11.3 Profiles of Happiness: What Is Important for Happiness to the Majority? Personal growth is important to the majority of singles; love to the majority of marrieds.

tional important factor for the divorced is sex. The majority of people in all categories exclude success, religion, and contribution to society from their assessments of what is important to happiness.

We have already noted the importance of health, friends, marriage, love, and children, and so the main surprise lies with those items not selected. Considering the image of the swinging single, it is surprising that the divorced are the only category in which the majority include sex on their list of what is important to happiness. The divorced, remember, are the ones likely to have had the most sexual partners. This high activity, then, may be a reflection of the high priority the divorced place on sex in regard to their happiness. And yet they are also the category least likely to be satisfied with their sexual lives (Chapter 7) and most likely to report sexual apathy (Chapter 9). It would seem possible that this high priority means that for some of the divorced sexual encounters fail to meet expectations, with consequent apathy, but that its importance is still noted by those who formerly had, presumably, a steady sex partner. The absence of personal growth as being important to the married is interesting in view of the fact that the sharing of marriage and personal growth would seem to be related. As one of the once-married women respondents wrote:

> I've been married six years, and I'm not the same person I was six years ago. I've changed quite a bit for the best, I've grown; I feel I'm a much better person and able to cope with things a lot better. I've found out that you can't be happy all the time; you can face a lot of problems much better if you realize you're not alone, and that there [are] a lot of people much worse off than you.

Perhaps the most surprising area that proved to be unimportant to happiness for the majority of respondents in every category is success. Americans are supposed to be success-oriented, but apparently success in itself is not considered important. But (being teachers) we never thought to ask about the importance of money to happiness!

We did ask about income, however, and responses there do seem to indicate that money is not important to happiness. Whether incomes are under $20,000, over $30,000, or in between, the happiness patterns did not vary much. At any income in any category more than two-thirds of the respondents reported that they were generally happy.

Only the remarried seemed to be affected by lack of income. Of the 27 remarrieds who reported incomes under $20,000, 6 indicated they were unhappy. None of the 15 with incomes over $20,000 reported unhappiness.

Two men in the Interaction group had opposite reactions on these results. "I don't think economics is nearly as important as it might on the surface appear to be," said a younger divorced man. "I think if you are genuinely happy with the other person, if you are truly married to that person, I think money has a decreasing importance, or decreasing slice of the marital pie, because that is not the source of the unhappiness or discontent, it is a vehicle on which to lay blame if things aren't going well. But in and of itself, I don't think money is the problem."

But an older divorced man did think it was a problem: "My ex always had enough or more than enough and when we got married, she still expected to live that way. It took me 20 years to get to the stage where I could afford to keep her in the style she was used to when she was younger, then she wanted to move further up because her friends were there."

Of course, it is not that all singles are poor and all marrieds are rich. Marrieds, too, are likely to be held down by lack of money as well as by commitments. As one married woman responded whimsically to the developmentary question about what she would do if she could change her life: "Liz Taylor — money, beauty, clothes, status, travel — opportunity to be a completely different personality." This comment could imply that money is important in obtaining items that might make one happy, but that it would be gauche to say so.

It is quite possible that freedom would have been included as important to happiness in the singles profile if it had been included in the questionnaire. The reason for thinking so is that "freedom" was the second most frequently mentioned word in connection with the word "single." And there were reinforcing comments when respondents were given a chance to comment on the advantages of being single: "Freedom" appeared again and again:

"Freedom to do as you please."

"FREEDOM."

"If something in your life displeases you, you can change without entanglements."

"Not having to answer or pamper anyone else."

And closely related to freedom was the idea of spontaneity, which emerged when singles were asked why they were not married:

"Spontaneity! When married always knew what was happening. Friday night was bowling and every other Sunday was bridge. Now never know and can change plans at last minute."

"Wading barefoot in the sand with someone."

The Extent of Happiness

ARE PEOPLE GENERALLY HAPPY?

They say they are. More than two-thirds of every category saw themselves as at least moderately happy. Fewer than 15 percent of any category saw themselves as unhappy (Table 11.2). Roughly the same results were obtained when we asked respondents whether they got a lot of fun out of life (Table 11.3). At least 70 percent in every category said they did, while no more than 30 percent in any category said they did not. The higher negative percentage of those not having fun may be accounted for by the fact that we had a neutral category (a neither happy nor unhappy) in our happiness question that was lacking in our fun question. It would seem that you could be happy without having much fun, or have a lot of fun without being particularly happy. But the respondents' answers were similar for both questions.

Marrieds have somewhat the better of happiness and fun. They are more likely to be happy than singles (86 percent versus 77 percent), but not less likely to be unhappy (6 percent versus 6 percent; Table 11.2). They are also more likely to have fun (83 percent versus 75 percent; Table 11.3).

Happiness and fun take on different aspects when the categories are further divided. The married once appear to be the most likely to report happiness (88 percent) or fun (85 percent), the divorced least likely (70 percent). But when you look at extremes of happiness, the picture changes somewhat. The never marrieds seem somewhat tepid, being less likely than anyone else to report either that they are very happy or very unhappy. And considering unhappiness, there is a surprising and important finding. While the divorced are most likely to report themselves very unhappy, the remarried score higher (14 percent versus 11 percent) on the overall unhappiness side of the scale (moderately and very unhappy combined).

Up until now, in terms of stress relief, sexual satisfaction, and belief in the importance of marriage, it has appeared that remarriage is a reasonable statistical solution for the problems

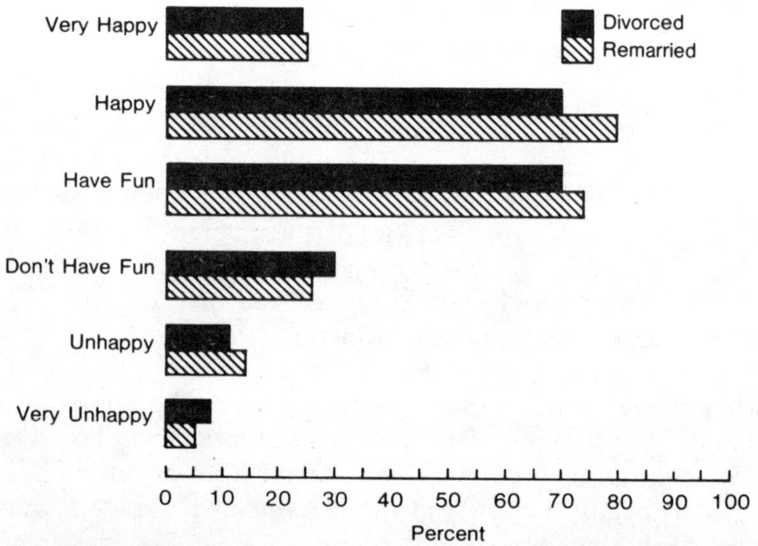

Figure 11.4 Will Remarriage Increase Happiness?
The odds are, somewhat, that it will, but the case is underwhelming.

of divorce. But if the ultimate criterion is considered to be happiness, remarriage may not prove to be the answer. Nonetheless, Glenn and Weaver have shown that the remarrieds are as satisfied with their marriages as are persons in a first marriage and that the present marriage is much better than the one that ended in divorce (cited in Albrecht, 1979: 860). Also, compared to the divorced, remarrieds are somewhat more likely to have fun. The differences, however, are not overwhelming (Figure 11.4).

Still, the answer to our question about whether the divorced will turn out to be the least happy must be a qualified yes, though they do not stand out as much as they have in some of the earlier chapters. They are, however, least likely to be happy, least likely to have fun, and most likely to be very unhappy. Even so, they are six times more likely to report themselves toward the happiness rather than the unhappiness end of the continuum (Table 11.2). A substantial majority of divorced, therefore, are likely to report themselves as being happy by several measures, but are less likely to do so than any of the other categories.

Perhaps the stereotype of the single having fun contributes to the higher percentage of divorced reporting that their lives lack fun. The stereotype could even contribute to divorce. As one woman in Interaction recalled, "I was married about 19 years, but I was miserable most of those years, and each year got worse. I decided I was doing 99 percent of all the work in the marriage, and I decided that if I was doing all the work—like being single — I might as well have the fun of being single."

A colleague reviewing this chapter wondered if age would be a factor in happiness. This proved to be so (Table 11.4). Singles at any age are less likely to report happiness than marrieds, but the gap widens as singles get older (Figure 11.5).

It would seem that the 30-50 age period might be one of greater stress for singles since this is a period when social pressures to be married are greatest and when one-parent families would be under the greatest stress. And, indeed, our divorced respondents meet expectations here, with only 53 percent of them reporting happiness at this age, compared to over 80 percent for all other categories. Social pressure, however, does not seem to bother the never marrieds in that age category. They are somewhat more inclined to report happiness than even the marrieds. But over 50, the percentage reporting happiness (35 percent) shifts dramatically against the never married, who, perhaps, begin to feel the need for a companion-caretaker as age-related illnesses make their pressure felt and finding a partner for social activities becomes more difficult.

HOW OTHERS SEEM

Incidentally, most people seem to see others as being less happy than themselves (Tables 11.5 and 11.6). Marrieds are more likely to perceive other marrieds or singles as less happy than themselves, which seems to confirm their own happiness

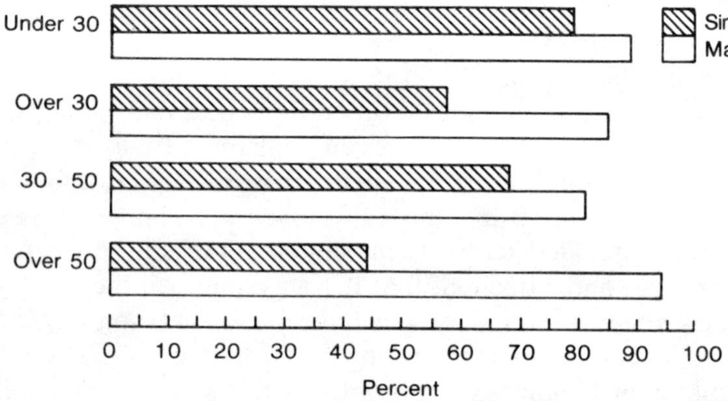

Figure 11.5 Happiness by Age

While marrieds tend to be happier than singles at any age, they are much more so after the age of 50.

rankings. Singles perceive marrieds to be less happy, but are somewhat more likely to perceive other singles as being more happy. This also seems to confirm their low ranking of marriage as important to their happiness and, perhaps, the stereotype of singles having more fun. Thus, singles may perceive their own unhappiness as something of a fluke, something not shared by other singles. These findings tie in with the conclusions of other studies (Glenn, 1975; Bradburn and Caplovitz, 1965) that marrieds are more likely to report themselves as being happy than singles and yet believe their single friends to be happier than their married friends. The marrieds, it would appear, are susceptible to the stereotype of the happy bachelor or the swinging single. Bradburn and Caplovitz note that a person's self-assessment may depend on relative assessment of positive and negative feelings. A married person may feel that the positive outweighs the negative, but still feel what Christopher Fry called "a space of heart" — something missing — in this case something perceived to be present in the single lifestyle.

There is also the possibility suggested by Jessie Bernard and illustrated by Marilyn French (1978: 212) in *The Women's Room:*

> She stood in the wide foyer, with its impressive chandelier and the winding staircase, and told herself she must be happy, she had to be. She had no other choice: there was a moral imperative on her to be happy.

Who Is Happier?

If it is possible that marrieds accept the stereotype that singles have more fun, why is it not possible that they, particularly married women, accept the stereotype that happiness is being married? The answer lies in finding some means for measuring "space of the heart."

It appears, then, that the priorities for happiness are quite different between marrieds and singles. Further, it would seem that more marrieds indicate that they are very or moderately happy most of the time and get a lot of fun out of life, but the differences are small. The divorced have the lowest percentage reporting happiness, but again the difference from other categories is minimal. People in general, regardless of civil status, usually report themselves to be happy.

Profile: The Happy Person

A glance at the significant figures for the happy person would show a close similarity to those for the sexually satisfied. Thus, if you see yourself as happy most of the time, you will also note fewer changes in moods, rarely be bored, be more likely to be satisfied with your day, see your single and married friends as less happy than yourself, and, in general, consider that you get a lot of fun out of life.

Profile: Happiness

	Happy Most of the Time		Lots of Fun Out of Life		Happy Person	
	Very and Moderately Happy	*Very and Moderately Unhappy*	*Most*	*Least*	*Very and Moderately Happy*	*Very and Moderately Unhappy*
Gender	male	female	little difference		little difference	
Civil status	married once	divorced	married once	divorced	married	divorced
Age	18-24	40-49	18-24	50+	50+	40-49
Education	college degree	high school	college degree	high school	college degree	high school
Political identity	neutral	liberal	conservative	neutral	conservative	neutral
Religious affiliation	Catholic	other	Catholic or Protestant	other	Catholic	other

Profile: Those Most and Least Likely to be Happy

	Most	*Least*
Gender	little difference	little difference
Civil status	married once	divorced
Age	18-24	40-49
Education	college degree	high school
Political identity	conservative	neutral
Religious affiliation	Catholic	other

Possibly because you are happy, you suffer less often from illnesses as a whole, do not take drugs very often, apparently have little reason for getting drunk (since your most likely answer to this question was "never"), and, since all of these conditions are true for you, you have never thought about suicide.

The reasons for your happiness may be related to your going out socially more often, spending more time with your spouse and friends, and spending the least time with television. Also, you engage in sexual intercourse more frequently and, although it is not directly related to frequency, you are more likely to be sexually satisfied.

Perhaps another reason for your current happiness is the fact that your current relations with your parents are warm. This may be an outcome of the fact that both parents were open in their emotions toward you while you were growing up.

Who this happy person is most likely to be is based on the composite high and low scores for three happiness items:

Do you get a lot of fun out of life?
Are you happy most of the time?
Do you consider yourself a happy person?

Our most happy person is most likely a young (18-24), married-once male or female, who has a college degree and is Catholic and politically conservative.

His/her opposite figure — the least happy person — is most likely to be a 40-49-year-old divorced male or female who has had a high school education, is neither Protestant nor Catholic, and is not politically affiliated. As noted in Chapters 9 and 10, it is the single parent of this age category that would be under the greatest stress, and so his/her appearance under the least happy person is no surprise.

Interestingly, though we have noted that in some ways divorced men seem under more stress than divorced women, and married men seem to benefit more from marriage than married women, on the bottom line of the happiness question gender does not seem to be a factor for either the typical happy person or the typical unhappy person.

Chapter 12

FIVE YEARS FROM NOW

Visions of Future Marriage

How do you see yourself five years from now? For the majority of the participants of Interaction, marriage was in the crystal ball:

50 percent thought they would be married;
36 percent thought they would be single;
6 percent were undecided.

(The rest were ambivalent or did not address the question.)

What did the future-married single see as going with marriage? Most frequently mentioned (Table 12.1) were:

happiness, 34 percent;
family (children, home), 30 percent;
working, 27 percent.

The next three aspects of a married life mentioned, but not nearly as often, were:

making money, 13 percent;
sharing, 9 percent;
travel, 9 percent.

WHAT THEY SAID

Typical visions of a married future were these:

"Am happily married and don't have to worry about finances."
"Living is good, married, helping child and grandchild."
"Married to a widower, enjoying and sharing life."

"Married, working space, plan child, sharing quiet pleasures."

"Happily married, looking forward to fun years in a nice home with travel occasionally."

"Children raised, married, working and enjoying my husband."

"Married to a very lively woman, working part-time."

"Happy, companionship, appreciated and security."

"Married, a happy couple, more children, working part-time."

"Hopefully married with children and comfortable finances."

"Married, reasonably happy, more prosperous, content."

"I hope that I will be happily married with 2-3 children. I would like to continue working on a part-time basis."

"Married to a doctor, lawyer, engineer, $150 to $200 thousand dream home; nice vacations; very active in community projects . . ."

"Probably married to a very gentle professional man. Each of us doing our own thing. Committed to caring about each other but with total independence."

PATTERNS IN THE VISIONS

Family connections were mentioned in many different ways. Some envisioned having a family of parents and children. Some envisioned having babies, or taking on the parenting of a spouse's children, or combining families in "yours, mine, and ours" style. Some focused on having a home. Some (6 percent) also looked forward to being free of children, who, in five years, would be on their own. These were not counted in ranking family second. We even considered subtracting them, but concluded that looking forward to children growing up is a natural part of the life cycle and does not imply hostility. As these positive comments about children indicate, the low ranking of children as important to happiness (Chapter 11) was probably due to the fact that they are not part of the current milieu of the singles.

The ranking of happiness as the quality most frequently associated with marriage by singles confirms the present self-conceptions of the respondents in the sample discussed in Chapter 11. Only one person in the sample anticipated an unhappy marriage, and that was a woman who feared she would have to marry her ex-husband "out of desperation." This, plus the fact that so many of the singles see marriage in their future, confirms our suspicion that marriage was not considered as important to happiness by the singles also because it was not a part of their current activity.

The high percentage of singles, most of whom are divorced, who see a future marriage and a happy one at that also belies the notion that the high divorce rate is a rejection of marriage. Rather, it would appear that divorce is a rejection of a particular mate, perhaps due to the various factors discussed in Chapter 1.

The next two associations with future marriages seem closely related: working and making money. Of the two, however, working was mentioned twice as frequently. Singles are hesitant even to dream about being affluent, apparently, but they can reasonably expect steady work, at least for one of the married partners.

That sharing should be a low fifth (9 percent) on the list is something of a surprise because the respondents in the sample, single and married, mentioned "companionship" more frequently than any other word in association with marriage, and "sharing" was one of the words we associated with companionship.

It was also something of a surprise that travel should be so low on the expectation list, since our stereotype was that one of the advantages of singlehood is freedom to travel. This had been reinforced by the mention of "freedom" as the word most frequently associated with singlehood by respondents in the sample and by the evidence in Chapter 6 that singles go out more frequently than marrieds.

I'll Still Be Single

For the respondents who expected to remain single, future associations were only slightly different from those of the respondents who expected that they would be married, except for one area: happiness (Table 12.1). The following were associated most frequently with future singlehood (Table 12.1):

family (24 percent)
making money (12 percent)
happiness (10 percent)
working (10 percent)
sharing (10 percent)

SOME VISIONS OF SINGLEHOOD

Typical visions of a single future were these:

"I've changed jobs to a good ($) promotion. Am still single and living with my sons who are now teens. Am 'going with' or seeing exclusively a . . ." (rest of response illegible).

"Single with children on their own."

"Probably living with male — possibly considering marriage."

"Hopefully I've grown and can share myself with someone special."

"Hope to have standard of living increased and possibly more social activity and dating."

"I'll either be single and unhappy or married and struggling to be happier."

"I hope to have found a permanent relationship, especially with someone with grown children; not having to work and enjoying life."

"Still single and loving it."

"Single and very lonely."

"About the same as now as the mate I want is already married and I don't care for anyone else — not my ex-husband either."

"A successful, financially secure therapist and engaged to a man who loves me."

"Financial independence to do as I please, free time."

"Self-employed single wih a home full of room and board elderly or foster children."

"Single, everything about the same."

The reasons for the relatively low association of happiness with singlehood are not clear from the comments. The one comment about not being able to marry a loved person is balanced among the future marrieds by a comment about having to remarry out of desperation. Other comments by singles anticipating continued singlehood seem relatively hopeful and upbeat about the future.

LESS HAPPINESS, LESS WORK

More than 20 percent of the singles mentioned happiness, family, and working in association with future marriage, but only the family was mentioned by more than 20 percent of those expecting to remain single (Figure 12.1). Family was mentioned in connection with children and home, as it was by those who expected to be married, but also in connection with living with one's parents. Exactly 20 percent of the singles thought they would be cohabiting with a person of the opposite sex, but we did not mention these in connection with family since, by that criterion, presumably almost all of the marrieds would be expecting to be cohabiting with a person of the opposite sex.

A distant second on the singles' list was money making, which was mentioned with about the same frequency as it was by the future marrieds. Close behind were happiness, working, and sharing, all at 10 percent. Even this much milder expectation of happiness was nullified because a still larger percentage (12 percent) of those who expected to remain single indicated that they also expected unhappiness, loneliness, despair, or even death. People were much less likely to associate work with future singleness than with future marriage (10 percent versus 27 percent). As for sharing, it was mentioned about as frequently by those expecting to remain single as by those expecting to marry (Figure 12.1).

NEITHER LOVE NOR SEX

What was rarely mentioned or not mentioned at all by the singles is also interesting:

- Love was mentioned only twice (and at that, once in connection with engagement, in the quotation above).
- Sex was mentioned only once in connection with each future, which ties in with its low ranking as important to happiness (Table 11.1, Chapter 11).
- Success was mentioned by 6-7 percent of each category.

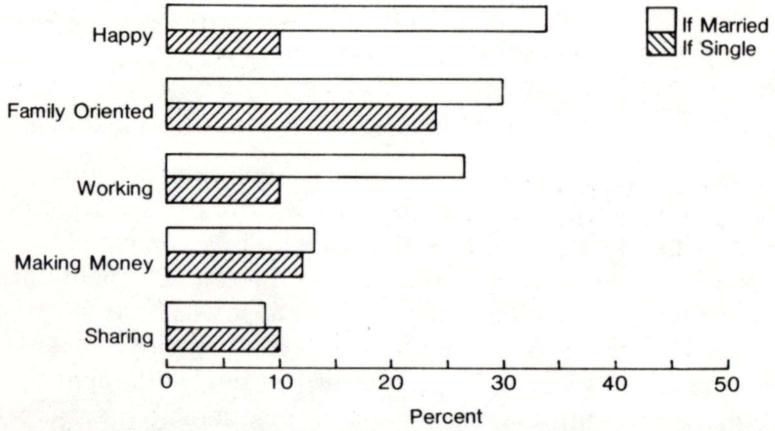

Figure 12.1 Five Years from Now, I Will Be (Married/Single) and . . .
According to the crystal ball, marriage will lead to happiness, family, and work.

- Social activitiy or visiting were mentioned by no more than 6 percent of each category.
- Loneliness was not mentioned once in connection with marriage, and only twice in relation to singlehood.
- Health was not mentioned, but was strongly implied; a feeling of optimism was pervasive in thoughts about a married future. Death was anticipated by two who expected to remain single.
- Personal fulfillment, considered important to singles for happiness, was mentioned only once in relation to future singlehood, and by 5 percent of the marrieds.
- The idea that marriage was natural or normal was mentioned only once.
- Freedom, the word most frequently mentioned in connection with singlehood by respondents, was mentioned by only 4 percent as an aspect of future singlehood and by 5 percent as a factor in marriage.

Is Marriage Natural?

The responses of the Interaction group were somewhat different when they were asked to discuss the future verbally. These differences may be accounted for partly by context. The questionnaire respondents were generally writing one line in response to a single question, but the Interaction discussion group was told what the respondents had answered and were reacting not only to the question but also to the answers of both respondents and their fellow members.

When asked, "Why do you desire to see yourselves married?" the subject of the naturalness of marriage soon came up, and was pursued with some vigor by the divorced members of the group.

"It's the desire and feeling you were put on earth for, I mean it's just a natural instinct, companionship, male and female," said an older woman. "And I mean with love. It's just humanly natural, because that's the beauty of togetherness."

"Whether we want to admit it or not," said a younger man, "men and women, that's what makes the world go round."

"That's Kurt's approach to things," an older man responded. "I might feel that it's man and several women that makes the world go round."

Others agreed that there were advantages to staying single.

"I don't know that I would never remarry," mused an older woman. "I may. I'm satisfied with what I'm doing and if somebody else comes along that I become involved with, you know, it would happen, but I don't feel that's an absolute must that I must include in my life."

"I think because I was so involved in marriage," said another woman, "that I never had time to be me. And after the divorce I've done all the things I wanted to do, and I've enjoyed them, and I realize I should have done them as a married person, I'm very involved with them and I'm just enjoying life."

A third woman added that when she said she was going to study early childhood, her sister replied: "'Don't do that, you'll never meet a man there' and you know, that's not what it's all about, you're not out there doing something just so you can meet a man."

Others agreed that being single could be a happy and fulfilling experience. When a younger woman associated happiness and fulfillment with marriage, a woman in her forties responded: "I think that seemed true when I first divorced. But the longer I've stayed single, the more fulfilled I feel as an individual."

"I've heard that from most divorced women," said another woman. "After about two years of being divorced, I became increasingly happy with my situation."

Thus singles responding in front of singles at a singles' organization were somewhat more positive about being single than they were in responding to the questionnaire.

Marriage: Past and Future

How would the future expectations of the singles compare with the past remembrances of the marrieds? Did people who are now married enter their present state for the same reasons that now seem important to singles? Apparently not.

When the most frequent reasons given by marrieds (from the sample) for having married are compared to the expectations of singles (from Interaction) for future marriage, there is quite a contrast (Table 12.2).

Love, which was mentioned only once by the singles, was by far the most frequent reason given among the answers to this question on why they married from the marrieds. To be sure, the intensity of the respondents varied from "I was crazy about her" to a more tentative "I thought I was in love." This infrequent mention of the term love by a singles sample that largely sees itself as married in the future implies, perhaps, that the romantic notion of marriage for love is replaced by more concrete ideas for this older, mostly divorced, singles' group. Love, then, may be the feeling for another person that leads to emotional envolvement, but the nitty-gritty reason for marriage given by our most previously married singles is a contemplated future happiness.

Ignorance, the second most frequent reason given for why the marrieds married, sums up a variety of responses that indicate that a person was too young to know better or was swept along because getting married was the thing to do. No other reason given by marrieds appears very frequently, but third on the list is family, which is mentioned three times as often by the singles. Indeed, family is the only subject to appear in both lists. A factor mentioned by marrieds, but not mentioned by singles, in connection with marriage includes escape from home as well as escape from an undesirable situation: unmarried pregnancy.

Happiness, the leading expectation of singles, does not appear at all in the recollection of marrieds. Nor does money, unless it is implied in security. The idea of improving or changing one's work situation as a result of marriage is frequently mentioned by the singles but never by the marrieds, perhaps because it is hardly an idea that would support the image of romantic love. The terms most frequently associated with marriage — the ideas of sharing and companionship — appeared with some frequency in the expectations of singles but are mentioned only twice in the recollections of the marrieds.

There may be a number of reasons for these differences. For one thing, most of our married respondents were married once, therefore most of them were recalling their outlooks when they were younger and before they had ever married. The Interaction participants, on the other hand, are mostly divorced and so were speaking from the experience of marriage and the anticipation of remarriage.

Another contrast is the greater emphasis on family by the singles. Those approaching first marriage were perhaps focusing on their beloved. Those anticipating remarriage may have been placing their expectations on the broader base of the family.

The disappearance of love in favor of happiness is probably the most striking difference in the two lists. Did the never married assume that love would come with happiness? Do the more experienced singles assume that happiness may be had without love if some combination of family, work, money, and sharing are present? On the other hand, the frequent mention of love by the marrieds, sometimes with doubt or irony, suggests that many marrieds may have been disappointed in love.

The references to ignornace took different forms. "I was young and it was part of the social structure." "Everyone was doing it." "Seemed like a good idea at the time." "It was the natural and expected thing to do." "Too young, followed the crowd." There was no expectation among the singles that ignorance would play any role in future marriage. We hope we learn from experience. And ignorance, like innocence and virginity, can be lost but once. Or, perhaps, ignorance is something that can be perceived only after the fact.

There are some shared absences on both lists. Singles and marrieds alike did not place much emphasis on sex, success, visiting, loneliness, health, freedom, or social life in connection with marriage. We have seen in Chapter 11 that sex was ranked high for happiness only by the divorced and in Chapter 9 that the divorced were most likely to be dissatisfied with sex. Failure to associate sexual satisfaction with future marriage suggests that the divorced are contemplating remarriage to fulfill needs of happiness, family, and sharing, but not necessarily sexual needs. The absence of loneliness and freedom is no surprise, since these were attributes associated with singlehood in a question on this regard. The absence of social life and visiting apparently reflects a realistic appraisal of the difference in lifestyle (Chapter 6). The absence of health, regarded by all as most essential to happiness (Chapter 11), and in most respects more frequently found in marriage than in singlehood (Chapters 9 and 10), may indicate that there is not much perception of a relation between health and civil status, or it may be that healthy people — and most respondents were healthy — do not look forward with anticipation to something they already have. The absence of success confirms the findings in Chapter 11: Most of the respondents, supposedly success-oriented Americans, did not place an extremely high priority on success. Also, success may be associated more with occupation than with marriage.

In any event, there seems to be a striking difference between one set of respondents, looking back at themselves in younger courtship days, and the other set, older now than the marrieds would have been in the days of their recollections. For the first set of people love was all-important, while happiness, perhaps, was taken for granted. For the second set happiness has become the most important desire, with love, perhaps, a lucky dividend if it happens to come along.

PART V

Assessments and Projections

Chapter 13

MYTHS AND REALITIES

When we listed stereotypes at the beginning of this book, we thought that most of them would prove to be myths and that singles would turn out to be similar to marrieds. Along the way, however, it has become apparent that there are quite a few differences, that some of the myths are supported by the data, or partly supported, or supported for one of the subgroups. In other cases it has turned out that there are differences, but it is the marrieds, or one of the married subgroups, who come closer to the stereotype. In this chapter we are going to sift through the data again, and try to sort out the myths from the realities.

In the final chapter we ask two questions that seem to be out of order: "What next?" and "What now?" "What next?" refers to the unanswered questions, or to questions that have been raised by this study. What kind of research needs to be done to answer these questions? "What now?" refers to what can be done with present information, not so much as a matter of social policy as on an individual and small-group basis. How can we or should we, as singles and marrieds, modify our outlooks and lifestyles? How can we or should we relate to each other?

Myths

SINGLES ARE TIED TO MOTHER'S APRON STRINGS

You see a bachelor, who should be married by now, and he tells you he is going to visit his mother over the holidays. And you think, "Uh, huh, that's the problem. Hasn't been able to let go of those strings."

It is even worse if the single person is living with a parent, particularly a mother. A man becomes a figure of faint tragedy and ridicule. A woman is perceived as an old maid who might have flourished if she could have gotten away from her possessive mom.

But even if they aren't living "at home" you wonder if an attractive man or woman has failed to find a partner because of unresolved relationships with a parent. And "failed to find," of course, presumes that a search was attempted.

The data from this study do not support this image. There is little difference between never marrieds and marrieds in their perceptions of relations and their parents. They do not differ in their perceptions of warmth or openness, nor are they much different about parental conflict (Figures 5.1 and 5.2).

There was a difference in perceptions of parental openness between the divorced and other categories, but when we discuss apron strings we are talking about the never married, not the divorced. Moreover, the problem for the divorced is not one of being tied to apron strings. Rather it may be a problem of apron strings not having been available during a stage of development when they were really needed, since the divorced were far more likely to have closed communications than any other subcategory with either their mother or both parents.

SINGLES ARE SELFISH

The stereotype is that singles do not get married or get divorced because they are too centered on themselves. Having only themselves to think of, they become egocentric, and being egocentric, they remain single. Or, if they do marry, they are unable to enter into a shared relationship and divorce results.

To be fair, another image also exists, that of the single who, not having family to give to, is loving toward larger groups of people: children, minorities, old people, nations, humankind. Jesus was a single and Buddha left his family because it would distract him from a greater work.

In attempting to answer this question from the data accumulated, we are going to assume that sinners outnumber saints, and that in a sample of 400 people in Dayton, Ohio, one saint would be an unusually high number to find. Even if he or she is there, the statistics will not be much affected.

Assuming the dominance of sinners, then, what can we tell from this study? We thought something might be learned from Table 6.1 on social outings. Is it not less selfish to visit Grandma than to go to Club 99? Then there might be something to learn from the statistics on community service in Table 6.4, particularly if compared to outlooks on the same in Table 11.1. We considered willingness to have sex without love, in Table 7.4, but ruled it out because it involves only singles, and, even as a measure between marrieds and divorced, the way the question is asked does not involve exploitation and is as much concerned with loneliness, desperation, and moral philosophy as with selfishness. We did include the "most are alone" question in Table 8.2, since a view that aloneness is normal would not encourage much altruism. And finally we looked at some of the items that are important to happiness, thinking that valuing friends, love, and community service might indicate tendencies toward selfishness.

We realize that any of these indicators could be subject to different interpretations. A given person striving for personal growth may be a generally selfless person seeking self-improvement for selfless ends or may perceive increased generosity and giving as part of that personal growth. But all the same, we felt that if we could build up a consistent picture of the selfish single, we would have established an area worthy of further study in terms of use of in-depth interviews and other techniques.

But the selfish single does not emerge from the examination of the data mentioned here. In some areas the single appears to be more selfish, in some more selfless.

We found that singles indeed were more likely to visit Club 99 than to visit Grandma (38 percent versus 16 percent), while for marrieds it was the other way around (19 percent versus 42 percent). Also singles value success (36 percent versus 30 percent) and growth (56 percent versus 47 percent) more than marrieds, while marrieds value love (63 percent versus 45 percent) and community service (28 percent versus 24 percent). Singles, however, value friends more than marrieds (56 percent versus 35 percent) and, most important, in the only area in which action is involved, prove to be greater contributors to community service. Of those contributing 2 or more hours to community service weekly, the ranking among our 4 aggregates were as follows:

never married:	20 percent
divorced:	18 percent
remarried:	13 percent
married once:	9 percent

So, even though marrieds are likely to value community service more, the singles deliver. Do actions speak louder than words?

SINGLES ARE RICH

Singles ought to be richer than marrieds. They have no spouses and children to support, they can live in condominiums or bachelor pads. The Internal Revenue Service takes this image into consideration in taxing them. The supermarket does too, in setting its bargains for large family sizes.

The questionnaire did ask about income. It turned out that over 20 percent of the married in both categories placed their incomes above $20,000 a year. Under 10 percent of the singles in both categories said they were making that much. Of the divorced, only 6 percent reached that figure (Table 6.7).

Looking at the low side of income, those under $10,000, the percentages seem to run high. More than 50 percent of all singles failed to make $10,000, and the figure reached 60 percent for the never married. Only the remarried were distinctly fewer, at 30 percent. It seemed as if age might be a factor here, but comparing marrieds and singles between the ages of 30 and 50 brought similar results. In that age bracket almost 60 percent of the singles reported incomes under $10,000 a year, compared to the 40 percent of the marrieds. Under 10 percent of the singles in this age bracket reported incomes over $20,000, compared to over 20 percent of the marrieds. No matter how you look at it, singles are not rich.

Certainly the Joe Namath image does not seem to be realized by most singles. Many are young, at the bottom of the economic ladder. Others are divorced, trying to support children and two households. On the whole, the marrieds are better off economically than singles.

SINGLES ARE HAPPIER

On happiness we asked two questions that allow us to check the validity of the stereotype. We asked (Table 11.4) whether people thought other singles and marrieds are happier than they are. It turns out that in this case the stereotype itself may be a myth. Singles tend to think that marrieds are unhappier than singles, and marrieds tend to think that singles are unhappier than marrieds. When we turned it around, it turned out that marrieds also think other marrieds are less happy, but that singles, by a narrow margin (26 percent to 23 percent), think other singles are happier than themselves. How much this proves about people is hard to say, for it is probably healthy to think yourself happier than other people. But it certainly appears that the stereotype we are about to destroy is not a stereotype in the first place. Marrieds do not think that singles are happier in their lifestyle than they are in their own lifestyle.

In any event, some married people do perceive singles to be happier and more carefree than marrieds. The image of the happy bachelor is found in the titles of popular magazines (Chapter 3), and even in our study marrieds were more likely to think their single friends happier than their married friends, though they were also likely to think of themselves as happier than either.

Generally most people say that they are happy most of the time. But on a number of specific questions about areas that would seem to contribute to happiness, the responses indicate there is more unhappiness than would be expected from the answer to the general question, and on most of these the indications are that singles are less happy than marrieds.

For instance, there are the loneliness questions (Figures 8.1 and 8.2). Singles are more likely to be depressed when alone (24 percent versus 15 percent) and they much more often feel they have no one with whom they can really share (71 percent versus 44 percent) or discuss (66 percent versus 49 percent). So, we have 77 percent of the singles seeing themselves as really happy, even though 71 percent have no one with whom they can really share. It would seem that some compartmentalizing may be going on in these areas.

Health may be a significant area to look at in relation to happiness, though no one area provides indisputable evidence. In fact, marrieds are more inclined than singles to have headaches (27 percent versus 21 percent), insomnia (18 percent versus 14 percent), or ulcers (7 percent versus 4 percent; Figure 9.1). Yet, when you turn to personal feelings, the singles are more likely than marrieds to feel anxious (25 percent versus 17 percent), guilty (21 percent versus 11 percent), despondent 18 percent versus 10 percent), and worthless (19 percent versus 10 percent; Figure 9.2; Table 9.1).

There are many possibilities here. It could be that the marrieds are less happy than they say they are, but their unhappiness is repressed and asserts itself only in physical forms. It could be that the greater expression of psychological stress by the singles actually represents problems of growing up for the never married; that is, a difference in stage of development, rather than a difference in civil status. These possibilities would reduce the stress difference between the marital categories.

The greater physical difference, however, could also be explained by the fact that one can discuss one's headache with one's spouse and, in making more fuss about it, be more aware of it. And the idea that the greater expression of psychological stress is a function of growing up is considerably undercut by the fact that feelings of despondency, worthlessness, and loneliness are higher in the divorced than in the never married — a younger category (Figure 4.3). These possibilities would increase the stress difference between the marital categories.

Two possible signs of trying to compensate for unhappiness might be the use of pep pills and getting drunk often (Table 9.2). Sure enough, singles are more likely than marrieds to use pep pills (11 percent versus 4 percent) and more likely to get drunk once a week or more (21 percent versus 7 percent). Of course some of that drinking could be the experimental drinking of the young, but the divorced are more inclined to get drunk that often than the never married (24 percent versus 20 percent).

A final check was on suicide, where in every category the singles are higher than the marrieds (Figure 9.5, Table 9.3). In total contemplated or attempted suicides, singles were higher — 55 percent to 35 percent. Again, one can speculate that suicide is more often contemplated by the young, but the older marrieds also had once been young.

All in all, regardless of reservations, there is very little here to support the idea that singles are happier than marrieds, and much to suggest that they are, by several measurements, considerably less happy.

SINGLES ARE INCREASING IN NUMBERS

This is literally true in America, if we are considering numbers. But usually we are not counting numbers; we are considering that within a group of a certain size we notice more singles than there used to be, or else we mean that the number is rapidly growing. Either way, it is clear that this is not so.

In a roomful of people, there were likely to be more singles in 1980 than there would have been in 1960, but not than there would have been in 1940 or 1920 or 1900. We have seen from our demographic study that the percentage of singles was over 40 percent from 1900 through 1940, but had dipped to 32 percent by 1960, rising back toward 40 percent by 1980 (Figure 2.3). Only those of us over 60 can make a meaningful comparison with 1940 in our own memories, and not only was 1940 a long time ago, but we would not have been aware of the idea of "singles" at that time. Our more recent memory span tells us that singles have been increasing, so it is not surprising that we would think there are more singles than ever in the sense that there are more in social groups or at the office than there used to be. In the short run this has been true.

Since we are also much more aware of the concept of singles, of a singles lifestyle, and of the rapid increase in divorce, it is not surprising that we should suppose that the percentage of singles in the population is rapidly growing and that the family is a declining institution. Our demographic survey, however, has given us good reason to believe that the growth of singles in the 1960s and 1970s was largely a function of the baby boom of the forties and fifties, and that even if the percentage of divorced population continues to increase, it is not likely to compensate for the decrease in the percentage of young adults (Table 2.5).

There are more singles than ever. But the percentage of singles is lower today than it was at any time before World War II and today's percentage appears to have peaked and to be approaching decline. It could be that even in numbers singles will be declining by the late eighties or early nineties.

BEING SINGLE IS ACCEPTABLE

Regrettably, perhaps, this is a myth advocated but not accepted by singles. A theme of the 1970s articles (see Chapter 4) is that parents ought to teach that marriage is one desirable option and singleness another, and when the child grows up, he or she may choose. Perhaps parents should do this, but most of them are married and apparently they do not. In any event we found, in a supplementary questionnaire administered to our singles groups, that the great majority saw themselves as being married in five years (Chapter 12). Marriage is in their future.

Our review of titles through the century indicated that there has been little change in the preoccupation of singles with marriage. Titles about mate finding were as prevalent as ever in the 1970s, and so were articles about making the best of it, implying that singleness is a regrettable condition that one must endure if one can not change it (Tables 3.3 and 3.4).

Whether the present emphasis on singleness as a desirable alternative will produce results in the next generation will have to wait for a survey of the 1990s articles.

THERE IS SOMETHING WRONG WITH SINGLES

> This was Barrington Erle, a politician of long standing, who was still looked upon by many as a young man, because he had never done anything to compromise his position in that respect. He had not married, or settled himself down in a house of his own, or become subject to gout, or given up being careful about the fitting of his clothes. No doubt the grey hairs were getting the better of the black hairs, both on his head and face, and marks of coming crows' feet were to be seen if you looked close at him, and he had become careful about his great-coat and umbrella. He was in truth much nearer fifty than forty; — nevertheless he was felt in the House and among Cabinet Ministers, and among the wives of members and Cabinet Ministers, to be a young man still. And when he was invited to become Secretary of Ireland it was generally felt that he was too young for the place. He declined it, however, and when he went to the post-office, the gentlemen there all felt that they had had a boy put over them. Phineas Finn, who had become Secretary for Ireland, was in truth ten years his junior. But Phineas Finn had been twice married, and had gone through other phases of life, such as make a man old [Anthony Trollope, *The Prime Minister,* 1876].

Barrington Erle, then, was perceived to be incomplete, perhaps immature, not developed. Were the wives of the Cabinet Ministers correct in their perceptions?

We have already concluded that singles are not particularly tied to parents' apron strings, nor especially selfish when compared to marrieds. What else can be wrong? We had, in our historical review, detected a note of defensiveness or apology on the part of the singles themselves. But this defensiveness was in response to a social expectation, not the result of any inherent problem within the singles themselves. And in the

1970s it appeared they were losing interest in defenses. The best defense was to cease defending. To respond defensively to a negative label is understandable, but hardly wrong. To overcome or circumvent that label through collective action seems undeniably right.

But by measures of happiness or loneliness, singles may not be as well off as marrieds. However, there is nothing wrong with being lonely or sad some of the time, or more often than your neighbor. By measures of freedom, singles may be better off than marrieds, but that does not make it wrong to marry. A married person may sometimes or often wish for freedom from the responsibilities of marriage but on the balance may consider it better to remain married. So may a single consider it better on the balance to remain single, even if loneliness is a price to be paid.

Are singles harmful to society, or do they become harmful if they reach a certain mass? It is hard to see how. We have seen that they are more likely than marrieds to contribute to community welfare. We have seen that they are poor as compared to marrieds, but one reason for that poverty may be, as an Interaction member suggested, that they are contributing more to the economy. If they divorce, they consume more automobiles and housing. If they are seeking to date, marry, or remarry, they support the arts by buying more theater tickets than they can afford (Chapter 6). Is overpopulation a long-term threat? By marrying later or by divorcing, singles may contribute to population control.

But are they injuring themselves? Do they have psychological problems? Undoubtedly divorce is a traumatic experience, but the trauma begins with marriage. And the trauma tends to recede, apparently, whether or not remarriage follows. Also, the average divorced person retains that status for between three and four years. Divorce, therefore, can be seen as a regrouping for a better marriage. This is supported by the Interaction response to the future question: In five years the majority of the divorced expect to be remarried (Chapter 12).

All right, but what about the never married? Can you really say there is nothing wrong with a 35 year old who has never married? Well, you really can't say there is anyone who has nothing wrong. But within the range of normality, we find no apron strings attached to this person and, what is more, he or she appears to be happier than any 34 year old who has married or divorced (Table 11.4). He or she is, of course, in the minority, but if there is something wrong with being in the minority, then it is wrong to be a Catholic, a Republican, a golf player, or a male American.

No, there is nothing wrong with being single. The belief that there is, perhaps, is the most destructive and most elusive of all the myths.

Realities

SINGLES ARE DEVIANT

It may seem incongruous to state that the image that there is something wrong with singles is a myth, but that singles are nonetheless deviant. But deviance is a perception of others, and though the gentlemen at the post office may be shown to have been incorrect in their assessment of Barrington Erle, nevertheless they labeled him as different from (and inferior to) Phineas Finn.

It is still the case today, as it was in Trollope's time, that normality and deviance are defined by perceptions. To that extent, the stereotype influences the reality. And the stereotype perceives marriage as normal. As one never-married woman exclaimed at an Interaction meeting: "Have you ever seen a television commercial where everybody wasn't married? I mean, they are the most married people in the world. After watching TV, you feel the whole world is married!"

If deviance is a matter of the perception of others as well as self-perception, who among the singles are deviant? Probably those most frequently perceived as such are those between the ages of 30 and 50. Persons under 30 are presumed to be young people still in the process of mate selection. Their problems are as much the problems of youth as they are of civil status. The problems of those over 50 are those of later stages of development rather than of marriage. We do not expect persons of that age to have or adopt children, so that whether they marry is of less consequence to society. If we invite them to our houses, we no longer have to worry about matching them with some theoretically eligible person of the opposite sex. If they remain single after 50, we accept them more easily. We no longer say it is too bad they didn't marry, or at least we don't say it as often. They have established themselves to be what they are. (This explanation, however, does not account for the high percentage of never marrieds over 50, reporting themselves to be unhappy.)

The deviants, then, are singles who are (or are perceived to be) in the 30-50 age bracket, whether they have never married or are divorced or widowed. Singles in this age bracket in the twentieth century, as in the time of Barrington Erle, perceive themselves and are perceived to be deviating from social norms. Whether they are defending themselves for being single or professing happiness, or if they are so fortunate as to have transcended that sort of thing and are discussing taxes, housing, automobiles, or grapefruit (singles do not generally buy ten-pound sacks of grapefruit), they are discussing problems that arise because they are perceived as a deviant type, as in the case of taxes, or because they are not considered at all where the focus is on the normal and implicitly desirable, as in the case of the bargain-priced large family size. Singles in the 30-50 age bracket have been labeled deviant because they are not following the norm, not because their behavior can be demonstrated to be abnormal.

We have expressed some concern, in defining the category of singles, that we may be contributing to the creation of a deviant category that had not previously existed (see Chapter 1). But all of the deviant categories have existed under different names. There have been bachelors and spinsters instead of never marrieds, and young widows and divorcees have been considered deviants under those names. Labeling can be harmful if it creates problems that did not previously exist, as happened when the tracking system was developed in high schools, but it can be useful when it causes people who newly perceive themselves to be in a category to recognize the possibility of mutual support in dealing with problems that could not have been handled, perhaps could not even have been perceived, by unlabeled individuals.

SINGLES HAVE MORE TIME

The question of whether singles have more time has been posed in various ways. Do marital responsibilities take more time than is compensated for by the division of labor in the partnership? The married see themselves tied down by ferrying children and being parent-teachers during the week, and by home maintenance, church, and cultural safaris during the weekend. Singles see themselves tied down with having to do the household chores on top of the job, and then having to arrange social relationships besides.

The problem also has been posed a different way. The marital image is that singles are free. They come and go as they please. They don't worry about baby sitters, they sleep nights without having to wake for the children, they go on vacation where they like.

The freedom question is hard to answer. Certainly "freedom" is the word most associated with the word "single." It comes up about equally between never marrieds and those who were married once (24 percent and 23 percent), more for the divorced (31 percent), and less for the remarried (10 percent). One could surmise that a divorced person focuses more on freedom after a situation that had many negative aspects, whereas a person who remarried has decided that the freedom is not important or even desirable compared to other advantages of marriage. In any event, the association of freedom with singleness is a perception. It does not prove the validity of the perception.

Therefore, it seems safer to focus on time. And it does appear that singles have more time than marrieds, whether they perceive it or not. For instance, over 60 percent of the singles in our sample are likely to spend 2 hours or more per week visiting friends, compared to 40 percent or under for the marrieds (Table 6.4). If they stay home, more than 70 percent may spend

2 hours or more on hobbies, compared to under 60 percent of the marrieds. While only 20 percent of the singles see themselves spending 2 hours or more a week on community service, still the marrieds hover around 10 percent. The only leisure activity in which there is equality is watching television, where 69 percent of the never marrieds and marrieds alike may spend 2 hours. Here the divorced fall to 55 percent, and the remarrieds rise to 73 percent.

The data on social outings (Table 6.1) also indicate that the singles have more time. They are more likely than marrieds to be out twice a week (22 percent versus 16 percent) and much more likely to be out three times (30 percent versus 8 percent).

It looks as if the marrieds much more than the singles are likely to be home working. The singles have more time for optional activities. It may be hypothesized that they visit friends because of loneliness, pursue hobbies as therapy, or contribute to community service as a means of increasing social contacts, but even if these hypotheses could be supported — and we could not support them from our data — it still appears that singles can make more choices and give more time to the leisure activities they choose.

SINGLES HAVE MORE FUN

It may seem something of a contradiction to assert that while they are less happy, nevertheless singles have more fun, especially since they do not think so themselves (Tables 11.2 and 11.3). But it is possible that a person can go to dances, amusement parks, and nightclubs, get out bicycling and camping more, in general have high experiences, and still, on a day-to-day basis, feel less happy. The married person remembering these experiences may have nostalgia for them, forgetting the less spectacular unhappiness and remembering the fun. The single person may be struck on Monday morning, well, Monday evening really, with the feeling that the effort to achieve the fun is not worth the more steady rewards of marriage.

Then why do we say singles have more fun? Well, as we have just pointed out, they have more social outings. When they do go out (Table 6.3), they are more likely than marrieds to go to movies, nightclubs, and theaters, while marrieds go to social clubs or restaurants or else they visit relatives. There can be much happiness and pleasure in such activities for marrieds, but perhaps less fun.

Again, it may be a crass judgment, one that would require more refinement in verification, but singles are more likely to have had more sexual partners by a two-to-one margin (Table 7.1). That sounds like fun, though it may not mean happiness.

When singles do visit friends, they are three times as likely as marrieds to sit around smoking marijuana, a sharing, pleasurable experience, or getting drunk (Table 9.2), which may be fun while you are doing it, though it is not likely to contribute to your happiness the next day.

So even though marrieds are more likely to perceive themselves as having more fun than singles (83 percent versus 75 percent; Table 11.3), we think that perhaps singles actually have more fun. In most specifics in which we can imagine fun would be involved, the singles come out on top. It could be that people answer questionnaires in more reflective moments, and some may conclude that all the moments of fun have not been worth the effort involved.

SINGLES ARE SWINGERS

There has been some disagreement between the authors on how to place this one. One author leans toward the view that the stereotype is a myth, the other is inclined to think that the image is supported by the data. Since some reality can be interpreted from the data, we decided to be conservative and not contend that we have demolished a myth when it would be more appropriate to say, perhaps, that we've "detitillated" it.

To begin with, there was some disagreement about the adjective to be applied. One author, with some enthusiasm, suggested "singles are lecherous" for the stereotype. When the other author suggested "swingers" as being less judgmental, the first objected that one has to be married to be a swinger. A student suggested that the use of "swingers" for marrieds is a specific modern adaptation of a more general usage for any person, but usually a male, who goes out frequently and spends much time with persons of the opposite sex with sexual relations as one possible objective. From that standpoint it does seem that the singles find more partners, in fact have had more partners than the marrieds, who after all were once single themselves. It could be that memory plays tricks here, that for a single man, at any rate, there is more incentive to remember sexual partners of the past, while for a married there may be some incentive to forget them. In any event singles outscore marrieds in every category, 24 percent to 19 percent at 2-3 partners, 23 percent to 16 percent at 4-10 partners, and a decisive 19 percent to 6 percent at 11 or more partners (Figure 7.1).

These figures take on something of a different meaning, however, if the remarried are considered. They, after all, have either been divorced or widowed along the way. And, sure enough, it turns out that there is not much difference between them and the singles. They outscore the never married and divorced at 2-3 partners (38 percent to 24 percent) and at 4-10 partners (28 percent to 23 percent; Table 7.1).

If singles have the best of it in variety, marrieds score higher in frequency. They outscore singles 36 to 21 percent in sexual activity twice a week and 28 percent to 18 percent at 3 times or more (Figure 7.2). Though these figures say nothing about quality, they do meet the expectations that marrieds, who have available partners, would have greater frequency. After all, swinging takes more energy and effort than merely going to bed at the end of the day.

Even here, however, the figures take on a different meaning when subcategories are considered. This time it is the divorced who provide the anomaly. At twice a week, their percentage is comparable with other singles, but they are more likely than anyone to engage in sexual activity 3 or more times a week; 36 percent compared to 28 percent for the marrieds and only 12 percent for the never married (Figure 7.3; Table 7.1).

It appears, then, that if you are measuring by the Don Juan standard, number of partners, that a single is more likely to be a swinger than a married, whether you regard more than three or more than ten as the number of partners required to earn the status. By the same token, more than half of the singles and nearly two-thirds of the marrieds have had fewer than three partners and two-thirds of the married once have had only one. So the majority of singles are not swingers, although they are still likely to have had more partners than the marrieds.

Since the divorced and the remarried are likely to indicate having more had partners, and the divorced are most likely to indicate the highest current frequency, it seems possible to hypothesize that most of the activity takes place during the period of divorce, and, very possibly, as one of the Interaction members suggested, during the several months that immediately follow the divorce, as an expression of freedom, as a means of attempting to prove one's desirability, or as an unconscious process of mate searching that simmers down as the field narrows and a particular person comes to be considered.

The never marrieds, high in variety but low in frequency, may be part of changing standards about nonmarital sexual relations. The dating process includes sexual relations, but the frequency of dating is lower, the opportunities for consummation less frequent. The never married may have had more partners than the married once because standards have been changing and years ago intimacy was more frequently contained short of sexual intercourse. It may be also that the number of "conquests" is to some extent a matter of pride for male never marrieds, but something less dwelt on or somewhat suppressed by marrieds of both sexes.

SINGLES ARE LONELY

We had expected to find that singles are neither happier nor lonelier than marrieds. The evidence from this study indicates that our expectations have not been met on either count. They are both less likely to be happy and more likely to be lonely.

We have seen that sometimes people answer one way on a general question, but indicate something else on specifics. In this case we asked a set of questions on feelings about specific kinds of activities (Table 8.1), and these reinforced the impression that singles are more lonely than marrieds. Singles are much more likely to feel that they have no one to share with or to discuss matters with. They also are more likely to feel that most people are alone (Table 8.2). More singles than marrieds join social organizations because of loneliness. They are more likely to feel depressed just being alone (when they enter an empty room and especially when they dine alone). The only area in which marrieds indicate that they feel more lonely is in living alone, but, of course, for the most part this is a rare occasional experience for them.

Once again it proved to be worthwhile to break down our singles and marrieds into subcategories, for even in an area in which results are so definite and consistent, we found the picture modified. It turns out that on the important perception that there is no one to discuss problems with, there is little difference between the never married and the remarried. About one-quarter of each subcategory (24 percent to 25 percent) felt they had no one with whom to discuss problems. It was the high percentage of the divorced (49 percent) that brought up the singles total. Again, in the perception that most people are alone the divorced are three times more likely to have this perception than any other subcategory (31 percent to 11 percent). The divorced are also far higher on feeling that there is no one with whom they can share, on feeling lonely when entering an empty room, and on feeling negative about just being or living alone.

The high percentages of the divorced on these loneliness feelings caused us to look again at the never married, and it turns out they are not as lonely as it first appeared. As compared to marrieds they do feel they have no one with whom to share, and are more likely to be lonely dining alone, and to sometimes be depressed about being alone. But they do not feel that most people are alone, do not especially mind entering an empty room, and are more comfortable than any other group in living alone. They are, on the whole, more lonely than marrieds, but the gap is not as decisive as it seemed at first.

The high loneliness score of the remarrieds on the discussion question was not repeated in any other area. Generally they were a point or two higher on the scale than the marrieds. Thus, on the whole, it would appear that remarriage is an effective cure for loneliness in a divorced person. Though it is true that singles are more likely to be lonely than marrieds, this feeling is far more pervasive for the divorced than for the never married.

LIFE FOR SINGLES IS CHANGING FOR THE BETTER

In Chapter 4 we noted that the perception that things are changing for singles goes back through the century. Writers from each period felt there had been significant breakthroughs compared to a generation earlier. They were continually declaring that apologies were no longer needed, that old terms of obloquy were fading away, and that it had become easier for singles to live alone, easier for women to find work and remain single. Yet they continue to apologize and they continued to advise one another on how to find a spouse. The trend continues: Singles are still asserting forcefully that the life of a single was tougher in the fifties and sixties, when the marriage norm was unchallanged and before the awareness of singlehood per se had developed and support groups such as Interaction had come into existence. Do these perceptions represent reality, or is it wishful thinking, an assertion that the world is what it ought to be?

On the whole we are inclined to think that, while there always has been wishful thinking intermixed, life has been getting better for singles, and progress has been greatest in the past twenty years. While it was not true in earlier periods that the need to apologize had faded, it does appear to be true that housing situations improved and employment opportunities for women increased. But in the sixties and seventies changes came much faster. For better or worse, but mostly for better, the unmarrieds in the seventies were perceived as a single category and labeled as such. Before that, spinsters, bachelors, divorced, and widowed, young and old, were perceived as separate categories with separate problems (Chapter 3).

On the whole it seems that there is more support for the view that, despite such continuities as a continued anticipation of marriage in the future, life and perceptions were qualitatively different for singles in the seventies and eighties from what they had been in previous decades of the century. We have seen that the universal norm of marriage was being challenged for the first time in the 1970s. For example, a recently published singles' declaration resolved: "To make of my single status an incidental fact . . . to maximize the possibilities for growth and freedom within my singleness. I will keep my eye fixed on its positive aspects" (Declaration of Undependence, Appendix III). Then too, the fact that a single lifestyle could work for some was evidenced by the increase in the sixties and seventies of articles about single life, articles that took the lifestyle for granted and gave practical advice on the special problems of singleness, articles that editors perceived would have a sufficient market for publication (Table 3.5).

For example, singles have cut their apron strings. In articles by singles for singles in the seventies there is little discussion of "home" as a place where one's parents live. But before the seventies this factor was always there, stronger for women than for men, and stronger the further back in the century you go (Chapter 4).

Another example seems to be the reduction of sexual frustration in the 1970s. Sexual problems are openly discussed, and there are many experiential or vicarious alternatives. Though singles may not be as satisfied sexually as marrieds, the channels to satisfaction seem to be opening. The evolution from repression in the era of Freud, to honest discussion, to reasonable resolution in an imperfect world is clearly observable in the changes in subjects and content of magazine articles (Chapters 3 and 4).

Singles still have a slightly harder time living than do marrieds, in that their world is still constructed for the married; and the life of the divorced seems considerably more difficult. But the problems have surfaced, and where there is trouble there is also help. The singles themselves have done the most about solving their own problems by recognizing and supporting one another. It is even possible that some of their myths, such as singleness as a normal alternative to marriage, will become realities by gaining recognition as desirable goals, just as openness in sexual relations has become a reality out of the debates and struggles of the past.

While life for singles may be more attractive, there is little in the data from this study to support the perception that the family is disintegrating. The singles population is stabilizing and may decline, so it follows that the married population is also stabilizing and may increase as a percentage of total population (Chapter 2). While single life may be better than it was, married life still has many advantages in crucial areas: Marrieds are more likely to be happy and healthy, less likely to be lonely (Chapters 8 and 11).

Singles themselves tend to see themselves as married five years from now. Even if singles think they will remain single, they are very likely to associate themselves with family (Chapter 12). While single life may be more rewarding and less frustrating than it used to be, the alternative of marriage does not appear to have become less attractive.

Chapter 14

WHERE DO WE GO FROM HERE?

What Next?

DAYTON, AUSTRALIA

This study has come up with some answers. We have sorted out some myths from realities. But, as often happens when new areas are being opened up, as many questions have been raised as have been answered.

First, we have accepted the pollster's view that Dayton, Ohio, is a fairly typical American area. But we need some corroborative studies in Muncie, Indiana, or Rochester, New York, or Spokane, Washington. Sociologists need to get out of their classrooms and into their communities to gather more comparative data.

At the same time, we need to check other situations. Even if Rochester corroborates Dayton, New York City or Los Angeles may not. Perhaps life in the bigger city provides greater stress, or perhaps it allows singles to lead their lives without fear of offending public morality. And how about Yellow Springs, Ohio, or West Newbury, Massachusetts? Are they the reverse of the big cities?

We cannot remain so provincial, either. The senior author is currently in the process of replicating this study in Dayton, Australia. Not literally in Dayton, of course, but in what is considered a typical community in Australia. Similar studies should be conducted by other colleagues in the Western world as well, so that we can learn what factors are American and what factors are Western. Beyond that, the followers of William Goode, who are investigating other civilizations, underdeveloped as well as developed societies, can give us some insights on the effects of culture and economics on the choices between married and single lives.

Once we have some community studies from various areas, the next step would be to make a national study, which again would give us a picture of what is national and what universal. When an Australian study is available to compare to an American, we shall have some comparative national data.

It should be evident that one cannot make a comparative study of singles without also throwing a great deal of light on marriage. We are inclined to think, from this study, that marriage does involve a heavy investment in time, that it is less fun to be married, and that sexual fantasies are less likely to be fulfilled, for the married. But the married are compensated in that they are probably wealthier, less lonely, need to take less thought for the morrow, and in general are happier. No one studying marriage alone could make more than speculative statements on these matters.

FOUR TYPES OF SINGLES

Three kinds of singles have been identified in this study. They include all the kinds of singles there can be, and yet there is a fourth category that requires special attention. The four are:

the never married
the divorced
the widowed
the single parent

The never married have been perceived in different ways, as parts of other aggregates. They have been perceived simply as young people who, in the course of events, will marry. But after they pass a certain age they are perceived as anomalous people, single men or single women who, like Barrington Erle, simply have not had the maturing experiences they should have had. The divorced and the widowed have at least had that experience which marrieds deem normal and responsible.

The most interesting question to explore in greater depth is the passage from the one phase to the other. Is there usually a decision not to marry, as there is a decision to marry? What determines when the passage has been made? How reversible is the passage? Does the life of the never married (after 30) differ from that of the divorced or the widowed? In some respects, we have shown that it does. Does a never married settle in? That is, does the loneliness and unhappiness marked here constitute a phase in the life of a single? By some age has the never-married adult made an accommodation so that the decision not to marry, or the happenstance of not marrying, leads to the same kind of resolution that takes place in marriage?

And what of the old age of the never married? Do nephews and nieces adequately replace children? Do old never marrieds thrive as well as old marrieds? Do they perhaps thrive better when compared to the widowed, who have less experience to cope with renewed singleness?

The divorced have been much more thoroughly studied, but still there are some questions raised about the divorced by this study that seem worth investigating. We have seen in many ways that the divorced seem to be under greater stress than people in any other category. They have the trauma of the unsuccessful marriage and whatever feelings they may take from that; they may have children; they have added expenses of trying to provide for two households; they have brought troubles into marriage that would not be resolved by divorce.

From studying the divorced, can we learn something about their characteristics that would be useful to the never married? We have seen, for instance, that lack of parental openness is much more characteristic of the divorced than of any other group. If that is the case, should marriage counselors explore parental openness as a factor to be considered in the counseling of the unmarried? Are there other characteristics of the divorced that, taken together, might help the unmarried decide whether singleness is a better situation for them? A divorced person strapped with unwanted children, poverty, or alimony may well know that marriage was a bad decision. He or she may well say, "If only I knew then what I know now . . ." It is likely that there is much more that never-married persons could know about marriage that may prevent their making a mistake that will lead to divorce.

Again, we see that marriage appears to be a much better situation than divorce. Is there any way of knowing which unhappily married people would be more unhappy in divorce? Could we, from a larger sample, isolate the happy divorced? We discuss successful marriages, why not successful divorces?

Finally, we see that remarriage, while not as blissful as first marriage, still looks like a better alternative than divorce in terms of health and companionship, if not happiness. Can we not, by studying the characteristics of the divorced and remarried, develop a better idea of which of the divorced should remarry?

Members of the third category, the widowed, were rather neglected in our study. We saw that demographically they have constituted a fairly consistent segment of our population and that they have always outnumbered the divorced, though they have not received as much attention. Since widowhood is a normal problem of aging, it has received considerable attention in studies of aging. It also receives special attention in terms of female widowhood during wartime. But what is the meaning of the change in ratio during the century of widows to widowers from 2 to 1 to 5 to 1? Does this have to do with a decline in childbirth deaths, an increase in discrepancy between the length of lives of men and women, or an increasing propensity of men (or a decreasing propensity of women) to remarry? Then what of the young widow or widower? In what respects are their problems similar to those of other singles of similar age and sex, and in what respects are they different? A study of young widows and widowers in comparison to other singles aggregates is highly desirable.

Finally there are single parents, commonly known as parents without partners. We have failed to provide adequate information on their special problems because we neglected to ask the participants in our sample how many children they had. No excuses. Many people looked at the entire questionnaire and no one, not even the author with 3 children, noticed that we had not asked the question. (His wife probably would have noticed it!) We partly made up for this incredible gaffe in our supplementary questionnaire and interviews with the singles group, but the comparative data are lacking.

A study is needed that compares single parents with married parents. Our hunch is that single parents will turn out to have problems more like those of marrieds than do married people without children, except that the single parents will be more harassed, which would be one reason for the greater stress signs we found in the divorced, since most of them have at least one child. The chief factor may not be guilt or failure so much as the stress of managing children. The single parent would seem to have all the disadvantages of both marriage and singleness, at least during the years when the children are being raised.

In all of these areas of study we believe comparison is needed. The single person of one type should be compared to other types of single persons and also to married persons, with age, sex, and other relative contexts taken into consideration.

It should be evident, however, that a comparative study involving singles and marrieds also gives us information about marriage that can be obtained in no other way. Even family specialists, who exclude singleness as an area of interest, can learn something about marriage from considering singles in their studies.

FOUR TYPES OF MARRIEDS

This study suggests four kinds of marriage that might be investigated with reference to singles. Only two have been studied here. The four kinds are:

the once married
the remarried
partners without children
marrieds with children

Even without considering children, it is not easy to find studies focused on the once married. After all, that is the normal condition of marriage, and all of the many books about marriage take it for granted that such marriage is the norm.

Well, it must be the norm. Even if a third of all marriages will eventually end in divorce, that means that two-thirds do not. These must be the marriages that end in the death of one of the partners. We have seen that in many respects marrieds are under less stress than singles, and that those married once are happier than those who have remarried. It may be, therefore, that for all the stresses families endure, lifetime monogamous marriage provides the best of all solutions for most people. What are the special qualities of those who have been married once? Are they nicer people? Or just more stubborn? Or lucky? Many of these questions have been answered in various studies, but we do not know of any one study in which it has all been put together. Some particularly interesting comparisons might be made between the married once and the single once, that is, the never married, with focus on gender and age. How do these alternative styles change with age, and how well do they serve men and women at different ages?

The remarried constitute a different situation. They have been studied in relation to the divorced and the widowed, and much has been made about the failure of remarriage. Our study seems to indicate that remarriage is to divorce what marriage is to singleness. It does resolve some of the problems, particularly those of loneliness, though the resolution is not as successful as first marriage, but then the problems of the divorced are more severe than the problems of the never married. It would also be interesting to take a larger sample of remarried and factor for age, and see whether stresses for the remarried vary within certain age groups. The MDR patterns we have noticed in passing would also be worth further study.

The phrase "partners without children," of course, is a takeoff on parents without partners. If the latter are more like the married, the former are more like singles. In fact one author recalls that in earlier days of his marriage, when many of his married friends did not yet have children, they were often referred to as "the unmarried." They could go out whenever they pleased. If they fought, one could walk out on the other for a week with no damage being done to anyone else. If they divorced, no one else was hurt. It is really difficult to distinguish these people from singles living together, and probably this suggests the best beginning for a comparative study. If one does not have children, what difference, in a secular society, does marriage make? It is this very idea that lies behind Margaret Mead's (1966) suggestion of a marriage in two steps.

Finally, marrieds with children should be compared to singles with children. We have assumed in this section that singles are more harassed. But is that really so? If children cause conflicts between parents, might it be that it is really easier for one parent to raise children than for two? If we could factor out for incomes, would it turn out that it is poverty and guilt, and not children, that create the most hassles for the divorced?

From such a study, in any event, we could learn a great deal about roles. Which roles of parents are really essential? If parents change roles, will that matter? Where there is only a male parent or a female parent, either one parent is filling all necessary roles, or some are being neglected. From differences in children can we learn which really are the crucial roles?

What Now?

While long-term studies continue to gather information about singles in relation to marrieds, what do we do on Monday morning? Or, more important perhaps, Friday evening?

In typical American fashion, associations have been springing up that have contributed considerably to the consciousness raising of various aggregates: Interaction, a singles association with participants usually in the 30-50 age bracket; Marriage Encounter, an international movement focusing on relations between spouses; Parents Without Partners. Each of these associations involves sharing of problems among people in comparable situations, and each particularly stresses emotional support.

One thing that might be done within the present framework and without further study is the promotion of encounters among the different organizations, particularly at the grassroots level. Local Interaction groups could meet occasionally with Parents Without Partners, for instance, to share different perspectives on similar problems, and to gain an appreciation of differences. The childless Interaction participants could come away feeling that members of Parents Without Partners have more difficult problems; perhaps a baby-sitting system could be developed to enable such parents to get to Interaction meetings.

Again, local Marriage Encounter groups might meet with Parents Anonymous, a group made up of parents of children who suffer from child abuse, though that might be more difficult to arrange. Here the members of Parents Anonymous may gain some insight in relations between spouses that would reflect on relations with children, while their insights into the problems of children might be helpful to the spouses of Marriage Encounter.

And finally — what diplomatic nuances would this require? — Marriage Encounter-type communities might meet with Interaction-type communities. The married could learn more about the singles, perhaps become more inclined to think about them in future social arrangements, perhaps become more comfortable about them. The singles would learn more about marriage. The never marrieds could get beyond the "how to meet a man" kind of problem to the less romantic considerations of whether day-to-day life in normal marriage is really preferable to the life of the single. And the divorced, comparing these relations to their own experiences, might be better prepared for remarriage. The marrieds, in turn, might also learn something about divorce as a reasonable alternative.

All these processes are desirable and exclusive. We need to study the people in various categories in order to understand them and help them understand themselves. The categories need to organize as such in order to understand themselves and share experiences with people who will empathize. Singles and marrieds need to perceive themselves as such in order to gain context and perspective. And singles and marrieds need to increase understanding of each other, at both general and community levels, in order to better understand and more fully experience human patterns.

TABLES

TABLE 2.1 Number and Percentage of Marrieds and Singles: 1900-1979

Year	*Total Adult Population*[a]	*Singles* *No.*[a]	*%*	*Marrieds* *No.*[a]	*%*
1900	51.237	23.441	46.0	27.796	54.0
1910	64.152	28.195	44.1	35.957	55.9
1920	73.796	30.750	41.8	43.046	58.2
1930	89.007	36.424	41.2	52.583	58.8
1940	101.093	40.820	40.4	60.273	59.6
1950	111.703	37.260	33.4	74.443	66.6
1960	125.457	41.052	32.7	84.405	67.3
1965	135.844	46.439	34.2	89.441	65.8
1970	147.472	53.068	36.0	94.404	64.0
1975	159.948	59.994	37.5	99.954	62.5
1979	169.586	67.852	40.0	101.734	60.0

a. In millions.

TABLE 2.2 Never Married, Widowed, and Divorced as Percentages of Singles: 1900-1979

		Never Married		Widowed		Divorced	
Year	*Singles*[a]	*No.*[a]	%	*No.*[a]	%	*No.*[a]	%
1900	23.441	19.363	82.6	3.880	16.6	.198	0.8
1910	28.195	23.273	82.5	4.634	16.4	.288	1.0
1920	30.750	24.578	79.9	5.664	18.4	.508	1.7
1930	36.424	28.610	78.5	6.752	18.5	1.062	2.9
1940	40.820	31.529	77.2	7.844	19.2	1.447	3.5
1950	37.260	25.818	69.3	8.998	24.1	2.494	6.7
1960	41.052	27.651	67.4	10.561	25.7	2.840	6.9
1965	46.399	31.947	68.9	10.944	23.6	3.508	7.6
1970	52.863	36.841	69.7	11.750	22.2	4.272	8.1
1975	59.994	41.542	69.2	11.921	19.9	6.531	10.9
1979	67.852	46.625	68.7	12.395	18.3	8.832	13.0

a. In millions.

TABLE 2.3 Young Population: 1900-1979

Year	Total Adult Population[a]	Ages 14-24 No.[a]	Ages 14-24 %	Ages 14-34 No.[a]	Ages 14-34 %
1900	51.237	16.459	32.1	28.544	55.7
1910	64.152	20.754	32.4	35.906	56.0
1920	73.996	20.354	27.7	37.511	51.0
1930	89.007	25.226	28.3	44.179	49.6
1940	101.093	26.326	26.0	47.665	47.1
1950	111.703	24.219	21.7	47.860	42.8
1960	125.457	26.090	20.8	48.837	38.9
1965	135.844	32.598	24.0	54.579	40.1
1970	147.472	38.536	26.1	63.460	43.0
1975	159.948	43.051	26.9	73.143	45.7
1979	169.586	44.291	26.1	75.871	44.7

a. In millions.

TABLE 2.4 Demographic Changes in Singles Population: 1960-1979

	1960		*1979*			
	No.[a]	*% of Total*	*No.*[a]	*% of Total*	*Increase 1960-1979*[a]	*% of Increase*
Singles	41.052	32.7	67.852	40.0	26.800	65.3
Never married	27.651	22.0	46.625	27.5	18.974	68.7
Widowed	10.561	8.4	12.395	7.3	1.834	17.4
Divorced	2.840	2.3	8.832	5.2	5.992	211.9
14-24 year olds	26.090	20.8	44.291	26.1	18.201	69.8
Never-married 14-24 year olds	18.785	15.0	34.847	20.5	16.062	85.5

a. In millions.

TABLE 2.5 Increase in Singles Population Attributable to General Population Increase: 1960-1979 (in millions)

	Total, 1969-1979	*Attributable to General Population Increase*	*Attributable to Other Factors*
Never married	19	13.1	5.9
Divorced	6	1.1	4.9
Widowed	1.8	3.6	−1.8
Total	26.8	17.8	9
Percentage	100	66.4	33.6

TABLE 3.1 Number of Articles on Singles: 1901-1975

Years	*Never Married*	*Widowed*	*Divorced*	*Total*
1901-1905	3	2	40	45
1911-1915	16	7	66	89
1921-1925	8	3	61	72
1931-1935	10	3	61	74
1941-1945	9	—*	36	45
1951-1955	27	16	22	65
1956-1960	30	12	40	82
1961-1965	20	13	47	80
1966-1970	60	15	89	164
1971-1975	79	15	102	196

*Undetermined because of category confusion relating to World War II.

TABLE 3.2 Topics of Articles on Singles

Topic	*1900-1950*	*1951-1975*	*% Increase (Decrease)*
Getting married (how to find a spouse)	9	34	277
Happiness (state of being single)	7	8	14
Explanation (compensations for being single)	13	12	(8)
Difficulties (dilemmas of being single)	9	3	(200)
Old maids versus swinging bachelors (the double social standard)	19	1	(1800)
Living (housing, work, money)	5	17	240
Love and friendship (with the opposite sex)	7	4	(75)
Sex (whether and how)	0	8	800
Outside perceptions (coping with singles)	3	2	(50)
Total	63	55	(15)

TABLE 3.3 Sample Titles of Articles about Mate Finding

From the Seventies
"What Women Should Know About Single Men"
"*Bazaar's* A to Z List on Where to Find a Man"
"Humanizing the Meat Market"
"Eight Eligible Men"
"Eligible Girls of 1973"
From the Sixties
"How Come a Nice Girl Like You Isn't Married?"
"Men That Get Away and Where They Go"
"My Mother Said I Should Give It A Try: Hunt For A Husband in the Catskills"
"Let's Take a Sane Look at the Hysterical Quest for a Husband"
"Eligible Bachelors for 1965"
From the Forties and Fifties
"129 Ways to Get a Husband: Ideas from a Panel of Experts"
"How to be Marriageable: Results of a Marriage Readiness Course"
"Six Ways of Being an Old Maid"
"Six Ways to Meet a Man"
"There are Plenty of Bachelors"

TABLE 3.4 Sample Titles of Articles on Making the Best of It

From the Seventies

"Celebrate Singleness: Marriage May Be Second Best"
"Movin' On — Alone"
"For Singles, Life Isn't All Swinging"
"Women: On Hating or Loving Being Single; Symposium"
"The Dangers of Being a Single Male"
"49 Million Singles Can't All Be Right"

From the Fifties and Sixties

"Study Disputes Image of the Happy Bachelor"
"The Blessings of Bachelorhood"
"A Spinster's Lot Can Be a Happy One"
"When Being Single Stops Being Fun"
"How to Be Human Though Single"

From the Twenties Through the Forties

"I'd Rather Be a Spinster"
"The Dilemma of the Educated Woman"
"Does It Hurt to Be an Old Maid?"
"The Sorrowful Mayden and the Jovial Batchellor"
"Alarming Increase of Old Maids and Bachelors in New England"
"Family Parasites: The Economic Value of the Unmarried Sister"

Before the Twenties

"Why I Am an Old Maid"
"The Necessary Melancholy of Bachelors"
"In Defense of Widows and Spinsters"
"There Is No Place in Heaven for Old Maids"
"The Compensations of Spinsterhood"

TABLE 3.5 Sample Titles of Articles on Living for Singles

From the Seventies and Sixties

"Serving Singles — Don't Play Mix and Match"
"You Can Go Home Again: Singles Starting to Move Back Home"
"Labor Force Status Prior to Retirement of Non-Married Women"
"Sex as Athletics in the Singles Complex"
"What Singles and Married Couples Should Know About Each Other"
"Taxes and the Single Woman"
"Should a Single Person Buy a House?"
"Sexual Problems of Women Alone"
"Church and the Single Person"
"Contraceptives and the Single Person"
"Should Doctors Prescribe Contraceptives for Unmarried Ladies?"
"Boys and Girls Together: Apartments for Singles Only"
"The Pill and the Girl Next Door"
"Life Insurance for Single Women"
"How to Travel Alone and Like It"
"Six Rude Answers to One Rude Question"

Before the Sixties

"Life of a Bachelor"
"Money Talk for Single Women"
"Must Bachelor Girls Be Immoral?"
"Love and the Single Woman"
"Won't You Come Up and See My Twing Memorial Window?"
"Taxing German Bachelors"
"Few Bachelors Among Savage Peoples"
"Bachelor Wives"
"Unmarried Woman in France"
"Taxation of Spinsters"
"The Necessary Melancholy of Bachelors"
"In Defense of Widows and Spinsters"
"There Is No Place in Heaven for Old Maids"
"The Compensations of Spinsterhood"

TABLE 5.1 Respondents' Recall of Parental Relations

	Loving/Warm		*Conflicting/Cold*		*Single Parent*	
	No.	*%*	*No.*	*%*	*No.*	*%*
Never married	74	64	32	28	9	8
Divorced	17	47	15	42	4	11
Singles	91	60	47	31	13	9
Married once	129	63	60	29	18	8
Remarried	31	72	8	18	4	9
Marrieds	160	64	68	27	22	9
Total sample	251	63	115	29	35	9

NOTE: $\chi^2 < .4935$.

TABLE 5.2 Respondents' Recall of Parental Openness

	Both Parents Open		*Mother Open*		*Father Open*		*Neither Parent Open*	
	No.	*%*	*No.*	*%*	*No.*	*%*	*No.*	*%*
Never married	53	47	31	27	8	7	22	19
Divorced	14	39	5	14	3	8	14	39
Singles	67	45	36	24	11	7	36	24
Married once	99	49	48	24	12	6	44	22
Remarried	15	35	15	35	5	12	8	19
Marrieds	114	46	63	25	17	7	52	21
Total sample	181	46	99	25	28	7	88	22

NOTE: $\chi^2 < .1778$.

TABLE 5.3 Current Parental Relationships

	Warm/Stable No.	*Warm/Stable* %	*Cool/Stable* No.	*Cool/Stable* %	*Fights/Fights a Lot* No.	*Fights/Fights a Lot* %
Never married	50	46	29	26	31	28
Divorced	15	44	6	18	13	38
Singles	65	45	35	24	44	31
Married once	124	71	28	16	22	13
Remarried	24	65	8	22	5	14
Marrieds	148	70	36	17	27	13
Total sample	213	60	71	20	71	20

NOTE: $\chi^2 < .0004$.

TABLE 6.1 Number of Social Outings per Week

	Less than 1 No.	*Less than 1* %	*1* No.	*1* %	*2* No.	*2* %	*3 or more* No.	*3 or more* %
Never married	24	21	31	27	24	21	36	31
Divorced	11	30	9	24	9	24	8	22
Singles	35	23	40	26	33	22	44	29
Married once	84	41	74	36	31	15	17	8
Remarried	13	30	19	43	8	18	4	9
Marrieds	97	39	93	37	39	16	21	8
Total sample	132	33	133	33	72	18	65	16

NOTE: $\chi^2 < .0000$.

TABLE 6.2 Age and Frequency of Social Outings

Age and Civil Status	*0-1*		*3+*	
	No.	*%*	*No.*	*%*
18-29				
Never married	40	46	33	38
Divorced	10	53	4	21
Singles	50	47	37	35
Married once	49	69	6	9
Remarried	3	60	0	0
Marrieds	52	68	6	8
30+				
Never married	14	52	4	15
Divorced	10	56	4	22
Singles	24	53	8	18
Married once	109	80	11	8
Remarried	29	74	4	4
Marrieds	138	79	15	9
Totals				
Never married	54	47	37	33
Divorced	20	55	8	21
Singles	74	49	45	30
Married once	158	76	17	8
Remarried	32	73	4	9
Marrieds	190	76	21	8

TABLE 6.3 Places Preferred for Social Outings (First Three Selections)

	Friends		*Restaurants*		*Movies*		*Relatives*		*Nightclubs*		*Theater*		*Social Clubs*	
	No.	*%*	*No.*	*%*	*No.*	*%*	*No.*	*%*	*No.*	*%*	*No.*	*%*	*No.*	*%*
Never married	64	56	51	44	52	45	19	17	40	35	23	20	9	8
Divorced	19	51	14	38	12	32	9	24	15	41	5	14	3	8
Singles	83	55	65	43	64	42	28	18	55	36	28	18	12	8
Married once	108	52	116	56	47	23	86	42	36	18	23	11	24	12
Remarried	29	66	30	68	15	34	19	43	12	27	6	14	9	21
Marrieds	137	55	146	58	62	25	105	42	48	19	29	12	33	13
Totals	220	55	211	53	126	31	133	33	103	30	57	19	45	11
$\chi^2 <$	.0043		.0211		.0000		.0007		.0007		.4695		.2388	

TABLE 6.4 Hours Devoted to Leisure Time Activities During Workday

Activity and Hours Spent	*Never Married*		*Divorced*		*Singles (Totals)*		*Married Once*		*Remarried*		*Marrieds (Totals)*		*Totals*	
	No.	*%*	*No.*	*%*	*No.*	*%*	*No.*	*%*	*No.*	*%*	*No.*	*%*	*No.*	*%*
Watching television[a]														
0	8	7	2	6	10	7	18	9	3	7	21	8	31	8
1	28	25	14	39	42	28	46	22	9	21	55	22	97	24
2	30	26	7	19	37	25	56	27	12	27	68	27	105	26
3+	48	42	13	36	61	41	86	42	20	45	106	42	167	42
Visiting friends[b]														
0	7	6	3	8	10	7	36	18	7	16	43	17	53	13
1	32	28	9	25	41	27	87	42	20	47	107	43	148	37
2	31	27	16	44	47	31	46	22	7	16	53	21	100	25
3+	45	39	8	22	53	35	36	18	9	21	45	18	98	25
Hobbies, sports, etc.[c]														
0	9	8	4	11	13	9	32	16	4	9	36	15	49	12
1	22	19	8	22	30	20	57	28	15	34	72	29	102	26
2	32	28	14	39	46	31	60	29	13	30	73	29	119	30
3+	52	45	10	28	62	40	56	27	12	27	68	27	130	33
Community service[d]														
0	67	60	27	75	94	64	123	60	30	68	153	62	247	63
1	22	20	3	8	25	17	63	31	8	18	71	29	96	24
2	13	12	2	6	15	10	11	5	2	5	13	5	28	7
3+	9	8	4	11	13	9	7	4	4	9	11	4	24	6

a. $\chi^2 < .8339$.
b. $\chi^2 < .0005$.
c. $\chi^2 < .0078$.
d. $\chi^2 < .0998$.

TABLE 6.5 Age and Occupation (in percentages)

Age and Civil Status	*White-Collar*	*Blue-Collar*	*Home*	*Other*
18-24				
Never married	44	28	0	28
Divorced	40	20	0	40
Singles	44	27	0	29
Married once	63	15	15	7
Remarried	0	50	30	20
Marrieds	59	17	14	10
25-29				
Never married	56	26	0	19
Divorced	57	0	0	43
Singles	56	17	0	27
Married once	55	18	16	11
Remarried	67	33	0	0
Marrieds	55	19	15	11
30-39				
Never married	55	45	0	0
Divorced	60	20	0	20
Singles	57	33	0	10
Married once	53	9	22	16
Remarried	33	13	47	7
Marrieds	49	10	27	14
40-49				
Never married	50	50	0	0
Divorced	40	20	0	40
Singles	43	29	0	29
Married once	59	13	23	5
Remarried	62	23	8	8
Marrieds	60	15	19	6
50+				
Never married	36	7	50	7
Divorced	25	0	0	75
Singles	35	6	35	24
Married once	36	14	36	14
Remarried	22	11	44	22
Marrieds	33	14	37	16
Totals				
Never married	47	27	6	20
Divorced	50	11	0	39
Singles	48	23	4	25
Married once	52	13	23	12
Remarried	40	19	29	12
Marrieds	50	15	24	11

TABLE 6.6 Age and Education (in percentages)

Age and Civil Status	*High School or Less*	*Some College*	*College+*
18-24			
Never married	43	41	16
Divorced	40	40	20
Singles	42	41	17
Married once	52	30	18
Remarried	50	50	0
Marrieds	52	31	17
25-29			
Never married	19	44	37
Divorced	14	50	36
Singles	17	46	37
Married once	24	25	41
Remarried	67	33	0
Marrieds	36	26	38
30-39			
Never married	9	55	36
Divorced	50	38	13
Singles	26	47	26
Married once	23	24	44
Remarried	53	40	7
Marrieds	37	27	36
40-49			
Never married	50	0	50
Divorced	60	20	20
Singles	57	14	29
Married once	39	26	26
Remarried	46	23	31
Marrieds	48	25	27
50+			
Never married	57	7	36
Divorced	50	25	25
Singles	56	11	33
Married once	60	24	17
Remarried	78	11	11
Marrieds	63	22	16
Totals			
Never married	36	38	26
Divorced	36	39	25
Singles	36	38	26
Married once	44	25	31
Remarried	57	29	14
Marrieds	46	26	28

TABLE 6.7 Age and Income (in percentages)

Age and Civil Status	*Up to $9,999*	*$10,000-$19,999*	*$20,000 or More*
18-24			
Never married	64	31	5
Divorced	60	40	0
Singles	64	32	5
Married once	50	41	9
Remarried	100	0	0
Marrieds	54	38	8
25-29			
Never married	48	41	11
Divorced	57	36	7
Singles	51	39	10
Married once	28	53	19
Remarried	67	33	0
Marrieds	30	52	18
30-39			
Never married	55	27	18
Divorced	70	30	0
Singles	62	29	9
Married once	36	38	26
Remarried	57	21	21
Marrieds	40	34	26
40-49			
Never married	0	50	50
Divorced	60	40	0
Singles	43	43	14
Married once	26	46	28
Remarried	42	25	33
Marrieds	30	40	30
50+			
Never married	71	21	7
Divorced	0	67	33
Singles	59	29	12
Married once	18	54	28
Remarried	71	29	0
Marrieds	26	50	24
Totals			
Never married	59	32	9
Divorced	57	38	5
Singles	59	33	8
Married once	30	47	23
Remarried	58	24	18
Marrieds	35	42	23

TABLE 6.8 Civil Status and Income, Ages 30-49

	Up to $9,999		*$10,000-$19,999*		*$20,000-$29,999*		*$30,000 or More*	
	No.	*%*	*No.*	*%*	*No.*	*%*	*No.*	*%*
Never married	6	50	4	33	2	17	0	0
Divorced	10	67	5	33	0	0	0	0
Singles	16	59	9	33	2	8	0	0
Married once	19	36	20	38	10	19	4	8
Remarried	13	50	6	23	4	15	3	12
Marrieds	32	41	26	33	14	18	7	9
Totals	48	45	35	33	16	15	7	7

TABLE 7.1 Number of Sexual Partners

	0-1		*2-3*		*4-10*		*More than 10*	
	No.	*%*	*No.*	*%*	*No.*	*%*	*No.*	*%*
Never married	45	42	23	21	24	22	16	15
Divorced	5	14	11	31	9	25	11	31
Singles	50	35	34	24	33	23	27	19
Married once	127	66	29	15	27	14	10	5
Remarried	10	25	15	38	11	28	4	10
Marrieds	137	59	44	19	38	16	14	6
Totals	187	50	78	21	71	19	41	11

NOTE: $\chi^2 < .0000$.

TABLE 7.2 Number of Sexual Partners, by Gender

	0-1		*2-3*		*4-10*		*More than 10*	
	No.	*%*	*No.*	*%*	*No.*	*%*	*No.*	*%*
Female	117	58	47	23	25	12	13	6
Male	70	40	31	18	46	26	28	16
Totals	187	50	78	21	71	19	41	11

NOTE: $\chi^2 < .0001$.

TABLE 7.3 Number of Sexual Partners, by Age

	0-1		*23*		*4-10*		*More than 10*	
	No.	*%*	*No.*	*%*	*No.*	*%*	*No.*	*%*
18-24	35	40	19	22	23	26	11	13
25-29	38	45	30	24	14	17	12	14
30-39	44	49	18	20	19	21	9	10
40-49	27	49	11	20	12	22	5	9
50+	43	72	10	17	3	5	4	7
Totals	187	50	78	21	71	19	41	11

NOTE: $\chi^2 < .0027$.

TABLE 7.4 Beliefs About Number of Sexual Partners of Others in Same Category

	0-1		*2-3*		*4-10*		*More than 10*	
	No.	*%*	*No.*	*%*	*No.*	*%*	*No.*	*%*
Never married	14	12	40	35	35	31	24	23
Divorced	2	6	12	34	15	43	6	17
Singles	16	11	52	35	50	34	30	20
Married once	50	27	84	45	34	18	17	9
Remarried	5	13	16	40	11	28	8	20
Marrieds	55	24	100	44	45	20	25	11
Totals	71	19	152	41	95	26	55	15

NOTE: $\chi^2 < .0036$.

TABLE 7.5 Sexual Attitudes ("Yes" Responses)

	Sex to Keep Date?		*Have Sex Without Love?*	
	No.	*%*	*No.*	*%*
Never married	25	24	51	49
Divorced	8	24	15	46
Totals	33	24	66	48
χ^2	< .8543		< .4111	

TABLE 7.6 Frequency of Sexual Intercourse

	Once a Week or Less		*Twice a Week*		*Three or More Times a Week*	
	No.	*%*	*No.*	*%*	*No.*	*%*
Never married	74	67	23	21	13	12
Divorced	15	42	8	22	13	36
Singles	89	61	31	21	26	18
Married once	66	35	69	37	53	28
Remarried	17	43	13	33	10	25
Marrieds	83	36	82	36	63	28
Totals	172	46	113	30	89	24

NOTE: $\chi^2 < .0000$.

TABLE 7.7 Sexual Partners and Frequency, by Civil Status

Number of Partners	Frequency: Never Married, Up to 1/Week No.	%	3+/Week No.	%	Divorced, Up to 1/Week No.	%	3+/Week No.	%	Married Once, Up to 1/Week No.	%	3+/Week No.	%	Remarried, Up to 1/Week No.	%	3+/Week No.	%
0-3	52	77	5	7	11	71	4	24	52	33	42	27	14	54	4	17
11+	5	31	5	33	10	9	6	55	3	27	6	55	1	25	1	25
χ^2	.0000				.4326				.6658				.6845			

TABLE 7.8 Frequency of Sexual Intercourse, by Gender

	1-2 Times per Month		*1-2 Times per Week*		*3 or More Times per Week*	
	No.	*%*	*No.*	*%*	*No.*	*%*
Female	101	50	59	29	42	21
Male	71	41	54	31	47	27
Totals	172	46	113	30	89	24

NOTE: $\chi^2 < .0288$.

TABLE 7.9 Frequency of Sexual Intercourse, by Age

	1-2 Times per Month		*1-2 Times per Week*		*3 or More Times per Week*	
	No.	*%*	*No.*	*%*	*No.*	*%*
18-24	50	57	20	23	18	21
25-29	34	40	26	31	25	29
30-39	25	28	40	44	25	28
40-49	21	38	18	33	16	29
50+	42	75	9	16	5	9
Totals	172	46	113	30	89	24

NOTE: $\chi^2 < .0000$.

TABLE 7.10 Sexual Satisfaction

	Very Satisfied		*Somewhat Satisfied*		*Neutral*		*Somewhat Dissatisfied*		*Very Dissatisfied*	
	No.	*%*	*No.*	*%*	*No.*	*%*	*No.*	*%*	*No.*	*%*
Never married	26	23	29	26	36	32	13	12	7	6
Divorced	12	33	10	28	8	22	1	3	5	14
Singles	38	26	39	27	44	30	14	10	12	8
Married once	89	44	69	34	32	16	9	5	2	1
Remarried	22	52	13	31	5	12	2	5	0	0
Marrieds	111	46	82	34	37	15	11	5	2	1
Totals	149	38	121	31	81	21	25	6	14	4

NOTE: $\chi^2 < .0000$.

TABLE 7.11 Sexual Satisfaction, by Gender

	Very Satisfied		*Somewhat Satisfied*		*Neutral*		*Somewhat Dissatisfied*		*Very Dissatisfied*	
	No.	*%*	*No.*	*%*	*No.*	*%*	*No.*	*%*	*No.*	*%*
Female	87	41	66	31	41	20	9	4	7	3
Male	62	34	55	31	40	22	16	9	7	4
Totals	149	38	121	31	81	21	25	6	14	4

NOTE: $\chi^2 < .1416$.

TABLE 7.12 Sexual Satisfaction, by Age

	Very Satisfied		*Somewhat Satisfied*		*Neutral*		*Somewhat Dissatisfied*		*Very Dissatisfied*	
	No.	*%*	*No.*	*%*	*No.*	*%*	*No.*	*%*	*No.*	*%*
18-24	28	32	25	28	21	24	10	11	5	6
25-29	34	39	34	39	9	10	5	6	5	6
30-39	40	44	31	34	15	15	4	4	2	2
40-49	17	30	23	40	12	21	5	9	0	0
50+	30	46	8	12	24	37	1	2	2	3
Totals	149	38	121	31	81	21	25	6	14	4

NOTE: $\chi^2 < .0005$.

TABLE 8.1 Activities and Feelings of Loneliness ("Yes" Responses)

	Never Married		*Divorced*		*Singles (Totals)*		*Married Once*		*Remarried*		*Marrieds (Totals)*		$\chi^2 <$
	No.	*%*	*No.*	*%*	*No.*	*%*	*No.*	*%*	*No.*	*%*	*No.*	*%*	
Dining alone	54	47	16	44	70	46	70	34	14	33	84	34	.0868
Entering empty room	17	15	10	28	27	18	25	12	6	14	31	13	.1115
Join social organization	25	22	6	17	31	21	34	17	5	12	39	16	.4125
Depressed — alone	23	20	12	33	35	23	29	14	8	18	37	15	.0412
Living alone — unhappy	9	8	9	25	18	12	37	18	9	21	46	19	.0262

TABLE 8.2 Responses to Loneliness Items

	Never Married				*Divorced*				*Singles (Totals)*				*Married Once*				*Remarried*				*Marrieds (Totals)*			
	Rarely/ Sometimes True		*Often/ Mostly True*		*Rarely/ Sometimes True*		*Often/ Mostly True*		*Rarely/ Sometimes True*		*Often/ Mostly True*		*Rarely/ Sometimes True*		*Often/ Mostly True*		*Rarely/ Sometimes True*		*Often/ Mostly True*		*Rarely/ Sometimes True*		*Often/ Mostly True*	
	No.	*%*	*No.*	*%*	*No.*	*%*	*No.*	*%*	*No.*	*%*	*No.*	*%*	*No.*	*%*	*No.*	*%*	*No.*	*%*	*No.*	*%*	*No.*	*%*	*No.*	*%*
No one to share with[a]	93	82	21	18	27	75	9	25	120	80	30	20	186	91	18	9	39	89	5	11	225	91	23	9
No one to discuss with[b]	84	74	30	26	18	51	17	49	102	70	47	30	172	84	33	16	33	75	11	25	205	82	44	18
Most people are alone[c]	100	88	14	12	25	69	11	31	125	83	25	17	181	90	21	10	39	89	5	11	220	89	26	11

a. $\chi^2 < .0000$. See question 56 in Appendix I.
b. $\chi^2 < .0003$. See question 58 in Appendix I.
c. $\chi^2 < .0000$. See question 60 in Appendix I.

TABLE 9.1 Illnesses in Past Month

	Never Married		*Divorced*		*Singles (Totals)*		*Married Once*		*Remarried*		*Marrieds (Totals)*		$\chi^2 <$
	No.	*%*	*No.*	*%*	*No.*	*%*	*No.*	*%*	*No.*	*%*	*No.*	*%*	
Frequent headaches	26	21	7	19	32	21	56	27	12	27	68	27	.6075
Stomach ulcers	4	4	3	8	7	5	12	6	2	5	14	7	.6797
High blood pressure	12	10	5	14	17	11	25	12	9	21	34	14	.3883
Insomnia	23	20	2	5	25	17	33	16	11	25	44	18	.0946
Nightmares	10	9	5	14	15	10	12	6	6	14	18	7	.1913
Irrational fears	9	8	4	11	13	9	6	3	2	5	8	3	.1013
Crying spells	9	8	4	11	13	9	13	6	1	2	14	6	.4451
Constant worrying and anxiety	33	29	9	24	42	28	33	16	10	23	43	17	.0551
Often feeling guilty	22	19	11	30	33	22	19	9	8	18	27	11	.0032
Despondency	22	19	8	22	30	20	21	10	3	7	24	10	.0301
Lack of interest in sex	11	10	12	32	33	22	21	10	4	9	25	10	.0009
Often feeling lonely	24	21	14	38	38	25	16	8	4	9	20	8	.0000
Feelings of worthlessness	21	18	11	30	33	22	18	9	6	14	24	10	.0026

TABLE 9.2 Use of Drugs

	Never Married		Divorced		Singles (Totals)		Married Once		Remarried		Marrieds (Totals)		χ^2 =
	No.	*%*	*No.*	*%*	*No.*	*%*	*No.*	*%*	*No.*	*%*	*No.*	*%*	
Alcohol – How Often Drunk													
Once/week or more	23	20	9	24	32	21	13	6	5	12	18	7	.0024
Once/month	22	19	6	16	28	19	24	11	8	18	32	13	.0024
Rarely/never	69	61	22	59	91	60	168	82	31	70	199	80	.0024
Drugs – Frequent Use													
Tranquilizers	9	8	5	14	14	9	24	12	4	9	28	11	.6601
Sleeping pills	13	11	2	5	15	10	22	11	5	11	27	11	.7663
Marijuana	38	33	10	27	48	32	17	8	8	18	25	10	.0000
Heroin/cocaine	7	3	3	4	10	3	4	1	1	1	5	1	.0721/ .4606
Morphine/codeine	7	3	0	0	7	2	4	1	1	1	5	1	.7196/ .0826
Pep pills (amphetamine, dexedrine)	12	10	5	14	17	11	6	3	3	7	9	4	.0153
Psychedelics (LSD)	6	5	3	8	9	6	14	7	1	2	15	6	.6283

TABLE 9.3 Suicide Responses

	Never Married		*Divorced*		*Singles (Totals)*		*Married Once*		*Remarried*		*Marrieds (Totals)*	
	No.	*%*	*No.*	*%*	*No.*	*%*	*No.*	*%*	*No.*	*%*	*No.*	*%*
Never thought about suicide	52	46	14	39	66	44	144	71	26	59	170	69
Thought about suicide a few times	51	45	15	42	66	44	51	25	15	34	66	27
Thought about suicide often	5	4	5	14	10	7	3	2	0	0	3	1
Planned suicide	1	1	1	3	2	1	3	2	0	0	3	1
Attempted suicide	5	4	1	3	6	4	3	2	3	7	6	2
Totals	114	100	36	101	150	100	204	102	44	100	248	100

NOTE: χ^2 = .0000.

TABLE 10.1 Illnesses in Past Month

	Never Married				Divorced				Singles (Totals)				Married Once				Remarried				Marrieds (Totals)			
	Females		Males		Females		Males		Females		Males		Females		Males		Females		Males		Females		Males	
	No.	%	No.	%	No.	%	No.	%	No.	%	No.	%	No.	%	No.	%	No.	%	No.	%	No.	%	No.	%
Frequent headaches	12	26	10	18	5	20	2	18	17	24	12	18	34	30	21	23	10	39	2	11	44	31	23	21
High blood pressure	3	6	3	5	1	4	4	36	5	10	11	13	17	15	8	9	3	12	6	33	20	14	24	13
Stomach ulcers	2	4	1	2	1	4	2	18	3	4	3	4	4	4	8	9	2	8	0	0	6	4	8	7
Crying spells	7	15	2	3	3	12	1	9	10	15	3	4	13	11	0	0	0	0	1	6	13	9	1	1
Insomnia	9	19	10	18	2	8	0	0	11	17	10	15	19	17	14	15	9	35	2	11	28	20	16	15
Irrational fears	6	13	2	3	4	15	0	0	10	14	2	3	2	2	4	4	2	8	0	0	4	3	4	4
Nightmares	5	11	2	4	4	15	1	9	9	12	3	5	6	5	6	7	3	12	3	17	9	6	9	8
Constant worry and anxiety	14	30	14	25	7	27	2	18	21	29	16	24	21	18	12	13	6	23	4	22	27	19	16	15
Often feeling guilty	11	23	9	16	6	23	5	46	17	23	14	21	13	11	5	5	5	19	3	17	18	13	8	7
Despondency	7	15	12	21	6	23	2	18	13	18	14	21	13	11	7	7	3	12	0	0	16	18	7	6
Often feeling lonely	12	26	8	14	8	31	6	55	20	27	14	21	11	10	5	3	3	12	1	6	14	10	6	6
Feelings of worthlessness	5	11	12	21	8	31	3	27	13	18	15	22	11	10	7	8	3	12	3	17	14	10	10	9
Lack of interest in sex	5	11	2	4	10	39	2	18	15	21	4	6	12	11	9	10	3	12	1	6	15	11	10	9

TABLE 10.2 Use of Drugs, by Gender

	Never Married				*Divorced*				*Singles (Totals)*				*Married Once*				*Remarried*				*Marrieds (Totals)*			
	Females		*Males*		*Females*		*Males*		*Females*		*Males*		*Females*		*Males*		*Females*		*Males*		*Females*		*Males*	
	No.	*%*	*No.*	*%*	*No.*	*%*	*No.*	*%*	*No.*	*%*	*No.*	*%*	*No.*	*%*	*No.*	*%*	*No.*	*%*	*No.*	*%*	*No.*	*%*	*No.*	*%*
Drugs – Frequent Use																								
Sedatives/ relaxants sleeping pills, tranquilizers)	5	10	6	9	3	11	1	5	8	11	7	8	13	11	10	11	3	10	1	8	16	11	11	11
Amphetamines (benzedrine, dexedrine)	6	11	6	10	4	15	1	9	10	12	7	10	5	4	1	1	2	8	1	6	7	5	2	2
Marijuana	13	24	24	40	7	26	3	27	20	25	27	38	8	7	8	9	6	21	2	11	28	9	10	9
Psychoactive drugs exclud- ing marijuana (morphine, codeine, LSD, heroin, cocaine)	1	2	4	6	1	2	1	7	2	2	5	6	2	2	2	2	1	2	1	1	3	2	3	2
Alcohol – How Often Drunk																								
Once/week or more	3	6	20	33	5	18	4	36	8	10	24	34	5	4	9	10	2	8	3	17	7	4	12	11
Once/month	10	19	12	20	3	11	3	27	13	16	15	21	13	11	10	11	7	28	1	6	20	13	11	10
Rarely/ never	40	76	29	47	18	71	4	36	58	74	33	45	96	84	72	78	16	64	14	78	112	82	86	79

TABLE 10.3 Suicide Responses, by Gender

	Never Married				*Divorced*				*Singles (Totals)*				*Married Once*				*Remarried*				*Marrieds (Totals)*			
	Females		*Males*		*Females*		*Males*		*Females*		*Males*		*Females*		*Males*		*Females*		*Males*		*Females*		*Males*	
	No.	*%*	*No.*	*%*	*No.*	*%*	*No.*	*%*	*No.*	*%*	*No.*	*%*	*No.*	*%*	*No.*	*%*	*No.*	*%*	*No.*	*%*	*No.*	*%*	*No.*	*%*
Never thought about it	22	42	30	50	10	40	4	50	32	41	34	49	83	76	60	61	16	62	10	56	99	73	70	65
Thought about it	27	51	28	47	14	56	4	50	41	53	32	48	24	22	29	32	8	31	7	39	32	24	36	33
Attempted	4	8	1	2	1	4	0	0	5	6	1	2	2	2	1	1	2	8	1	6	4	3	2	2

TABLE 11.1 Factors Very Important to Happiness

	Never Married		*Divorced*		*Singles (Totals)*		*Married Once*		*Remarried*		*Marrieds (Totals)*		*Totals*		$\chi^2 <$
	No.	*%*	*No.*	*%*	*No.*	*%*	*No.*	*%*	*No.*	*%*	*No.*	*%*	*No.*	*%*	
Health	79	70	27	75	106	70	169	83	33	81	202	83	308	78	.0596
Marriage	24	22	8	23	32	23	140	69	32	78	172	69	204	53	.0000
Children	24	23	16	44	40	26	130	64	22	54	152	61	192	50	.0000
Friends	61	54	21	60	82	54	73	36	13	32	86	34	168	43	.0352
Love	48	43	15	43	63	42	128	63	26	63	154	61	217	55	.0000
Sex	43	38	18	51	61	40	85	42	17	42	102	41	163	42	.0133
Personal growth	58	51	20	57	78	51	99	49	16	40	115	46	193	49	.2084
Success	35	31	15	42	50	33	59	29	14	35	73	29	123	31	.2082
Religion	29	26	3	9	32	21	76	37	13	32	89	36	121	30	.0000
Contribution to society	27	24	7	21	34	22	57	28	9	22	66	27	100	26	.3423

TABLE 11.2 Happiness Self-Ratings

	Very Happy		*Moderately Happy*		*Neither Happy nor Unhappy*		*Moderately Unhappy*		*Very Unhappy*	
	No.	*%*	*No.*	*%*	*No.*	*%*	*No.*	*%*	*No.*	*%*
Never married	20	17	64	56	23	20	7	6	1	1
Divorced	9	24	17	46	7	19	1	3	3	8
Singles	29	21	81	56	30	17	8	4	4	2
Married once	57	28	124	60	18	9	5	2	3	1
Remarried	11	25	24	55	3	7	4	9	2	5
Marrieds	68	27	148	59	21	8	9	4	5	2
Totals	97	24	229	57	51	13	17	4	9	2

NOTE: $\chi^2 < .0061$

TABLE 11.3 Responses to "Do You Get a Lot of Fun Out of Life?"

	Yes		No	
	No.	*%*	*No.*	*%*
Never married	87	76	27	24
Divorced	26	70	11	30
Singles	113	75	38	25
Married once	171	85	31	15
Remarried	32	74	11	26
Marrieds	203	83	42	17
Totals	316	80	80	20

NOTE: $\chi^2 < .0833$.

TABLE 11.4 Happiness, by Age ("Yes" Responses)

	Never Married		*Divorced*		*Singles (Totals)*		*Married Once*		*Remarried*		*Marrieds (Totals)*	
	No.	*%*	*No.*	*%*	*No.*	*%*	*No.*	*%*	*No.*	*%*	*No.*	*%*
Under 30	66	75	11	84	77	79	65	91	4	60	69	89
Over 30	16	59	11	58	27	58	116	85	31	84	147	85
30-50	11	85	8	53	19	68	76	81	23	82	99	81
Over 50	5	35	3	75	8	44	40	95	8	89	48	94

TABLE 11.5 Respondents' Beliefs About How Happy Single Friends Are in Comparison to Themselves

	Much Happier		*Somewhat Happier*		*About the Same*		*Somewhat Unhappier*		*Much Unhappier*	
	No.	*%*	*No.*	*%*	*No.*	*%*	*No.*	*%*	*No.*	*%*
Never married	4	4	26	23	65	57	17	15	3	3
Divorced	2	5	9	24	16	43	8	22	2	5
Singles	6	4	35	22	81	54	25	18	5	3
Married once	6	3	20	10	114	58	52	26	6	3
Remarried	3	7	10	23	21	49	8	19	1	2
Marrieds	9	4	30	12	135	56	60	25	7	3
Totals	15	4	65	17	216	55	85	22	12	3

NOTE: $\chi^2 < .0947$

TABLE 11.6 Respondents' Beliefs About How Happy Married Friends Are in Comparison to Themselves

	Much Happier		*Somewhat Happier*		*About the Same*		*Somewhat Unhappier*		*Much Unhappier*	
	No.	*%*	*No.*	*%*	*No.*	*%*	*No.*	*%*	*No.*	*%*
Never married	9	8	26	23	47	41	23	20	9	8
Divorced	2	5	7	19	14	38	10	27	4	11
Singles	11	6	33	21	61	40	33	24	13	9
Married once	5	2	13	6	156	76	31	15	1	1
Remarried	2	5	5	11	27	61	9	21	1	2
Marrieds	7	3	18	7	183	73	40	16	2	1
Totals	18	5	51	13	244	61	73	18	15	4

NOTE: $\chi^2 < .0000$.

TABLE 12.1 Five Years from Now I Will Be . . .

	Married and		*Single and*	
	No.	*%*	*No.*	*%*
Happy	28	34	5	10
(Unhappy)	(1)	(1)	(6)	(12)
Family oriented	25	30	12	24
(Free of family)	(5)	(6)	(2)	(4)
Working	22	27	5	10
(Not working)	(2)	(2)	(2)	(4)
Affluent	11	13	6	12
(Poor)	(1)	(1)	(1)	(2)
Sharing	7	9	5	10
(Detached)	(1)	(1)	(0)	(0)
Traveling	7	9	2	4
Successful	6	7	3	6
Secure	6	7	2	4
Free	4	5	2	4
Fulfilled	4	5	1	2
Socially active	3	4	3	6

TABLE 12.2 Marrieds' Reasons Compared to Singles' Expectations

Marrieds' Reasons	*No.*	*%*	*Singles' Expectations*	*No.*	*%*
Love	23	46	Happiness	28	34
Ignorance	12	24	Family	25	30
Family	5	10	Work	22	27
Security	4	8	Money	11	13
Escape	4	8	Sharing	7	9

APPENDIX I: THE QUESTIONNAIRE

1. Sex:

_____1) Female
_____2) Male

2. Age:

_____1) 18-24
_____2) 25-29
_____3) 30-39
_____4) 40-49
_____5) 50 or above

3. Race:

_____1) Black
_____2) White
_____3) Other

4. Education:

_____1) Less Than High School Diploma
_____2) High School Diploma
_____3) Some College
_____4) College Degree
_____5) Some Graduate School
_____6) Graduate or Professional Degree

5. Occupation:

_____1) Professional (Doctor, Teacher, Engineer, etc.)
_____2) Business Official or Manager
_____3) Sales Person
_____4) Clerical Worker
_____5) Service Worker (Policeman, Fireman, etc.)
_____6) Skilled Worker (Draftsman, Machine Operator, etc.)
_____7) Unskilled Worker
_____8) Homemaker

_____9) Other (Please specify) ______________________
_____0) Currently Unemployed (Please specify usual occupation)
____

6. Religion:
_____1) Catholic
_____2) Protestant (Fundamentalist, Baptist, Pentecostal, etc.)
_____3) Protestant, All Others (Episcopalian, Methodist, Presbyterian, etc.)
_____4) Unitarian, Quaker
_____5) Jewish
_____6) Other (Please specify) ______________________
_____7) None

7. Religious Attendance:
_____1) Once a Week
_____2) 2 to 3 Times a Month
_____3) 4 to 6 Times a Year
_____4) Once a Year
_____5) Less than Once a Year
_____6) Not at All

8. Marital Status:
_____1) Single (Never Married)
_____2) Married, First Time
_____3) Married, More than Once
_____4) Separated
_____5) Divorced
_____6) Widowed
_____7) Single but Cohabiting on a Long-Term Basis

9. Living Arrangements:
_____1) Living in a Family as Its Head
_____2) Living in Family but not as Its Head
_____3) Living in a Nonfamily Household (Non-related)
_____4) Living Alone

10. How happy would you say you are most of the time?
_____1) Very Happy
_____2) Moderately Happy
_____3) Neither Happy nor Unhappy
_____4) Moderately Unhappy
_____5) Very Unhappy

11. Does your level of happiness change often or remain fairly constant?

_____1) It changes very often.
_____2) It changes often.
_____3) It rarely changes.
_____4) It remains quite stable.

12. Compared to you, how happy are most of your single acquaintances?

_____1) Much happier than I
_____2) Somewhat happier than I
_____3) About as happy as I
_____4) Somewhat less happy than I
_____5) Much less happy than I

13. Compared to you, how happy are most of your married acquaintances?

_____1) Much happier than I
_____2) Somewhat happier than I
_____3) About as happy as I
_____4) Somewhat less happy than I
_____5) Much less happy than I

14. How happy are you with the kind of person you are?

_____1) Very Happy
_____2) Moderately Happy
_____3) Neither Happy nor Unhappy
_____4) Moderately Unhappy
_____5) Very Unhappy

15. When you begin the day, do you generally anticipate that it will be:

_____1) Very Satisfying
_____2) Moderately Satisfying
_____3) Neither Satisfying nor Unsatisfying
_____4) Moderately Unsatisfying
_____5) Very Unsatisfying

16. How much of the time are you bored?

_____1) Frequently
_____2) Sometimes
_____3) Rarely
_____4) Never

17. I get a lot of fun out of life:

_____1) Yes
_____2) No

For each of the following issues, indicate how important it is to your own happiness, and how happy you have been with that issue over the past six months.

			I. Important for Your Happiness				*II. General Happiness Over Last 6 Months*				
			Very Important	Moderately Important	Slightly Important	Not at All Important	Very Happy	Moderately Happy	Neither Happy nor Unhappy	Moderately Unhappy	Very Unhappy
____	____	18. Recognition, Success	1	2	3	4	1	2	3	4	5
____	____	19. Children and Being a Parent	1	2	3	4	1	2	3	4	5
____	____	20. Personal Growth and Development	1	2	3	4	1	2	3	4	5
____	____	21. Religion	1	2	3	4	1	2	3	4	5
____	____	22. Being in Love	1	2	3	4	1	2	3	4	5
____	____	23. Your Sex Life	1	2	3	4	1	2	3	4	5
____	____	24. Marriage	1	2	3	4	1	2	3	4	5
____	____	25. Friends and Social Life	1	2	3	4	1	2	3	4	5
____	____	26. Health	1	2	3	4	1	2	3	4	5
____	____	27. Contributing to Society	1	2	3	4	1	2	3	4	5

28a. How often do you go out socially?

_____1) Less than Once a Week
_____2) Once a Week
_____3) Twice a Week
_____4) Three Times a Week
_____5) Four or More Times a Week

b. When you go out socially, you usually go to (rank those that apply)

_____1) Restaurant
_____2) Nightclub (Bar)
_____3) Movie
_____4) Theatre or Concert
_____5) Visit Friends
_____6) Visit Relatives
_____7) Social Club (Private club) ______________________________
_____8) Other (Please specify) ______________________________

On the average, how many hours each workday do you spend on the following activities:

29. Time with your spouse or partner.

_____ 0 1 2 3 4 5 or more

30. Time doing leisure activities, sports, and hobbies.

_____ 0 1 2 3 4 5 or more

31. Time with friends.

_____ 0 1 2 3 4 5 or more

32. Watching television.

_____ 0 1 2 3 4 5 or more

33. Time doing community activities.

_____ 0 1 2 3 4 5 or more

34. How satisfied are you with the allotment of your time?

_____1) Very Satisfied
_____2) Somewhat Satisfied
_____3) Somewhat Dissatisfied
_____4) Very Dissatisfied

35. Do you feel conspicuous dining alone in a restaurant?

_____1) Yes
_____2) No

36. Do you feel depressed when you are alone?

_____1) Yes
_____2) No

37. Are you apprehensive upon entering an empty room?

_____1) Yes
_____2) No

38. Have you ever joined a social organization to find companionship?

_____1) Yes
_____2) No

39. Do you equate living alone with a state of unhappiness?

_____1) Yes
_____2) No

40. Do you think there is something deviant about a person who chooses to live alone?

_____1) Yes
_____2) No

41. When you were growing up, your family was:

_____1) Lower Class
_____2) Lower Middle Class
_____3) Middle Class
_____4) Upper Middle Class
_____5) Upper Class

42. How would you describe your parents' relationship while they were together?

_____1) Very Loving and Stable
_____2) Generally Warm and Stable
_____3) Stable but Emotionally Cold
_____4) Generally Cold and Conflicting
_____5) Grew Up with One Parent Only

43. Were emotions freely expressed in your childhood home?

_____1) Both parents generally expressed their feelings openly
_____2) My mother usually expressed her feelings
_____3) My father usually expressed his feelings
_____4) Neither parent expressed emotions openly

44. How would you describe your current relationship with your parents?

_____1) Warm and stable, few conflicts
_____2) Cool and stable, few conflicts
_____3) Periods of closeness alternate with fights
_____4) We fight a lot
_____5) There was a big fight and currently are not speaking
_____6) I'm close to one parent but not the other

45. What is the first word(s) that comes into your mind when you hear the word "married"?

____

46. What is the first word(s) that comes into your mind when you hear the word "single"?

____

FOR SINGLES ONLY (If married, skip to question number 55)

47. Do you think that being single will be a permanent status for you?

_____1) Yes
_____2) No

48. Where do you meet people of the opposite sex? (Rank in order of importance)

_____1) School
_____2) Blind Dates
_____3) Church
_____4) Bars
_____5) Other (Please specify) ______________________________

49. How satisfying were these places?

a. 1st choice

_____1) Satisfied
_____2) Not Satisfied

b. 2nd choice

_____1) Satisfied
_____2) Not Satisfied

c. 3rd choice

_____1) Satisfied
_____2) Not Satisfied

50. Have you or would you accept a date with someone you are not attracted to?

_____1) Yes
_____2) No

51. Have you or would you engage in intimate relations with an escort to avoid losing his/her attention?

_____1) Yes
_____2) No

52. Do you feel that you have to be "in love" or care for someone deeply before you have sex?

_____1) Yes
_____2) No

53. Why are you not married (rank those that apply)?

_____1) Something is wrong with you
_____2) You never found the right person
_____3) You lost the right person
_____4) You did not want the responsibility of children
_____5) You are having too much fun
_____6) You love your freedom and privacy
_____7) Your career prevented this commitment
_____8) It never seemed like a desirable option
_____9) Other (Please explain) ______________________________
____

54. What pressures do you feel toward getting married? ____________
____

55a. Do you feel that something is wrong with you (those not married) because you (they) are not married?

_____1) Yes
_____2) No

If yes, why? ________________________________
____

b. For someone over 30, being married is the normal and healthy way to be?

_____1) Yes
_____2) No

56. There is no one with whom to share my happy and sad moments.

_____1) Rarely true
_____2) Sometimes true
_____3) Often true
_____4) Mostly true

57. I have friends that understand me.

_____1) Rarely true
_____2) Sometimes true
_____3) Often true
_____4) Mostly true

58. I cannot discuss my problems with anyone.

_____1) Rarely true
_____2) Sometimes true
_____3) Often true
_____4) Mostly true

59. You can count on most people you meet.

_____1) Rarely true
_____2) Sometimes true
_____3) Often true
_____4) Mostly true

60. Mostly people are pretty alone and friendless.

_____1) Rarely true
_____2) Sometimes true
_____3) Often true
_____4) Mostly true

61. Which of the following has been true of you in the past month? (Check all that apply)

_____1) Frequent headaches
_____2) Stomach ulcers
_____3) High blood pressure
_____4) Insomnia
_____5) Nightmares
_____6) Constant worry and anxiety
_____7) Often feeling guilty
_____8) Sometimes feeling you just can't go on
_____9) Irrational fears
____ 10) Crying spells
____ 11) Often feeling lonely
____ 12) Lack of interest in sex
____ 13) Feelings of worthlessness

62. Which of the following statements best describes your feelings about suicide?

_____1) I have never contemplated suicide
_____2) I have thought about it a few times
_____3) I have thought about it often
_____4) I have planned to commit suicide
_____5) I have attempted suicide once
_____6) I have attempted suicide more than once

63. Which of the following drugs do you take fairly often? (Check all that apply)

_____1) Tranquilizers
_____2) Sleeping pills
_____3) Pep pills, dexedrine, amphetamine, "uppers"
_____4) Morphine or demerol
_____5) Codeine
_____6) Cocaine
_____7) Heroin or methadone
_____8) Marijuana
_____9) Psychedelics (LSD, Mescaline)

64. How often do you get drunk?

_____1) Every day
_____2) Several times a week
_____3) Once a week or so
_____4) Once or twice a month
_____5) Rarely
_____6) Never

65. In general, how satisfied are you with your sex life?

_____1) Very Satisfied
_____2) Somewhat Satisfied
_____3) Neutral
_____4) Somewhat Dissatisfied
_____5) Very Dissatisfied

66. During the last six months, how often have you had sexual intercourse?

_____1) Never or almost never
_____2) Once or twice a month
_____3) Once or twice a week
_____4) Several times a week
_____5) Daily or more often

67. With how many sexual partner(s) have you had sexual intercourse?

_____1) None
_____2) 1
_____3) 2 or 3
_____4) 4 to 6
_____5) 7 to 10
_____6) 11 to 20
_____7) more than 20

68. How many sexual partners do you think most people your age, sex and marital status have had?

_____1) None
_____2) 1
_____3) 2 or 3
_____4) 4 to 6
_____5) 7 to 10
_____6) 11 to 20
_____7) more than 20

69. Political Orientation

_____1) Very conservative
_____2) Somewhat conservative
_____3) Moderate (neutral)
_____4) Somewhat liberal
_____5) Very liberal

70. What was your total personal income before taxes?

_____1) Less than $10,000
_____2) $10,000-$19,999
_____3) $20,000-$29,999

______4) $30,000-$39,999
______5) $40,000-$49,999
______6) $50,000 or more

71. If you could change lives with another person, would you do it?

______1) Yes
______2) No

Why? ____

APPENDIX II: THE SAMPLE BREAKDOWN

Civil Status and Gender

	Females		*Males*	
	No.	*%*	*No.*	*%*
Never married	53	24	61	34
Divorced	26	12	11	6
Singles	79	36	72	40
Married once	114	52	92	51
Remarried	26	12	18	10
Marrieds	140	64	110	60
Totals	219	95	182	45

Civil Status and Age

	18-24		*25-29*		*30-39*		*40-49*		*50+*		*Totals*	
	No.	*%*	*No.*	*%*	*No.*	*%*	*No.*	*%*	*No.*	*%*	*No.*	*%*
Never married	61	53	27	24	12	10	2	2	13	11	115	29
Divorced	5	14	14	38	9	24	5	14	4	21	37	9
Married once	27	13	44	21	55	27	29	19	42	11	207	51
Remarried	2	5	3	7	16	36	14	32	9	20	41	11
Totals	95	24	88	22	92	23	60	15	68	17	403	101

Civil Status and Education

	Less than High School		*High School Diploma*		*Some College*		*Degree or More*		*Totals*	
	No.	*%*	*No.*	*%*	*No.*	*%*	*No.*	*%*	*No.*	*%*
Never married	9	8	32	28	44	38	30	26	115	29
Divorced	7	19	6	17	14	39	9	25	36	9
Married once	24	12	67	32	52	25	64	31	207	52
Remarried	8	18	16	36	14	32	6	14	44	11
Totals	48	12	121	30	124	31	109	27	402	101

Civil Status and Occupation

	White-Collar		*Blue-Collar*		*Homemaker*		*Other*		*Totals*	
	No.	*%*	*No.*	*%*	*No.*	*%*	*No.*	*%*	*No.*	*%*
Never married	54	47	32	28	6	5	23	20	115	29
Divorced	18	49	4	11	0	0	15	41	37	9
Married once	108	52	28	14	47	23	23	11	206	52
Remarried	19	45	8	19	12	29	3	7	42	11
Totals	199	50	72	18	65	16	64	16	400	101

Civil Status and Religion

	Protestant		*Catholic*		*Other*		*None*		*Totals*	
	No.	%	*No.*	%	*No.*	%	*No.*	%	*No.*	%
Never married	62	54	19	17	10	9	24	21	115	29
Divorced	15	41	7	19	3	8	12	32	37	9
Married once	124	60	56	27	6	3	20	10	206	51
Remarried	28	64	5	11	4	9	7	16	44	11
Totals	229	57	87	22	23	6	63	16	402	100

Civil Status and Political Identity

	Conservative		*Neutral*		*Liberal*		*Totals*	
	No.	*%*	*No.*	*%*	*No.*	*%*	*No.*	*%*
Never married	23	20	48	42	43	38	114	29
Divorced	7	19	19	53	10	28	36	9
Married once	69	35	78	39	52	26	199	51
Remarried	18	42	15	35	10	23	43	11
Totals	117	30	160	41	115	29	392	100

Civil Status and Income

	Less than $9,999		*$10,000-$19,999*		*$20,000-$29,999*		*More than $30,000*		*Totals*	
	No.	*%*	*No.*	*%*	*No.*	*%*	*No.*	*%*	*No.*	*%*
Never married	68	60	35	31	9	8	1	1	113	30
Divorced	20	57	14	39	1	3	1	3	36	9
Married once	58	30	89	46	35	18	10	5	192	90
Remarried	22	55	10	25	5	13	3	8	40	11
Totals	168	44	148	39	50	13	15	4	381	100

APPENDIX III: THE DECLARATION OF UNDEPENDENCE

More than 50 million strong, let the single community resolve together to mark this day as the beginning — or the affirmation — of an undependent life.

(1) I resolve to think for myself in all situations rather than allow an "expert" to decide the course of my life. While I will remain open to wise counsel, I will make the final decision in personal matters and make myself heard when there are shared decisions to be made.

(2) I resolve to remain aware of my identity and my wholeness at all times, particularly when in a coupled relationship. I will exercise my need for personal space without impinging on others.

(3) I resolve to be a loving friend and to nurture worthwhile friendships, realizing my self-sufficiency is not equivalent to isolation. I will cultivate relationships with those of all ages, occupations and marital statuses as long as they meet my needs.

(4) I resolve to become acquainted with the other gender burdened with a minimum of bias, recognizing they are neither alien nor enemy. I will focus on our similarities and develop real relationships with them, establishing authentic intimacy rather than superficial sexuality.

(5) I resolve to plan my own life for myself insofar as is possible; career goals, family future, my personal ambitions to develop and grow.

(6) I resolve to make of my single status an incidental fact. I will remember that first of all, I am a distinct and unique person that happens also to be unmarried. There are times when being single is an advantage, and others when it is not. Yet when I consider myself in a total picture, marital status will not be a prime consideration. Involvement will.

(7) I resolve to go with my occasional loneliness, remembering not to flee nor wallow nor make impulsive decisions in the midst of it. I

will bear in mind that everyone feels momentary twinges of loneliness, whether married or single it may well be a dimension of humanness. I will make it a point to note the difference between loneliness and aloneness, appreciating that being in my own company can be a wise choice.

(8) I resolve to maximize the possibilities for growth and freedom within my singleness. I will keep my eye fixed on its positive aspects.

Interaction Newsletter (June 1981)

REFERENCES

ACKERMAN, NATHAN W. (1972) pp. 10-26 in Harold Hart (ed.) Marriage: For and Against. New York: Hart.

ADAMS, MARGARET (1976) Single Blessedness: Observations on the Single Status in Married Society. New York: Basic Books.

ALBRECHT, STAN L. (1979) "Correlates of happiness among the remarried." Journal of Marriage and the Family 4 (November): 857-867.

America (1958) "Feature X." 4 (January): 398.

Anonymous (1934) "A spinster I." Atlantic (May): 540-546.

BELL, ROBERT (1972) pp. 79-99 in Harold Hart (ed.) Marriage: For and Against. New York: Hart.

——— (1966) Premarital Sex in a Changing Society. Englewood Cliffs, NJ: Prentice-Hall.

BERNARD, JESSIE (1979) "Marriage: his and hers," pp. 114-120 in Leonard Cargan and Jeanne Ballantine (eds.) Sociological Footprints. Boston: Houghton Mifflin.

BIRD, CAROLINE (1972) pp. 168-186 in Harold Hart (ed.) Marriage: For and Against. New York: Hart.

BRADBURN, NORMAN and DAVID CAPLOVITZ (1965) Reports on Happiness. Chicago: Aldine.

BRAITO, RITA and DONNA ANDERSON (1978) "Singles and aging." Presented at the meetings of the Society for the Study of Social Problems, September, San Francisco.

BRODY, JANE E. (1979) "Marriage is good for health and longevity, studies say." New York Times (May 8): C-1, C-4.

BROOKS, ANDREE (1981) "Single at midlife: divorce suburban style." New York Times Magazine (May 24): 30-31, 66-70.

CARTER, HUGH and PAUL C. GLICK (1970) Marriage and Divorce: A Social and Economic Study. Cambridge, MA: Harvard University Press.

CHIRIBOGA, DAVID A. (1978) "Psychological study of adaptation to divorce." Journal of Divorce (Winter):

Christianity Today (1979) "Celebrate singleness — marriage may be second best." 20 (May): 26-27.

DAVIS, ALAN G. and PHILLIP STRONG (1977) "Working without a net: the bachelor as a social problem." Sociological Review 25 (February): 109-130.

DEEGAN, DOROTHY Y. (1969) The Stereotypes of the Single Woman in American Novels: A Social Study with Implications for the Education of Women. New York: Octagon.

DUBERMAN, LUCILLE (1977) Marriage and Other Alternatives. New York: Praeger.

EDWARDS, MARIE and ELEANOR HOOVER (1974) The Challenge of Being Single. Los Angeles: New American Library.

FIELDS, CHERYL M. (1980) "Faculty stress is found to be highest among married women, single men." Chronicle of Higher Education 21 (September): 1, 6.

FISHER, ESTER OSHIVER (1972) pp. 152-166 in Harold Hart (ed.) Marriage: For and Against. New York: Hart.

FRENCH, MARILYN (1978) The Women's Room. New York: Jove.

GAGNON, JOHN H. and CATHY S. GREENBLAT (1978) Life Designs: Individuals, Marriages and Families. Glenview, IL: Scott, Foresman.

GALLUP, GEORGE (1976) "Pollster visits nation's 'barometer'." Dayton Journal-Herald (June 22).

GILDER, GEORGE (1974) "In defense of monogamy." Commentary (November): 31-36.

GLENN, NORVAL D. (1975) "The contribution of marriage to the psychological well-being of males and females." Journal of Marriage and the Family 37 (August): 594-600.

——— and C. M. WEAVER (1977) "Marital happiness of remarried divorced persons." Journal of Marriage and the Family 39, 2: 331-337.

GLICK, PAUL (1975) "A demographer looks at the American family." Journal of Marriage and the Family 37 (February): 15-26.

GOVE, WALTER (1979) "Sex, marital status, and psychiatric treatment: a research note." Social Forces 58 (September): 89-93.

——— (1973) "Sex, marital status, and mortality." American Journal of Sociology 79 (July): 45-67.

HETHERINGTON, E. MAVIS, MARTHA COX, and ROGER COX (1977) "Divorced fathers." Psychology Today 10 (April): 42, 44-46.

HUGHES, MICHAEL and WALTER R. GOVE (1981) "Living alone, social integration, and mental health." American Journal of Sociology 81 (July): 48-74.

HUNT, MORTON (1974) Sexual Behavior in the 1970's. Chicago: Playboy.

ISR Newsletter (1979) "Americans seek self-development, suffer anxiety from changing roles." 7 (Winter): 4-5.

JACOBY, SUSAN (1974) "49 million singles can't all be right" New York Times Magazine (February 17).

KAIN, EDWARD L. (1981) 'Social determinants of the decision to remain never-married." Presented at the meetings of the American Sociological Association, Toronto.

KINSEY, A. C., W. B. POMEROY, and C. E. MARTIN (1948) Sexual Behavior in the Human Male. Philadelphia: W. B. Saunders.

KUHN, MANFRED (1955) "How mates are sorted," in Howard Becker and Reuben Hill (eds.) Family, Marriage, and Parenthood. Lexington, MA: D. C. Heath.

LEAR, MARTHA WEINMAN (1980) "Loneliness: more common than the common cold." Redbook (November): 33, 202, 204, 206.

LIBBY, ROGER W. (1978) "Creative singlehood as a sexual lifestyle: beyond marriage as a rite of passage," in Bernard I. Murstein (ed.) Exploring Intimate Lifestyles. New York: Springer.

MACKLIN, ELEANOR D. (1978) "Review of research on nonmarital cohabitation in the United States," in Bernard I. Murstein (ed.) Exploring Intimate Lifestyles. New York: Springer.

MAYNARD, FREDELLE (1974) "Must divorce be so painful?" Reader's Digest 105 (July): 98-101.

MEAD, MARGARET (1966) "Marriage in two steps." Redbook (July).

MILTON, MARGE (1915) "Why I am an old maid." Independent (June 7): 399-404.

MONEYMAKER, JAMES and FRED MONTANINO (1978) "The new sexual morality: a society comes of age," in James M. Henslin and Edward Sagarin (eds.) The Sociology of Sex. New York: Schocken.

MURSTEIN, BERNARD I. (1978) "Swinging and comarital sex," in Bernard I. Murstein (ed.) Exploring Intimate Lifestyles. New York: Springer.

Newsweek (1978) "Saving the family." May 15: 63-90.

——— (1973) "Games singles play." June 16: 52-58.

NYE, F. IVAN (1967) "Values, Family, and a Changing Society." Journal of Marriage and the Family 29 (May): 241-248.

O'BRIEN, PATRICIA (1973) The Woman Alone. New York: Quadrangle.

PEARLIN, LEONARD I. and JOYCE S. JOHNSON (1977) "Marital status, life strains, and depression." American Sociological Review 42 (October): 704-715.

PICKHARDT, CARL E. (1981) "Working it out." Single Parent (January/February): 26-27.

RAMEY, JAMES (1978) "Lifestyles of the future," in Bernard I. Murstein (ed.) Exploring Intimate Lifestyles. New York: Springer.

RAWLINGS, ELEANOR M. (1966) "Family situations of married and never married males." Journal of Marriage and the Family 28, 4: 485-490.

REISS, IRA L. (1972) pp. 234-251 in Harold Hart (ed.) Marriage: For and Against. New York: Hart.

ROSENBLATT, ROGER (1977) "The self as a sybarite." Harpers (March): 12-14.

RUBIN, ZICK (1979) "Seeking a cure for loneliness." Psychology Today (October): 82, 85-86, 89-90.

SKOLNICK, ARLENE and JEROME SKOLNICK [eds.] (1977) Family in Transition. Boston: Little, Brown.

SMITH, HAROLD IVAN (1979) "Sex and singleness the second time around." Christian Century (May 22): 16-18.

SOMERS, ANNE R. (1979) "Marital status, health, and use of health services." Journal of the American Medical Association 241 (April 27): 1818-1822.

SPREITZER, ELMER and L.E. RILEY (1974) "Factors associated with singlehood." Journal of Marriage and the Family 36, 1: 533-542.

STARR, JOYCE and DONALD CARNS (1972) "Singles in the city." Society 9: 43-48.

STEIN, PETER (1978) "The lifestyles and life chances of the never-married." Marriage and Family Review 1 (July/August): 1-11.

——— (1976) Single. Englewood Cliffs, NJ: Prentice-Hall.

TAVRIS, CAROL (1978a) "40,000 men tell about their sexual behavior, their fantasies, their ideal women, and their wives: Part I." Redbook (February): 111-113, 176-181.

——— (1978b) "40,000 men tell about their sexual behavior, their fantasies, their ideal women, and their wives: Part II." Redbook (March): 99, 109, 193.

U.S. News and World Report (1977) "The ways 'singles' are changing the U.S." January 31: 59-60.

——— (1975) "For singles, life isn't all 'swinging'." December 8:

VILLET, GREY (1959) "The blessings of bachelorhood." Life (January 26): 95-98.

VERBRUGGE, LOIS N. (1979) "Marital status and health." Journal of Marriage and the Family 41 (May): 267-285.

VON TUNGELIN, ANNIE LAURIE (1955) "How to be human though single." Today's Health 33 (January): 22-25.

WALLIN, PAUL (1954) "Marital happiness of parents and their children's attitudes toward marriage." American Sociological Review 19 (February): 20-23.

WHYTE, WILLIAM (1957) Organization Man. New York: Simon & Schuster.

ZELNIK, MELVIN and JOHN F. KANTNER (1977) "Teen girls' premarital sex up 30%." Dayton Journal-Herald (April 8): 26.

ABOUT THE AUTHORS

LEONARD CARGAN is Associate Professor of Sociology at Wright State University in Dayton, Ohio. He received his doctorate in sociology from Wayne State University in 1968. He has published scholarly articles and book chapters on community structure and power, abortion attitudes, student rights, and school busing, as well as the area of family studies. The second edition of his book, *Sociological Footprints* (coedited by Jeanne Ballantine), has recently been published by Wadsworth. Dr. Cargan founded in 1973, and remains a trustee of, a discussion-social program for singles in Dayton called Interaction.

MATTHEW MELKO, Professor and Chairman of the Department of Sociology and Anthropology at Wright State University, received his Ph. D. in 1959 from the London School of Economics and Political Science. His most recent book-length publication (with Richard Weigel), *Peace in the Ancient World,* was published by McFarland in 1981. Dr. Melko's studies of systems, civilizations, and peace have appeared in such diverse journals as *Bulletin of the Atomic Scientists, Journal of World History,* and *Quarterly Journal of Ideology.*